Stormy Lives

A Journey Through Borderline Personality Disorder

Dr. Tennyson Lee

muswell hill press
London • New York

First published by Muswell Hill Press, London, 2016

© 2016. Tennyson Lee

Tennyson Lee has asserted his right under the Copyright, Design and Patents Act 1988 to be identified as the author of this work. All rights reserved. No part of this publication may be reproduced without prior permission of Muswell Hill Press.

www.muswellhillpress.co.uk.

British Library CIP Data available
ISBN: 978-1-908995-16-2
Printed in Great Britain

Contents

Acknowledgements xiii

Forward by Professor Kamaldeep Bhui xv

Introduction xvii

Part One: What is Personality Disorder? 1

Chapter 1: What Is Wrong With Me? 3
Nina's Story Part 1–The Trouble With Nina 3
What is Personality Disorder? 6
A Short History of Personality Disorder:
Mad, Bad or Simply Sad? 8
How do I know if I may have a Personality Disorder? 10
Should the Diagnosis of Personality Disorder Be Abandoned? 12
What is Borderline Personality Disorder? 13
Two Approaches to Personality – the 'Deficit' and
'Conflict' Debate 15
More Questions on Personality Disorder 18
Questions to Consider When Starting Treatment 19
How is Personality Disorder Viewed by the Law and Society? 22
Key Points 24

Chapter 2: Can You Help Me? 25
Nina's Story Part 2–Help I Need Somebody 25
Nina's 5th Appointment 25
Will I Get Better? 26
Can You Help Me? 27
Can You Cure Me? 28
Key Points 29

**Chapter 3: How did I get here? Why do I have a
Personality Disorder? 31**
Nina's Story Part 3–Getting to Know Her 31
Why do I Have a Personality Disorder? 33

Attachment: What's the Big Thing About It? 36
So How Does All This Link With Treatment? 40
Is My Personality Disorder Due to My Sexual Abuse? 41
Why Has it Taken So Long for Me to Get Help? 41
Key Points 42

**Chapter 4: Stop Messing Around. What is Really the
           Matter With Me? 45**
Nina's Story Part 4–Getting to Know Her More 45
The Psychological Formulation: How Can I Understand What Is
Wrong With Me? 45
Am I Too Defensive? What Do You Mean by
'Defence Mechanism'? 47
Why do I Have All These Other Problems – like Depression,
Anxiety, Drinking and Eating Difficulties? 50
What's the Difference Between Borderline Personality Disorder and
Other Psychiatric Disorders? 50
Anxiety Disorders Versus Borderline Personality Disorder 51
Mood (Affective) Disorders Versus Borderline
Personality Disorder 52
Schizophrenia Versus Borderline Personality Disorder 55
Why Do I hear Voices – Does it Mean I'm mad? 57
Why Do I Harm Myself? 58
What is Repetition Compulsion? 59
The Treatment Contract: What is it and Do I Need To
Agree to it? 60
Why Must I Stop Using Street Drugs? 61
Responsibility: What's the Big Deal About It? 63
Kate is 16 – Could She Have Borderline Personality Disorder? 65
Commentary 66
Key Points 66

**Chapter 5: What is Wrong With the Others? Different Types of
           Personality Disorder 69**
Nina's Story Part 5–Why Pick on Me? 69
Meeting Some Other Patients 69
Paul's Story 70
Gregory's Story 71
Description of Specific Personality Disorders 71
Paranoid Personality Disorder 72
Schizoid Personality Disorder 74
Schizotypal Personality Disorder 75
Histrionic Personality Disorder 76

Dissocial (Antisocial) Personality Disorder 77
Anankastic (Perfectionist) Personality Disorder 79
Anxious (Avoidant) Personality Disorder 80
Dependent Personality Disorder 82
Narcissistic Personality Disorder 84
Commentary 86
What's In a Name – Is It a Disorder? 87
Who Gets the Diagnosis? 88
So why do I have Personality Disorder and she doesn't? 89
I tick all the boxes- am I a Superpoly Personality Disorder and
Really Messed Up? 89
Key Points 90

Part Two: What is the Treatment? 91

Chapter 6: The Treatment 93
Nina's Story Part 6–Treating Nina 93
Evidence Based Psychological Treatments 95
Common Characteristics of Psychological Treatments 95
Extra Content: Brief Descriptions of the Different Evidence Based
Treatments for Borderline Personality Disorder 95
Mentalization Based Treatment 97
Transference Focused Psychotherapy 103
Schema Focused Therapy 106
Dialectical Behavioural Therapy (DBT) 108
Cognitive Analytic Treatment (CAT) 111
What About Psychoanalysis? 113
Which Treatment Should I Choose? 113
Who Should I Go To When I Seek Treatment for Borderline
Personality Disorder? 114
How do I Actually Choose My Therapist? 115
Should I Go for Group or Individual Therapy? 116
Are Hospital Admissions Helpful for People With Borderline
Personality Disorder? 118
Do Health Workers Cry? An Illustration of the
Countertransference 119
What do You Mean I Don't Have Depression and
You Won't Give Me Pills? 120
What About Medication for Borderline Personality Disorder? ... 121
Key Points 121

Chapter 7: Moving Life Forward 123
    Nina's Story Part 7–Love, Work and Play 123
    How Can I Progress In Love, Work And Play When I Haven't
    Loved, Worked or Played For Years? 124
    Commentary 125
    Key Points 127

Chapter 8: What Can Family and Friends Do? 129
    Nina's Story Part 8–With a Little Help From My Friends 129
    Commentary 130
    Be Realistic, Go Slow 131
    Looking After the System/Family Environment 132
    Looking After the Person with Borderline Personality Disorder 134
    Looking After Yourself 140
    Key Points 142

Chapter 9: What Happens in Therapy 145
    Nina's Story Part 9–The Long and Winding Road 145
    Commentary 151
    Meeting the Treatment Team 154
    Has Nina Made Any Progress in Changing? 158
    Commentary 163
    Key Points 164

Chapter 10: So What happened? 165
    Following Up the Lives of Nina's Fellow Patients 165
    Commentary 166
    Nina's story Part 10–Goodbye to Nina 167
    Commentary 168
    Key Points 169

Chapter 11: Epilogue 171
    Nina's Story Part 11–A Life in Flow 171

Annexure 173

  Acronyms 175

  Glossary 177
    Ambivalence 177
    Cognitive Behavioural Therapy (CBT) 177
    Countertransference 178
    Defence Mechanisms 178
    Dissociation 179
    Evidence Based Medicine 179

Formulation 179
Mentalizing 179
Mindfulness 180
Object 180
Presentation 180
Projection 180
Projective Identification 180
Psychiatrist 181
Psychoanalyst 181
Psychoanalytic 182
Psychodynamic 182
Psychopathy 182
Psychotherapist 182
Psychologist 182
Schema 183
Splitting 183
Trait 184
Transference 184
Treatment frame 184
A Final Question on Different Disciplines: After All Your
Explanation I Remain Confused About the Different Disciplines.
Why Is That? and Does It Matter? 184
Does It Matter? 185
References 186

Key Facts and Figures 187
Suicide 187
Borderline Personality Disorder 188

**ICD–10 Classification of Mental and Behavioural Disorders
Diagnostic Criteria for research World Health Organization,
Geneva, 1993 .... 189**
F60 – F69 DISORDERS OF ADULT PERSONALITY AND
BEHAVIOUR 189
F60 SPECIFIC PERSONALITY DISORDERS 189

The Treatment Contract 191
Treatment Contract at DeanCross Personality Disorder
Service, East London Foundation NHS Trust 191

Relevant Resources 195
Books 195
Internet 196

Notes and References 199

Index 205

List of Tables

Table 1	Borderline Personality Disorder Dimensions	14
Table 2	Links between the Infant Strange Situation, Adult Attachment Interview and DSM-5	39
Table 3	Classification of Personality Disorder in DSM-5 and ICD10	72
Table 4	Common Characteristics of Evidence Based Treatments for Borderline Personality Disorder	96
Table 5	Evidence based Treatments for Borderline Personality Disorder	98

Acknowledgements

To the patients I have worked with whose stories, humanity and humour have inspired this book. There are moments in therapy when the patient reaches some real and life changing emotional understanding. This book is dedicated to the courage and sweat required on both the patient's and clinician's part to get to this point.

To the clinicians, colleagues and teams who have either trained, inspired or continue to stimulate me clinically. The National Health Service in the UK has exposed me to too many dedicated and gifted colleagues to individually list, but clinicians who have particularly influenced my practice and thinking are: Elizabeth Bishop, Julia Bland, Tony Davies, Sue Davison, Frank Denning, Julia Fabricius, Patrick Grove, Eileen McGinley, Duncan McLean, Stirling Moorey, Wil Pennycook, Nikolas Ragiadakos, and Clare Tanner.

The following units and services have shaped my thinking or continue to do so:

- The Cawley Centre, Maudsley Hospital
- The Psychotherapy Department, Maudsley Hospital
- The Intensive Psychological Treatment Service, Guys Hospital
- DeanCross Centre, Tower Hamlets Personality Disorder Service, East London Foundation NHS Trust
- Consultant Psychiatrists in the Tower Hamlets Mental Health Service, East London Foundation NHS Trust

And finally to my family: Lucian, Sophie, Charlotte and Päivi.

Foreword

Balance & Bridges

One of my favourite novels 'A Fine Balance', by Rohinton Mistry, outlines the tragedy, destruction and violence experienced by people living in slums in India. The mutilation of young children to offer them a prospect of earning money as beggars, coupled with the desolation of material poverty are located within sub-cultures and relational networks in which people still live their lives to the full; they love and play and lose and gain.. The balance between the material and psycho-spiritual world in order to maintain delicate and fragile relationships helps them to navigate, tolerate and even accept adversity.

Dr Tennyson Lee's remarkable book reminds me of this balancing act, and of the hazards that some people endure in order to school, mature and age while living life to the full. Lee focuses on helping the patient and the professional achieve a balance in the therapeutic relationship, through sharing information about personality disorders. Hence, patient and professional come to hold the same narrative of the malady that both seek to remedy. All patients struggle with the conventional asymmetry afforded by the encounter between a patient and the doctor or therapist. These struggles are made even more acute for people with personality difficulties, where there is exquisite sensitivity to the imbalance in knowledge and power and psychological functioning. The added exposure of intimate feelings and precious private moments may be experienced as loss events leading to psychological reactions and defences against the cause of the perceived loss, namely the therapy and therapist. This book will help to restore balance by offering patients a professional guide and professionals a patient guide, to help both in their journeys in medical practice and psychotherapy.

Personality difficulties may form due to trauma or attachment problems in childhood. Sometimes there is no explanation for emotional instability and mood problems. Sharing such experiences helps to achieve a shared narrative, but this ideal may never be fully met. The struggle to do so despite interruptions and eruptions in therapy is more important and perhaps the active ingredient. Achieving a shared narrative is no easy task, as professional bodies of knowledge triumph in esoteria, acronyms, rituals and codes, not to mention scientific references to authorized sources of knowledge that determine what is 'true'. Lee does away with these conventions and reveals to the patient and the public the contested nature of the diagnostic categories called *personality disorders*. The limitations of the classifications and, at the same time, the value of these classifications present a paradox. Lee responds with careful narration to turn plain speaking science into common sense. He walks through different personality types illustrating the multiple dilemmas faced by the patient, the therapist and the doctor with incisive case studies that speak to the reader.

Kamaldeep Bhui
Consultant Psychiatrist, East London Foundation Trust
Professor of Cultural Psychiatry & Epidemiology,
Wolfson Institute of Preventive Medicine,
Queen Mary University of London
Editor of British Journal of Psychiatry, and International
Journal of Culture and Mental Health

Introduction

Most of us are interested in people – we get intrigued by the inner lives of others – we're interested in personality. But what exactly is personality? We would probably say that personality is how someone usually is – how they think, respond emotionally, behave, and what their relationships are like. This is a useful framework to conceptualise personality: how one thinks, feels, behaves and is in relationships. When these aspects of personality constantly lead to problems for the individual or those around them, this may indicate a *Personality Disorder.*

My personal interest in Personality Disorder was sparked in my first 6 months of training as a psychiatrist. There was a particular patient who was dreaded by the team. She had (literally) kicked the consultant psychiatrist around the block. She had repeated emergency admissions to the psychiatric ward because of concerns she would harm herself. Her husband constantly called the ward, and was clearly at his wits end trying to cope with his wife and their two young children.

So I approached my first meeting with her with some anxiety. And I found her likeable and engaging. I was left thinking 'What was all the fuss about – the patient just needs the right approach.' But at a point in the meeting her manner switched with the speed of a light being flicked off. I had been asking how she was feeling in the ward at the moment. 'I don't see the point of that question – why do you ask that?' Flustered I responded that I just wanted to see if she was feeling all right. She looked at me contemptuously and wordlessly walked out of the room. From what had seemed a reasonable discussion I suddenly felt cut down, shunned and bewildered. That sense of 'what just happened there? I thought we were getting on and you've just annihilated me' has never left me. Trying to work out a psychological reason for that emotional swerve keeps me drawn to working with people who have these difficulties. Many years later, when I met my previous consultant again and asked after the patient I was glad to hear that she (and he) had weathered through. Her marriage had remained intact and she had been able to mother her young children in a more caring way. She remains a patient of his service but is more stable now with far fewer psychiatric admissions. The complexity and power of that clinical encounter drew me into working in this area.

The concept of *Personality Disorder* is often questioned, and we'll address some of these issues in the book. 'Personality Disorder' as a term needs considerable unpacking and explanation. Over and above the terminology however, Personality Disorder is a difficult condition to navigate. I hope that this book will help anyone who wants to go below the surface and gain a deeper understanding of this fascinating group of conditions.

The book is aimed at three audiences. Firstly the individual who thinks he may have a Personality Disorder or has been diagnosed as having the Disorder. Secondly to the family or friends of the individual concerned. And finally to the many clinicians, including general practitioners and general psychiatrists who frequently meet patients with this disorder. I have tried to provide a useful framework to approach Personality Disorder at these three levels.

The book has a number of objectives:

1. To give a sense of what is happening in the mind and heart of the person with Personality Disorder and how they may affect those around them.
2. To give an example of the trajectory of the individual in treatment.
3. To describe what Personality Disorder Services do, why they do it, and how they may be able to help. What happens in treatment may be perplexing to the public, and professionals in other services, and the book tries to give a behind the scenes look at it. I hope this will make experiencing this condition more understandable, and the thinking of clinicians less impenetrable.

The book is aimed at the interested general reader. I have tried to avoid too much theory. Where the theory remains dense, I invite you to skip that section and simply move on. It is the general sweep of the book rather than any specific detail that is more important.

We'll follow the progress of Nina, a young woman who has been diagnosed as having a Personality Disorder. We'll track how she got to the health service, her pathway through it, and what happens to her. Along the way we'll meet her family, the professionals who come into contact with her, and some of the individuals who she meets in the treatment programme she enters. There are some dramas along the way and we'll see how Nina responds to these and how her story ends. In the course of this hopefully you'll get some sense of the interaction between past and present, genes and environment, and Personality and what has been termed as Personality Disorder.

The breakdown of the book is as follows. Part One covers what Personality Disorder is. Chapters 1–5 follow Nina's introduction to the Personality Disorder service. Through her story and questions, the book covers the 'what' and 'why' questions relating to Personality Disorder. Part Two covers the treatment of Personality Disorder. Through Nina's story and questions as she progresses through treatment this section covers aspects of how Personality Disorder is treated, and what the outcome of the treatment can be. Chapter 8 specifically addresses what the role of family or friends of someone with Personality Disorder can usefully be.

As you will see, Nina has a diagnosis of Borderline Personality Disorder (BPD). Nina is the person we follow most closely in the book and similarly, most of this book will be addressing Borderline Personality Disorder, however we will also deal with other types of Personality Disorder (PD). Nina, as are the other people described in the book is a composite of a number of different individuals and no one character in this book is based on a specific person in real life. However the fictionalised individuals in the book are inspired by patients whose thinking and qualities have touched me. Nina per se is a distillation of several patients. I have chosen her as the main person as she illustrates most clearly aspects of Borderline Personality Disorder through her life history, typical ways of thinking and responding to situations, current difficulties, and relationships.

Each chapter will start with Nina's narrative. A more factual commentary will follow, relating Nina's issues to wider aspects of Personality Disorder. The Frequently Asked Questions format contain actual questions which have been asked by patients in my service. Each chapter ends with some key points. Where possible I have tried to indicate if my statements are evidence based, or generally accepted clinical opinion, or just my opinion.

A Note on Terms Used

Different services and clinicians use different terms for the concept *patient* such as *client* or *service user*. My use of the word *patient* is a conscious one, and one I believe appropriate for individuals who have severe problems related to their personality. My view is that if someone wants to seriously address and possibly change aspects of their personality, this is major piece of work warranted by the individual believing that there is something wrong with them – that there is at some level an *illness*. This implies a level of seriousness and responsibility both on the part of the individual seeking treatment and the treating clinician which I feel is better captured by the term *patient* than, for example, *client*.

I have referred to the patient as *he* when not specifically describing Nina or a female patient. Similarly I have referred to the clinician as *he* unless specifically describing a female clinician.

I've used the heading 'Extra Content' to indicate sections of the book which are not critical to read to get the main message of the book.

PART ONE

What is Personality Disorder?

CHAPTER 1

What Is Wrong With Me?

Nina's Story Part 1–The Trouble With Nina

The woman sitting with the psychiatric nurse has sharply cut hair, and a small turquoise tattoo of a hawfinch bird on her left forearm. Her name is Nina.

She fiddles with her mobile phone and glances regretfully at her pack of cigarettes. She looks troubled. She is talking about Kate, her 16 year old daughter.

Nina is barely audible as she says 'I'm so worried about Kate – that she's getting more and more like me – messed up – that's the last thing I want. Her teacher's been contacting me that she's been missing school. She goes out with boys who are a lot older than her. She stays out late and I hate to think what she gets up to. She never introduces me to these friends of hers. The other night I found a bag of cannabis in her jeans.' She starts weeping. Linda, the nurse working in the Personality Disorder service feels moved. She wonders what to say.

The pathway Nina Kelman took to get to this point is a long one. She is a 34 year old white British woman. She has three children, sixteen year old Kate, four year old Jamie, and Natasha who's three. The two younger children were fathered by Eddy, who is in an on-off relationship with Nina. Presently it is on.

Nina has gone to the Emergency Room at hospital twice in the last 12 months.[1] She had gone to the Emergency Services the first time because of a strong urge to take an overdose of medications. She had become so alarmed that she may follow through on this urge that she had phoned her twin, Claire. Claire had immediately gone over to Nina's house and taken her to the Emergency Room.

The second time, after an argument with Eddy, Nina had locked herself into the bedroom and had swallowed her remaining sleeping tablets.

Eddy had become anxious when Nina refused to open the door and he had broken it down. Nina tearfully told him she'd taken an overdose and Eddy had called for the ambulance to take her to hospital.

After the hospital had checked that there were no serious medical complications from the overdose, a psychiatrist met with Nina. When Nina admitted that she had been self harming since her teens and how she experienced these dramatic and sudden drops in her mood, he suspected that she may be suffering from a Personality Disorder. Nina was now settled enough to go home. The psychiatrist told her he would like to refer her to a service he thought may have a more definitive treatment for her difficulties. He then referred her to the local Personality Disorder service.

We now fast forward 2 months. Nina missed the first two appointments at the Personality Disorder service. Then when she did finally attend an appointment, she left early as she felt the nurse she met was critical of her, especially over the mothering of her children. But she continued to struggle with her relationship with Eddy and the children and out of desperation she decided to try again and she came to the fourth appointment. We join her in this meeting where she was able to stay and talk about her difficulties. I will use Nina's own words to capture the flavour of the issues that were troubling her.

> 'I don't know who I am. I feel like I'm dissolving – one minute I think I know who I'm about, but it doesn't last and I end up feeling all mixed up about me – who I am. For once in my life I wish I could just stand still and have a sense of who I am…. to know me as me.'
>
> 'I end up doing the most crazy things – last month, this man started chatting me up. I'd just dropped off the children at my mother and I felt so spare and empty and didn't know what to do with myself. So when he said 'how about a drink' I knew where this was heading but felt so empty I thought why not? We ended up at some bar – next I know I'm in a taxi and I can't remember much what happened after, but I woke up in some hotel the next day with this total stranger. I'm 35 – I've got 2 young kids that I adore – of course I love Kate too but she's not as cuddly now is she? I can't keep on doing this. Sometimes when I'm bored, I just go out to the high street and buy clothes for myself and the children on credit – I'm getting more and more into debt.'

Nina goes on to talk about Eddy, her partner:

> 'I can't stand it when Eddy's away – I always think he's not going to come back – that he'll leave me. I get this voice saying 'Think he's interested in you? What a joke – look at you. He's probably going to meet some other woman now he's away from you and he'll think she's a lot nicer. Who'd want

you anyway?' Sometimes I phone him 20 times a day – it drives him crazy. I've always been like this – I always think my boyfriend is going to dump me.'

'Eddy and I are like a roller coaster – we argue a lot and we've split up so many times, I can't count them anymore. It's mainly me – I either think Eddy's great and the love of my life and there's never been a better man for me and the next moment I think he's a horrible bastard who keeps on letting me down. Sometimes I know what's set me off – but more often it just seems to come out of the blue. I get so angry with him – like there's this rage. But it's not only with him – it's with the kids, my family, people I don't even know – shop assistants – the anger just spills out.'

'I've been suicidal since I was in my teens – I've always cut myself – but I've taken overdoses too. Now, when I feel stressed I go into the bathroom and cut myself and then I feel lighter…but last night Natasha was outside the bathroom and was calling for me. She's only three but I think she knows something's wrong – she was saying 'Mummy come out. And there I am saying to her 'in a moment sweetie' and I'm bloody bleeding all over…I can't go on like this.'

'The last time I took an overdose was when Eddy was away and he hadn't called back and I was hearing this voice saying out loud to me 'go on, take it- he doesn't love you anyway, no one will ever love you – what's the point?'. I started believing this more and more until taking the overdose seemed the most logical thing to do – it's scary when I just go into that mood and there's nothing I can do about how I feel.'

'My mood is all over the place – one minute I'm happy and then suddenly I feel like everything is spoilt and pointless and I'm a waste of space. I don't know why this happens – it just happens. Last weekend the kids and I were making a cake and my mother phoned. She said something about how I never quite get my cakes to taste like hers (my mother won prizes for her cakes). We chatted a bit more and after I put the phone down, I just said to the children: 'That's it I'm going to have a lie down.' Then Natasha started crying because she wanted to make the cake – I don't know what happened –my mother was just joking wasn't she? I just wanted to shut myself in the room by myself. Why do I keep doing things like this? I'd promised Natasha for weeks that we would make a cake – she'd been singing all week 'me and mummy are going to make a cake' the way kids do, and then I go and spoil it all because of some stupid call from my mother.'

Linda the psychiatric nurse establishes that these difficulties started in Nina's teens and have been present throughout her life. They have adversely affected her in all aspects of her life – in her personal relationships, at school, and at work.

At school Nina had had fractious relationships with teachers, often feeling they were unsympathetic and hard on her. The staff room had had very divergent views on her, some teachers feeling protective towards her

'Oh Nina, she's a handful and can be quite a rebel – but deep down she's a nice kid.' There was however another group of teachers who thought her unacceptably rude and touchy – 'She needs a firm hand or she'll take advantage of you and the situation'.

After finishing school, Nina had shown promise as a teaching assistant and had been offered support for further training. However Nina fell out with her head teacher due to feeling criticised. She had had such an angry outburst one day that she felt too embarrassed to return to work. She regrets this now – 'I loved teaching – the head teacher was fine really – I don't know why I lost it with him – I keep on falling out with people.'

Towards the end of the interview Nina straightens up, looks Linda in the eye and says 'I heard the doctor in the Emergency Services say it's one of those Personality Disorder patients again. What did she mean. Do I have a Personality Disorder? She said it like I have a bad smell.' Linda in turn straightens up, gulps a bit, thinking 'How am I going to respond to this now?'

What is Personality Disorder?

- What's wrong with me?
- Am I mad?
- If I hear voices does it mean I'm mad?
- Is Personality Disorder the same as madness?

These are some of the questions that I will try to answer in this book. In brief, Personality Disorder is not *madness* in the sense that someone is *psychotic,* namely being out of touch with reality as psychiatrists would define it. But some forms of Personality Disorder do show such extremes of thinking, or feelings, or behaviour that people have seriously questioned whether the individual concerned may be frankly out of touch with reality or psychotic. We'll return to this in the brief historical section.

To come to Nina: the difficulties Nina describes suggest she may have a *Borderline* Personality Disorder. This is dealt with in the following section but before we just accept this diagnosis, it's useful to review what is meant by personality and by the term Personality Disorder.

What is Personality?

Personality may be thought of as the consistent patterns of thinking, perceiving and feeling and how these traits are organised to make up a person.[2]

Personality may be understood as the aspects of each of us that make us unique individuals. It is the particular way in which each of us thinks, responds emotionally, behaves and relates to other people – in summary the *pattern* in which we think, feel, behave and relate. The term pattern indicates that we have a usual repertoire of thinking, feeling, behaving and relating. When these patterns are so extreme and/or inflexible that it starts causing distress to the individual or those around him we sometimes consider this person to have a Personality Disorder.

We all have personalities but not all of us have Personality Disorder, although we all probably have some personality traits that can make things difficult for ourselves or those around us. There has been no piece of research which has been able to demonstrate a cut off point at which someone is *Personality Disordered* versus *Not Personality Disordered*. The above two points may be useful in preventing an 'us' vs. 'them' attitude to creep in towards those with Personality Disorder. We all have personalities which can be rather disordered at times. If you think of what you may have said the last time you were stressed in an argument with a loved one you may agree with this point. You may have said: 'I know you don't really love me because if you did, you would have come with me to that work function/family gathering/friend's party' or 'I feel that you don't want to come with me, even if you say you do, and I just know you don't want to come because that's what I feel'. Or you may not have said it – but you may have felt it. And felt it strongly enough that it in some way affected what you then did.

What is Personality Disorder? and What Role Does Culture Play?

The ICD-10 criteria for diagnosing a Personality Disorder is given in the annexure.[3] In essence it requires that the individual's usual way of experiencing and responding to events differs markedly from the cultural norm. This difference from the cultural norm in an individual may be shown in one or more of the following areas – his thoughts, emotions, behaviour and interpersonal relationships. There should also be evidence that there has been an early onset of these differences, that they have persisted throughout the person's life, and that they impact significantly in all parts of his life especially in the big three areas of love, work and play.

Although the previous statements indicate the importance of identifying an individual's difference to the particular culture within which he exists, little research has been done on culture, race and ethnicity in Personality Disorder. The concept of dependence is a good example of this. The concept of dependence is based on social relationships. In

Western societies, individual independence and autonomy are highly valued. In contrast, Japanese society places a value on collective rather than individual action. So what a psychiatrist in London may diagnose as *dependent* may be considered completely normal by a Japanese psychiatrist. Indeed a Japanese psychiatrist may consider *independence* as a disorder.

Again using Japan as an example, cultural factors seem to affect how individuals with Borderline Personality Disorder present. In Japanese society, suicide is more permissible and substance use is uncommon – accordingly Borderline Personality Disorder patients in Japan report more suicidal behaviours and less substance use.[4]

Nina's question as to whether Personality Disorder equates with madness is one which has fascinated clinicians for centuries and is dealt with in the short historical section which follows.

A Short History of Personality Disorder: Mad, Bad or Simply Sad?

Personality has interested us for a long time. Hippocrates, born 460 years BC, described the four *humors,* which are linked with particular personality types:

- black bile with *melancholic* – people who tend to be introverted, serious, and cautious.
- yellow bile with *choleric* – people who tend to be extroverted, excitable, and impulsive.
- phlegm with *phlegmatic* – people who tend to be thoughtful, reasonable, calm, and caring.
- blood with *sanguine* – people who tend to be optimistic and warm-hearted.

The humors were used to explain emotional states in physical terms. For example, when a patient was melancholic, it was assumed that his feelings of sadness and depression resulted from the physical excess of black bile. Likewise if someone was angry and impulsive this was attributed to an excess of yellow bile.

When these humors were in balance the individual was considered to be healthy – when out of balance, disease took over. The aim of medical therapy was to restore humoral equilibrium through diet, exercise, and managing the body's products (for example its blood, urine etc.).

For centuries European society excluded people who were regarded as insane from society. But for people with Personality Disorders, doctors began to realise that some of these patients did in fact have a grasp of reality – it was the intensely strong emotions they experienced, which they felt unable to control, that impacted so destructively on themselves or others.

Thus in the early 19th century, the French psychiatrist Pinel described *manie sans delire* which he felt applied to patients who had tendencies of outbursts of rage and violence but who were not deluded (namely not out of touch with reality).

In 1835 Prichard, referring to Pinel's *manie sans delire*, coined the term *moral insanity* which he defined as a 'morbid perversion of the natural feelings, affections, inclinations, temper, habits, moral dispositions and natural impulses without any remarkable disorder or defect of the intellect or knowing or reasoning faculties and in particular without any insane delusions or hallucinations.'[5] Similar to Pinel these were also individuals who were clearly not insane but who had abnormalities in their feelings, temper, and moral disposition. Some of these individuals would now be considered to have an *Antisocial Personality Disorder*. It is this thread of abnormality within the context of sanity that will continue through the book with the ongoing debate about both the treatment of such patients and the attitudes to them displayed by society and the legal system.

The 'mad', 'bad' or 'sad' tags are sometimes used to characterise the Clusters A, B and C in Personality Disorder diagnoses (see annexure). We can see these tags also describe a way that Personality Disorder has been viewed historically. Firstly, considering if these individuals are 'mad' in a psychiatric sense. Secondly, when madness was ruled out then moving to considering if individuals are 'bad' as lacking some moral capacity or 'sad' as in having depressive aspects to them.

More recently a review of the literature revealed that Personality Disorders, in general, are associated with impairments in:

1. A sense of self. This involves a self understanding or self knowledge, a coherent sense of one's identity and the ability to set and attain satisfying personal goals that give direction, meaning and purpose to life or one's self-directedness.
2. Interpersonal functioning. This involves the capacity for empathy, intimacy and social behaviour.

This is a useful framework for understanding personality and Personality Disorder – how we feel about ourselves and how we get on with others. If we think of how Nina described her problems at the start of this chapter, we can see how she is describing problems in her sense of herself and in her interpersonal functioning.

How do I know if I may have a Personality Disorder?

Nina's questioning of whether she has a Personality Disorder has stymied the best minds in psychiatry for a long time. There have been many problems with the diagnosis and classification of Personality Disorder to date.

With regards to classification these problems include:

1. Most patients diagnosed with one Personality Disorder meet criteria for more than one Personality Disorder. The least we expect out of a classification system is that it places different conditions into different boxes. We would want to know, for example, if someone has asthma rather than pneumonia because the treatment of these two conditions is different. Personality Disorder classification does not allow this.
2. Worse still, even patients diagnosed with the *same* Personality Disorder are very different to one another. If you take a look at the list for diagnostic criteria for Borderline Personality Disorder, you will see that 5 out of 9 criteria are required to make the diagnosis. This means that any two patients may only share one common criterion – and that there are 151 possible combinations of criteria to make the diagnosis! This suggests considerable differences within the group of patients who have a diagnosis of Borderline Personality Disorder.
3. The threshold for making a diagnosis is arbitrary. The threshold of 5 out of 9 criteria needing to be present to diagnose Borderline Personality Disorder was set for DSM-5 simply because 5 is more than half of 9.
4. The criteria for making a diagnosis are difficult to apply with certainty or accuracy. This leads to low agreement between different clinicians on not only the type of Personality Disorder but whether the individual has a Personality Disorder at all!
5. When retesting whether an individual still has a Personality Disorder, very poor stability of diagnosis is found. Yet we know that personality traits are reasonably stable, and that individuals no longer meeting diagnostic criteria are still significantly impaired. This suggests a significant problem as to how the diagnosis is made.

The two major western classification systems are the American Diagnostic and Statistical Manual of Mental Disorders (DSM) and International Classification of Disease (ICD). The ICD is developed by the World Health Organisation and is the system used in the UK.

The ICD system is currently being revised. Proposals for Personality Disorder in the ICD11 are to provide guidelines for the severity of Personality Disorder. There is also a proposal to reduce the number of diagnoses into 4 main domains – dissocial, anankastic (perfectionist), detached and emotional distress or negative emotional.

Although the NHS in the UK uses the ICD system, the DSM system has a major influence on how mental health is thought about, assessed, treated and researched both in the UK and internationally.

While the classification systems are useful to standardise terms, they are also fraught with political, financial and academic agenda. For example, 18 out of 27 of the members of the DSM-5 taskforce had direct links to the pharmaceutical industry.[6]

The proposals in the DSM-5 have also been criticised for medicalizing mental health.[7] Previous definitions described major depressive disorder (MDD) as a persistent low mood, loss of enjoyment and pleasure, and a disruption to everyday activity. However, these definitions also specifically excluded a diagnosis of MDD if the person was recently bereaved. This exception has been removed in DSM-5. The concern is that DSM-5 is *medicalizing grief* – that grief is a normal human process that should not require treatment with drugs such as antidepressants.

Some experts were concerned that the DSM's most recent proposals were too complex, incoherent and inconsistent. Classification systems do offer benefits – notably helping to ensure that the same condition is being discussed – but should not be reified. The recent DSM-5 panel did not manage to agree on a new classification system on Personality Disorder. As a result the DSM-5 section on Personality Disorder is unchanged from the DSMIV section on Personality Disorder. This indicates the complexity and early stage of classification of Personality Disorder. An illustration that classification systems are limited by the context and state of knowledge at the time, is that homosexuality was listed as a 'sociopathic disorder' and remained so until 1973.

To make matters worse, Personality Disorder is not only a contested diagnosis; it is also a stigmatising one. The stigma attached to the diagnosis is starkly shown in a landmark 1988 study on attitudes to Personality Disorder performed on 240 psychiatrists randomly selected from the membership list of the Royal College of Psychiatrists.[8] These psychiatrists were randomly allocated one of 6 case histories and asked how they would manage the patient and how they felt about him. The case history essentially described the same patient who complained of feeling depressed, was requesting a hospital admission, and had thoughts of killing himself by taking an overdose of tablets. A key difference however was that some patients were described as having been previously diagnosed with Personality Disorder, while others were not. Patients who had been given a previous diagnosis of Personality Disorder were seen as more difficult and less deserving of care compared with patients who had not received this diagnosis. Psychiatrists regarded the Personality Disorder cases as manipulative, attention seeking, annoying and in control of their suicidal urges and debts. The authors suggested that Personality Disorder appears to be an enduring pejorative judgement rather than a clinical diagnosis and concluded that the diagnosis of Personality Disorder should be abandoned.

Should the Diagnosis of Personality Disorder Be Abandoned?

My own view is that there will always be a need for a way to conceptualise the condition which is presently captured by the term Personality Disorder – it is part of the human condition. We may coin another term to capture the concept, for example *personality difficulties* or *people with complex needs*. But these terms are just as likely to acquire a pejorative sense if they merely replace the term Personality Disorder.

If we accept there should be a term that captures the condition, then should the term be medicalized into a clinical diagnosis? There is a similar objection to diagnosing bereavement as a medical condition in the DSM-5. Given that people with Personality Disorder seek help from health services and there are now some treatments that have been shown to be effective for the condition, there seems to be some justification for retaining the clinical diagnosis of Personality Disorder. Also, as Personality Disorder is associated with a higher risk of having other psychiatric diagnoses, such as depression, they will need to be screened and treated within the health system.[9]

Regarding Borderline Personality Disorder more specifically, the diagnosis has met the usual standards of validity of a psychiatric disorder. Research has shown the disorder can be discriminated from other disorders, and has its own course, and specific treatment.[10]

In my own clinical practice the usual response of the individual on being informed of their diagnosis is one of relief that there is some formal recognition and understanding of what he has been grappling with for many years. Some of these people have told me that looking at the diagnostic criteria and finding that it matches what they had thought was their unique problem, has been reassuring. This has resonated with the experience I have had in running psychoeducation groups for patients in preparation for joining my Personality Disorder service. To quote a patient: 'I feel so relieved to be with a group of people who have also been diagnosed with Borderline Personality Disorder. Before I thought I was a freak and the only person to have these problems – but to hear that others go through the kinds of experiences that I do makes me feel less as though I'm all on my own'.

However, many individuals do find the experience of being labelled as having a Personality Disorder difficult. This is particularly so with some diagnoses, particularly Narcissistic and Paranoid Personality Disorder. This is possibly related both to the individuals' traits which contribute to the diagnosis being made, and to the more stigmatising and misunderstood nature of these particular disorders.

Since the time of the publication of the article by Lewis and Appleby there have been important developments. There has been a large number of initiatives to further the treatment of Personality Disorder in the UK, resulting in the roll out of numerous Personality Disorder services. The Department of Health documents with titles like 'Personality disorder: no longer a diagnosis of exclusion' encapsulates the more recent progressive approach to Personality Disorder.[11] Thus, contrary to the call to abandon the concept of Personality Disorder, the concept has instead focused thinking, and harnessed resources. There has also been an increasing evidence base for the treatment of Personality Disorder (more on this later).

What is Borderline Personality Disorder?

The criteria required to make the psychiatric diagnosis of Borderline Personality Disorder according to DSM-5 are as follows.[12]

Borderline Personality Disorder is manifested by a pervasive pattern of instability of interpersonal relationships, self-image, and affects, and marked impulsivity, beginning by early adulthood and present in a variety of contexts, as indicated by five (or more) of the following:

1. Frantic efforts to avoid real or imagined abandonment. Note: Do not include suicidal or self-mutilating behaviour covered in (5).
2. A pattern of unstable and intense interpersonal relationships characterized by alternating between extremes of idealization and devaluation. (This is called "splitting.")
3. Identity disturbance: markedly and persistently unstable self-image or sense of self.
4. Impulsivity in at least two areas that are potentially self-damaging (for example, spending, sex, substance abuse, reckless driving, binge eating). Note: Do not include suicidal or self-mutilating behaviour covered in (5).
5. Recurrent suicidal behaviour, gestures, or threats, or self-mutilating behaviour.
6. Affective instability due to a marked reactivity of mood (for example, intense episodic dysphoria, irritability, or anxiety usually lasting a few hours and only rarely more than a few days).
7. Chronic feelings of emptiness.

Table 1: Borderline Personality Disorder Dimensions.

Dimension	Criteria
Thought	Identity, paranoia or dissociation
Affect	Instability, emptiness, anger
Behaviour	Impulsivity, self harm
Relationships	Fear of abandonment, unstable

8. Inappropriate, intense anger or difficulty controlling anger (for example, frequent displays of temper, constant anger, recurrent physical fights).
9. Transient, stress-related paranoid ideation or severe dissociative symptoms.

As written earlier, personality may be thought of in 4 main dimensions. If we reorganise the above in terms of these dimensions then Borderline Personality Disorder may be mapped as in Table 1.

The above is a psychiatric perspective on Borderline Personality Disorder and it could be criticised for being a *cookbook* approach. While reorganising Borderline Personality Disorder into the above table helps in conceptualising the disorder, it still doesn't really explain the disorder in a psychological way. There have been many different attempts to describe Borderline Personality Disorder by understanding the psychological mechanisms involved.

The concept of a 'borderline' condition, somewhere between neurosis and psychosis, was already emerging in the 1880s in psychiatric attempts at classification.[13] However it is psychoanalytic thinking that has really contributed to a more detailed appreciation of the condition. This is well captured in Henri Rey's description of people with this condition being on the borderline of psychosis and neurosis, between male and female, between fear and need for the other person.[14]

Rey's description captures the condition poignantly: 'They complain of an inability to make contact with others and find it impossible to maintain any warm and steady relationship. If they actually manage to enter into a relationship it rapidly becomes intensely dependent and results in disorders of identity. They seldom establish a firm sexual identity and vacillate in their experience of maleness and femaleness...their feelings are dominated by phantasies of relative smallness and bigness. When threatened by feeling small and unprotected and in danger they may defend themselves by uncontrollable rages and various forms of impulsive behaviour. Other aspects of their abnormal affectivity are reflected in the sense of futility they complain of...Together with this deadness there is a search for stimulants and production of sensory experiences by means of alcohol, drugs, cutting themselves, perversions, promiscuity etc. Their underlying state of perplexity and confusion is frequently apparent.[15]

The problems experienced by individuals who have this condition with their sense of their own identity is captured in the terms used by other psychoanalysts to describe them. They have been described as the *as if* personality[16] or the *false self*,[17] Deutsch described the *as if* personality in those people whose superficial social appropriateness hid very disturbed personal relationships. These individuals tended to adopt the qualities of others as a way of keeping their love, giving an as-if or non-genuine feel to their personality.

By now you may be realising that the concept of Borderline Personality Disorder is not an easy one to grasp. We may be helped by using another way of looking at things, namely two mainly psychoanalytic approaches to understanding psychological problems: the *deficit* view versus the *conflict* view.

Two Approaches to Personality – the 'Deficit' and 'Conflict' Debate

The Deficit View

The deficit view points to some lack in the individual which accounts for the difficulties in Borderline Personality Disorder. This brings us to another important concept – that of mentalization.

Mentalization

The deficit or lack may be in *mentalization,* which is the process by which we make sense of ourselves and each other. A *mentalizing* capacity that is very vulnerable to social interactions is a core feature of Borderline Personality Disorder. In other words, the individual with Borderline Personality Disorder has a decreased ability to identify what is in his own mind regarding his thoughts and feelings and what may be in the mind and feelings of the person he is interacting with.

Mentalizing theory is based in the theory of attachment which was developed by the British psychoanalyst John Bowlby. According to attachment theory, the development of the self occurs in the context of early relationships. It follows then that problems in early attachment leads to problems in the development of self. To achieve a normal experience of self, the infant needs his emotional signals to be accurately mirrored by an attachment figure.[18] If this has not been the case, the individual's ability to accurately identify what is in his mind and the nature of his emotions is decreased.

The deficit in identifying what is in the mind or emotional world of the other may arise as follows: the individual with Borderline Personality Disorder has had such an aversive experience with his early carer that it is protective for him to not identify what is in the carers' mind. For example, for the child who is being sexually abused by his father, it seems quite understandable that it may be protective for him to not know what is going on in his father's mind. Unfortunately what was initially a coping mechanism for the child becomes a handicap. In negotiating normal life it is more helpful to know what is in the mind of the other than not to know! For example, when meeting your prospective mother in law it helps if you can have some sense of what is in her mind regarding her view of you as a family member.

Nina's Story Continued

At a time when Nina and Eddy were going through a particularly difficult period, Nina became increasingly frightened that she would be abandoned by him. This had come to a head when Nina wanted Eddy to stay with her and not report for a job which would take him away from home for a few days. We join them at a particularly tense point of their conversation.

> Eddy: I don't know what's got into you, we've known this job has been planned for weeks now, I can't just pull out.
> Nina: But I just know that you're not going to come back.
> Eddy: Why do you say that? I know things have been difficult but at least we've been talking about it – and we've both been saying we want to work on this relationship – that it matters – it does matter to me, I'll be back same as usual when this job's done.
> Nina: But I just feel you won't. That if you leave now, it'll be all spoilt. I know it will. But if you don't go to this job then I'll know you're really committed to staying with me and the children. Don't go Eddy, please.

The discussion goes on for a long time. Nina's position changes. She suddenly becomes very encouraging of Eddy going. Rather mystified at the change in Nina, Eddy asks:

> 'So are you sure it's okay for me to go now?'
> 'Yes of course. I don't mind. I've just been silly. No problem.'

The above description of Nina provides examples of the main deficits in mentalizing. Developers of this theory, Peter Fonagy and Anthony Bateman have used rather technical terms as described below. The concepts themselves though make a lot of sense when applied in our everyday lives.

1. *Psychic equivalence mode:* This is a mode of thinking in which reality is equated with mental states. This is where the person believes that what he is thinking or feeling is unequivocally the truth, the only way to view the situation and that no other perspectives are possible. Nina says there is no doubt Eddy is planning to leave her because she simply feels he will. Nina's belief becomes reality for her, there is no capacity for doubt.
2. *Teleological mode:* When there is an overemphasis on the physical rather than the mental – thus experience is only felt to be valid when there is some physical *proof* of it. Nina requires as proof that Eddy is not planning to abandon her, that he gives up on this work assignment and stays with her instead.
3. *Pretend mode:* When the person's thoughts and feelings lose touch with each other, and with reality. This may result in intellectualising or speaking in a meaningless way. Nina suddenly says its 'not a problem' that Eddy will be going away. We can understand this as Nina still feeling deep down as strongly that she doesn't want Eddy to go away but that there is a disconnect with this feeling and what she thinks and says.

Nina has a mother who was too self absorbed with her own needs and a father who was too absorbed in attending to his wife's needs. This meant that she was raised with insufficient care and attentiveness to adequately develop a sense of herself with an ability to accurately identify her own thoughts and feelings. We develop a sense of ourselves through interaction with others. Think of the delight an infant takes in experiencing his mother's delight in him. His sense of himself as an entity who can be loved is forged in this experience.

The Conflict View

We've just described the deficit view and the way in which Mentalization theory contributes to our understanding of it. Let us now turn to the conflict view.

Otto Kernberg is a prominent psychoanalyst who prefers the conflict view of Borderline Personality Disorder. If we think about it, we all have a mixture of positive, loving and negative, hostile feelings – although it may be more difficult for us to own up to the hostile feelings than the warm loving ones. The conflict for the individual is represented by the positive loving feelings versus the negative aggressive feelings. The person with Borderline Personality Disorder tends to manage this conflict badly – being unable to take a balanced view, he takes either one side or the other.

This split view has a number of consequences which accounts for the psychiatric description of Borderline Personality Disorder above. It leads to identity diffusion which is a difficulty in having a coherent sense of oneself. The split can be so extreme that it can lead the person to temporarily lose touch with reality – leading to severe dissociation or what seems like psychotic episodes. This failure to process aggressive feelings leads to the intense anger and affective instability. The split also leads to a very characteristic tendency for relationships to be unstable, as the individual with Borderline Personality Disorder has very split views of the other person, moving rapidly between idealising to devaluing the other. Thus in Nina's presentation we see her identity diffusion (not knowing what her aims are in her career), her aggression, and very split views of Eddy – one minute he's the most wonderful partner, the next a cheating liar.

So Should I Choose a Conflict or a Deficit Based Approach to My Treatment?

This shouldn't be too much of an issue for the patient when he is seeking treatment. While there are debates about whether the deficit or conflict approach is best, in reality the most effective treatments probably combine elements of both.[19] The ongoing technical debate relates more to the relative proportion and the timing of these two main approaches. What is more important is the coherence achieved by following a particular model and the supervision required to follow a particular model rather than a spurious argument regarding which evidence based intervention is better.

A pragmatic treatment approach may be to keep in mind the importance of attachment. Clearly a degree of attachment is important for the therapy to progress – it will be very difficult otherwise for the patient to discuss painful issues in an open way unless there is some attachment to the therapist or service. Given that the person with Borderline Personality Disorder has a disorganised way of forming attachments and that he may lose the ability to mentalize if attachment issues become too intense, the attachment of the patient to the clinician or the service becomes very important whichever approach is taken.

More Questions on Personality Disorder

So do I only have Borderline Personality Disorder – am I a 'pure' Borderline Personality Disorder?

As described above, most patients with one Personality Disorder meet criteria for more than one Personality Disorder. In Nina's case she does in fact only meet diagnostic criteria for Borderline Personality Disorder.

Ok so I have a Personality Disorder – do I need treatment for it?

This is a difficult question to answer. Reasons for this difficulty lie in the components of the question – what is the nature of personality and Personality Disorder, who is deciding there is a need for treatment, and the nature of the treatment.

Personality (and Personality Disorder) may be viewed as a complex and lifelong way an individual has developed for coping with the world. This would then mean that a lot of these coping mechanisms are *syntonic*, meaning that we are at ease with them; many of them even temporarily lower our anxiety. This means the individual will have an investment in maintaining the status quo and keeping his personality, or his Personality Disorder, intact.

Regarding need, the person concerned may not identify a need for treatment, although others around him may. Thus for example, individuals with an Antisocial Personality Disorder or a Narcissistic Personality Disorder may not themselves identify a need for treatment, or may not put themselves forward for it, while others, like family or professionals, may have a strong view that the individual needs treatment. Even if the individual does himself identify a need, this perception may wax and wane, as may the motivation to address the need.

Regarding the treatment – at present this is a psychological treatment. By its very nature, a psychological treatment does mean that the individual has to contribute actively to the endeavour – it cannot be done passively. Treatment for Personality Disorder is not like simply taking medication in the way that taking an antihypertensive tablet may lower blood pressure.

Given the two above points, (the fact that individuals would often not identify a need to change or would resist changing, and that even if the individual feels the need to change, his motivation may drop), the active contribution of the individual may be too low for him to benefit from a psychological treatment.

Questions to Consider When Starting Treatment

Taking the above factors into account, questions I would ask an individual considering whether to start a therapy are:

What is Troubling You?

If it is something within you or regarding your relationships with others, then this is something which may be addressed in therapy. If on the other hand, what is troubling you are the shortcomings of others – that they are too uncaring/stupid/foreign/unsupportive/ and that the change that is required is that they/the world needs to change then you are not a candidate for therapy which aims to lead to real psychological change in you.

What is the Nature of Your Difficulty?

If you view it as something which is psychological, and which may have some links to your earlier experiences, again this may be addressed in therapy. If you view it as due to physical reasons it is difficult to see how a psychological treatment can address this effectively.

What is the Impact of these Problems?

Is it a big enough problem that you have sufficient motivation to take on therapy? Therapy is difficult. You need to make a commitment to regular attendance for a lengthy period even when you don't feel like attending. After all who really wants to put themselves forward to discuss the things that they find the most difficult and would prefer to keep secret?.

Is it a big enough problem to be worth the potential impact that therapy will have on your life? It will be emotionally draining, and you will feel worse at times. Also if we are talking about changing something as fundamental as your personality, it may have knock on effects on your relationships. You may decide you no longer want to be with your partner. It may however also really deepen your relationship with your partner.

What Do You Expect of Treatment?

Do you expect that it is about addressing something that you will change in yourself and that you will be an active part in achieving this change? Again if your expectation if of a more passive role for yourself this may not auger well for a psychological treatment.

All these questions are not with the aim of putting someone off, or an excuse to not offer therapy. Rather they are asked because the decision to start a therapy is a serious one as it is potentially a life changing one. Therapy can also be a serious waste of the individual's time if they do not enter it with some idea of what it entails. In this case they may either not stick the course, or dutifully stick the course but in such a passive way that they gain little from it. Therapy is more than just attending as in 'punching the clock.' Essentially what the therapy entails is a commitment at both a practical and an emotional level.

Should I Start Therapy Now?

Your question may be: 'Ok, now you've convinced me therapy is a serious business – but should I start it now? I need to get on with my life/work/university course and don't want to delay things by starting on a therapy.'

This is a question that gets asked a lot. And the answer will differ according to the unique circumstances of each person asking the question. It needs a realistic assessment of the impact of the person's present difficulties on their life. If the impact is big enough, it may mean that the individual will need to put his external development on hold so that he can attend to his internal development.

Here are two recent encounters I've had that shed some light on this issue.

Bernard is a 23 year old medical student at Oxford. He came from a family of high achievers and became increasingly stressed that he was not top of his class and struggling with some of his course work. He began to miss lectures and had stopped attending altogether by the time he was assessed in the Personality Disorder service. He was feeling suicidal but did not feel he was at risk of acting on any of these thoughts of harming himself. After his assessment was completed he was offered a treatment but turned it down as he felt he 'had lost a year already and needed to get back on track.'

Mandy is a 35 year old teacher who had been referred to the Personality Disorder service after taking an overdose. She was assessed as having a Borderline Personality Disorder. She had a very critical view of herself which led to sudden drops in her mood. This had a profound impact on both her, and those around her, and she was offered a treatment. However at the final meeting we had arranged to discuss practicalities, she withdrew from the offer of treatment. She had found a private therapist who, although not following an evidence based medicine approach, she felt was helping her. Her boyfriend remained highly supportive, she had successfully started doing some volunteer teaching and she was enrolled onto an advanced teachers course which would make her more competitive on the job market.

Which of these were the correct decisions? I am unsure as both vignettes are partly based on individuals I have seen quite recently. I certainly had more anxiety about Bernard – his desire to return to his studies seemed more based on his need to achieve – which is what had been at the core of why he had developed his problem. I had less anxiety about Mandy's decision – her desire to get back on track was similar to that of Bernard but she seemed to have more realistic reason for thinking she may be able to manage. Her social set up was more secure and full and she had actually taken some positive action. I admit to having qualms about both decisions though. These vignettes do illustrate the principle that the individual has to feel that the time is right for them to enter therapy and this cannot be foisted on him.

How is Personality Disorder Viewed by the Law and Society?

Personality Disorder and the Law

People with Personality Disorder are largely judged by the law to have *capacity*. They therefore do not have the special protections offered to those considered to be insane.

Capacity is the ability of a person to make decisions that may have legal consequences for themselves and/or for others affected by the decision. An example of this approach is the Mental Health Act within the UK.[20] The Act sets out the test for assessing whether a person is *unable to make a decision* and therefore lacks capacity. Four reasons are given why a person may be unable to make a decision:

If they are unable:

1. To comprehend the information relevant to the decision;
2. To retain this information for long enough to make a decision;
3. To use and weigh it to arrive at a choice;
4. To communicate the decision in any way.

This thinking has a link with the evolution of thinking around Personality Disorder. The doctors we mentioned earlier, Pinel and Prichard, were pointing to those individuals who performed extreme, often violent acts which seemed *mad* while retaining their full faculties. If Pinel and Prichard were practising today, and had assessed these individuals for capacity, they would have found it.

The law holds that someone with Personality Disorder has responsibility for their actions and is therefore answerable to the law courts if they commit a crime. The outcome of the trial of Anders Breivik, the mass killer in Oslo in 2011 is a case in point. The initial expert psychiatrists diagnosed that Mr Breivik had a psychotic illness and therefore needed to be placed in a hospital rather than in prison. The psychiatrists who then reviewed Mr Breivik diagnosed a Narcissistic Personality Disorder and found that he did not have a schizophrenic illness.[21] On the basis of this, Mr Breivik faced the criminal Courts. It is useful that the law and psychiatry hold a similar view that individuals with Personality Disorder are responsible for their actions. On another point, this case is a cautionary note regarding the lack of certainty surrounding psychiatric diagnoses.

Personality Disorder and Society

The aspect of personality which has most exercised the public, and hence the politicians' minds, has been the role that personality plays in offending. A telling example of this is the coining of the term *dangerous and severe Personality Disorder* (DSPD) within the UK. Many regard the impetus for the introduction of this new term as political; resulting from high profile cases of extremely violent offending by individuals considered to have a Personality Disorder.

Within the UK, the Dangerous and Severe Personality Disorder programme was established, which allowed for the detention of those suspected of having Dangerous and Severe Personality Disorder if they satisfied all three of the following criteria:

1. They are more likely than not to commit an offence within five years that might be expected to lead to serious physical or psychological harm from which the victim would find it difficult or impossible to recover;
2. They have a significant disorder of personality;
3. The risk presented appears to be functionally linked to the significant Personality Disorder.

This programme is problematic for a number of reasons. Firstly the assessment of risk is notoriously difficult, never mind attempting to predict risk over a 5 year period. Secondly the link between risk and significant Personality Disorder is a difficult one to claim with any certainty. Hence a suspect concept allows for the detention of individuals who are deemed to be at risk of violence. It has been estimated that between 6 and 8 people would need to be detained unnecessarily under this programme in order to detain one who would generally satisfy the risk criterion.[22] This blurs the role of the medical profession –asking them to be custodians of society – to keep it safe rather than focussing on an individual patient and attending to him as clinically appropriate.

The successes and failures of the DSPD programme were reviewed a decade after its introduction. The conclusion was that although much had been gained from the experiment – particularly in developing services for those with personality disorder in general – it has been less effective in managing those whom it was primarily targeting and may not have been cost-effective.[23]

Early on in the book we described a thread that runs through the history of Personality Disorder, namely the difficulty in conceptualising a disorder with extreme emotions and behaviour in which the individual was not psychotic. The controversy around the diagnosis of Dangerous and Severe Personality Disorder and its management shows that society continues to struggle with this dilemma.

Key Points

- The concept of Personality Disorder is one that has been contested. It has many conceptual flaws and requires much more research and refining.
- There is an ongoing debate whether Personality Disorder is a mental disorder. Suffice to say it is not a *madness* as in a chronic psychotic disorder where the problem is an enduring loss of contact with reality.
- With increasing evidence for successful treatment of some Personality Disorders, doctors will be more prepared to view Personality Disorder as a disorder of mental health.
- The label is stigmatising – often intensely so.
- The diagnosis is therefore potentially problematic to make by the clinician, and to receive by the patient and should thus be done with extreme care.
- Whatever problems exist with the concept of Personality Disorder as a diagnosis, there will always be an ongoing need for some shorthand term to describe a group of individuals whose thoughts, feelings and behaviour cause suffering to themselves or to those around them.

CHAPTER 2

Can You Help Me?

Nina's Story Part 2–Help I Need Somebody

Nina is seen over several meetings to complete the assessment. The assessment aims is to get sufficient understanding of what her difficulties are, and what treatment may be helpful. She is asked what are her main problems, how severe are they and how does she hope that treatment can help? These are difficult questions for any of us to answer coherently. They can also be probing and highly personal and stir up a lot of feelings. This indicates why an assessment of someone's psychological difficulties can be a lengthy one.

In Nina's case the process is particularly lengthy for a number of reasons. She can be very prickly in the meetings and it is difficult to get a coherent sense of her story. We have excerpts from the 5th and 6th appointments Nina has with the Personality Disorder service.

Nina's 5th Appointment

Nina arrives 20 minutes late for this appointment. She is unapologetic and sullen. Linda, the psychiatric nurse, is at a loss; she tries various openings but Nina remains detached. Suddenly:

Nina: I don't know why I came today – after last time and what you said.
Linda: I'm glad you did come. What did I say that upset you?
Nina: You can't even remember! Why do you do this job then?
Linda: I'm sorry I upset you. It really wasn't my intention. [pause] can you help me though – can you tell me what I did?
Nina: Well you were having a go at me weren't you.
Linda: I'm not aware of that – can you tell me what I said?
Nina: You told me I had a Personality Disorder!
Linda: I'm very sorry if you felt I was having a go at you. It really wasn't my intention. But I can see that I really upset you. Can we just go back to that meeting to see if we can understand a bit better what was going on?

After a while Nina becomes less angry – and after exploring her experience of the last meeting, it emerges that she felt hurt, rejected and misunderstood – a common experience for her. She had felt so strongly that by informing her that she had a Personality Disorder, Linda was saying something was wrong with her and that she only had herself to blame for this, that she became convinced that Linda was criticising her. This is a common problem in mentalizing – we feel so strongly about something that we convince ourselves it is true. As described previously, this is an example of *psychic equivalence*. We've also come across Nina illustrating this particular problem in her mentalizing earlier in the book, when she had taken as fact, based solely on the strength of her feeling, that Eddy was going to abandon her when he accepted an out of town work assignment.

Nina's 6th Appointment

Nina is less hostile. She has been shouting at her children. She has nearly smacked Natalie on two occasions. She has been self harming more frequently.

Nina leans towards Linda: Ok so I have a Personality Disorder – why has it taken so long for me to get help? Will I get better? Can you help me?

Linda feels grateful that Nina seems less intent on having a fight today and gathers herself to answer.

Will I Get Better?

Nina's questions go to the heart of how Personality Disorder has been viewed in the past and how it can be viewed in the light of present information. Lets address them in turn.

Overall the news is good. Follow-up studies show that that Personality Disorder is less unchangeable and fixed than described in the DSM-5. These studies also suggest that individuals with Personality Disorder tend toward improvement or recovery. A recent study has shown that half of people with Borderline Personality Disorder recovered from the disorder in 2 years; the researchers defined recovery as no longer meeting the criteria to allow the diagnosis of Borderline Personality Disorder, having at least one emotionally sustaining relationship with a close friend or life partner/spouse, and being able to go to work or school consistently, competently and on a full time basis.[24] The same study reported over 90% showed an improvement of symptoms of Borderline Personality Disorder lasting for at least 2 years.

We should however not get carried away by the good news. Another study suggests that while Borderline Personality Disorder consists of symptoms which resolve, other symptoms are more difficult to get rid of.[25] Symptoms reflecting core areas of impulsivity such as self-mutilation and suicide efforts and some interpersonal difficulties such as problems with entitlement seemed to resolve the most quickly. In contrast, emotional symptoms reflecting areas of long term sense of unhappiness such as anger and loneliness/emptiness and interpersonal symptoms of dependency and abandonment such as intolerance of being alone seemed to be the most stable.

Can You Help Me?

There is now evidence that treatment is effective for Borderline Personality Disorder. This has been shown in a study which reviewed 25 studies.[26] Both Cognitive Behavioural Therapy (CBT) and psychodynamic therapy was found to be effective (we'll cover more on treatment later). The improvement (the effect size) from these psychological treatments was of a size which would are as good as, or far better than very impressive drug trials.[27]

There have also been studies reported on specific treatment approaches which have shown that people with Borderline Personality Disorder benefit from treatment. This is relevant because if you, or someone you know, are seeking treatment for Borderline Personality Disorder, it is important to know if there is an evidence base for the approach the therapist is using. So there is an evidence base for Transference Focused Therapy (TFP), Mentalization Based Treatment (MBT), Dialectical Behavioural Therapy (DBT), Schema Focused Therapy (SFT) and Cognitive Analytic Therapy (CAT). Transference Focused Psychotherapy and Mentalization Based Treatment are psychodynamic therapies, Dialectical Behavioural Therapy and Schema Focused Therapy are forms of cognitive behavioural therapy, and Cognitive Analytic Treatment is a combination of both psychodynamic and cognitive behavioural approaches.

Within the UK, the Department of Health has issued guidelines on Borderline Personality Disorder and Antisocial Personality Disorder (ASPD).[28,29] The guidelines are infused with a sound psychological understanding of Borderline Personality Disorder. For example it emphasises that care should be person-centred, and take into account patients' needs and preferences. It stresses the need for informed decisions, good communication, and families' and carers' involvement. It lays importance on access to services, autonomy and choice. Its emphasis on developing an optimistic and trusting relationship, managing endings and transitions underline the importance of attachment difficulties in individuals with Borderline Personality Disorder. It also brings general Mental Health Services firmly into the frame, recommending that general psychiatric teams have a role in the assessment and treatment of patients with Personality Disorder. It recommends that psychological treatment needs to have an explicit and integrated theoretical approach, be well structured and have a coherent theory of practice. It also recommends that brief psychotherapy (of less than 3 months) should not be considered.

Whatever the form of treatment, one of the most important ingredients for successful psychological treatment is the willingness of the individual to undertake difficult emotional work. After all, the treatment is about undoing aspects of one's personality – ways of thinking, feeling, behaving and relating which have become very familiar old ways of coping, even if not the most helpful. If you, or a family member is considering treatment it is worth recognising that there will both be some resistance and ambivalence to change. This will occur during periods of the treatment even with the best intentions and effort at change.

It may also be worth recognising that psychotherapy is about the individual changing certain aspects of himself rather than an expectation that others around him will change. What then requires consideration is whether the individual feels sufficiently unhappy with how he is that he wants to enter into what will be very difficult work. If we don't feel sufficient discomfort, there's insufficient incentive to persevere with the difficult task of changing aspects of ourselves. It is not easy work to face reality – to face hurtful thoughts and feelings that would be far easier to avoid, either consciously or unconsciously.

It does point to how brave it is for individuals to put themselves forward to do difficult psychological work. It could be considered as the psychological equivalent of what one has to do to earn the Victoria Cross.

So the question that may be best asked is 'Can you help me to help myself?' (and for this to occur requires some ability to take responsibility).

Can You Cure Me?

This is a question that is often asked in my service. It is an interesting question and depends on what you mean by *cure*.

Maria, a 47 year woman originally from Southern Spain, had a lengthy assessment in the Personality Disorder service. The main reasons for the length of the assessment was the number of missed appointments as she said she was feeling physically unwell, although it was difficult to get a clear understanding of what the ailment actually was. The assessment was finally completed and Maria was recommended for therapy. On attending the first meeting of the psychoeducation group, the preparatory stage of the treatment, Maria enthusiastically said she expected a complete change in her personality to occur in the treatment, akin to having a brain transplant. Indeed she became transfixed on the thought of having a brain transplant, believing that the therapeutic work would be the psychological equivalent of physically having a brain transplant. The therapist pointed out to her that even if it were physically feasible to have a brain transplant it would rather defeat the purpose as Maria would no longer be Maria. She seemed strangely unphased at the prospect.

It transpired that Maria had such a critical view of herself that the thought of losing the essence of herself was a welcome prospect. She also had such a hopeless and pessimistic view of her ability to effect any change herself that she was hoping for cure to be effected in some magical way upon her in which she would be a passive recipient. Maria dropped out of therapy after a desultory 5 months. In retrospect the treating team thought that the main reason for the failure of her treatment had been in a mismatch in terms of what Maria had defined as 'cure' and the expectations of her treating team.

So if you mean by *cure* 'can you change me completely, make me a new person' the answer is a clear 'no'. Our personality traits are deeply embedded – the aim in therapy is to either moderate them or make you sufficiently aware of what you may be inclined to think, feel or do, so that you are more able to consider alternatives. In any case this is not what I'd be aiming to do as a psychotherapist treating a patient. Aspects of our personality constitute the essence of us – what makes us unique – so the approach is rather to build on the positive aspects and take more control of the negative aspects.

If you mean by *cure* can therapy help me to make significant qualitative changes to my life – in how I manage being in a loving relationships, or in how I work, or in how creative I am with my leisure time my answer is 'yes' – with the rider that for this 'cure' to occur, requires a lot of motivation and work from the individual. There is no guarantee of this 'cure' but my experience has been that when individuals really do make an effort within a good treatment setting, they do improve.

Key Points

- Personality is stable but we are not set in stone – there is always the possibility of change.
- Personality Disorder can 'burn out' in some (but not all) individuals. What therapy can achieve is to shorten the time period during which the

disorder has the most devastating impact on the individual, making it less damaging for themselves and those around them.
- There is evidence for effective treatment of Personality Disorder.
- Before starting therapy it is worthwhile asking yourself.
    - Are you really up for what will be difficult work.
    - Are you really up for a treatment that may lead to major changes in your life. This may include how you relate to your family or even lead to decisions. about starting or ending the relationship with your partner. After all we are talking about changing fundamental aspects of your personality.
    - Have you thought what it is you want to get out of therapy? If not, it still may be helpful to meet with a health professional to help you formulate what it is you want to address.

CHAPTER 3

How did I get here? Why do I have a Personality Disorder?

Nina's Story Part 3–Getting to Know Her

Nina is telling her therapist about some of her early background. It is an account which is far more entangled than the rather neat summary below. Nina delivers it with hesitations, whispers, tears, detours – all the accompaniments of a painful hurting life in all its intimate details.

Her parents are Cressida, a 56 year old teacher at secondary school and Richard, 59 an accountant. Nina has a twin sister Claire and younger brother, Paul, 30. Claire is the success of the family, a solicitor with 2 young children and in a stable marriage. Paul is a clerk in his father's business. He is back living with his parents after a failed relationship ended 3 years ago.

Nina describes an early memory of her mother:

> 'My mother always wanted to be so proud of me. In primary school I was once Mary in the Nativity play. I was so excited to be chosen, and so was my mother – she told all the neighbours. But on the day I felt ill and didn't want to do it but Mum said she'd be so disappointed if I didn't so l said that I would. But I was running a temperature and wasn't enjoying it and then I forgot my lines. Mum was sitting in the front row – I looked at her because I was feeling so upset – just wanting her to say it's ok. But her face was horrified and furious. I've never forgotten that look on her face. She was still angry with me on the way home, saying she'd never felt so embarrassed and I'd let her down in front of the whole school. I still remember her words: 'I was really so proud of you Nina – for once you were doing something good – and then you mess up the chance – well that's just typical of you isn't it – making me look a fool in front of all those parents'. I felt so ashamed of myself. I let her down – but I was just a child and I was sick – I really was – I couldn't help it could I? Maybe it is my fault though – maybe I could have tried harder as my mother said I should – I don't know..if only I hadn't forgotten my lines – or felt sick on that day of all days.'

Nina's father seems to have been eclipsed by his wife. Nina has few distinct memories of him in her early childhood. She remembers one incident when she had returned from school at the age of seven, flushed with excitement at having learnt a new ballet step. Her mother had initially attended to her. But when Nina carried on and on, as young children do, her mother had snapped 'Oh for god's sake Nina I've looked already, can't you see I'm busy now' Nina, stung at being shouted at when she had been so proudly dancing, looked to her father for support. Her father had said 'listen to your mother Nina, there's a good girl' and had gone into the study to read, as he often did when there was tension in the household.

Nina has warm memories of her grandparents on her father's side. Her Finnish grandmother would knit her jumpers with images of reindeer that she loved. Her grandfather would take her into his shed where he kept his beloved books on birds and open up a magical world for her with his interest in wild life. Nina had the tattoo of the hawfinch done a few months after he died – it had been his favourite bird and even now she draws comfort from looking at it.

At the age of nine Nina was sexually abused by her uncle Lawrence, her mother's younger brother. The abuse continued for several months before Nina felt able to tell her mother. Cressida disbelieved Nina at first but when Nina's twin sister, Claire, also said that Lawrence had abused her in the past she finally accepted this as true and cut off ties with her brother.

Nina had initially enjoyed school but around of the time of her sexual abuse, she started missing classes and never quite fitted in again. She still has fond memories of her primary school head teacher, but she hated her secondary school. She limped along academically, achieving grades well below her potential. She and Claire had managed to remain close even though teachers often used to say to Nina despairingly 'Why can't you be a bit more like Claire?'

Nina gravitated towards the wilder set at school, experimenting with street drugs and drinking heavily. During this period she started cutting her wrists at times when she felt very upset. A teacher noticed this once and enquired about it. Nina denied anything was wrong, or that she had done anything to herself and the teacher, flustered, had dropped the issue. She then started cutting on her thighs to avoid detection. Around this time Nina was also marched off to the family medical practitioner by her worried mother. This doctor had known the family for years and was fond of Nina but was unable to get to the bottom of things with an adolescent who was now sulky and withdrawn. The doctor started her on antidepressant medication which Nina took irregularly.

Despite being an erratic student, Nina managed to get reasonable grades in her final school exams. She worked as a voluntary teaching assistant for a few months but fell out with the head teacher. She then applied for a place to study English at university. She started off with great anticipation but, as had happened at school, she developed difficult relationships with the faculty department, fell behind in her assignments and dropped out after the first 9 months. She met and moved in with one of her lecturers, and became pregnant with Kate at age 18. The relationship was violent and stormy and ended after 5 years. Since then Nina has had numerous partners, the relationships marred by turbulence, and a constant fear that she would be abandoned. She met Eddy 5 years ago and has had her two younger children with him. Jamie was conceived a week after she met Eddy.

A constant source of support throughout this time was the ongoing close relationship she has with Claire. Nina has always been able to be quite open with her, even at times when she felt her life was in a mess.

Why do I Have a Personality Disorder?

Patients in my service often ask this question. Here is an account of my recent encounter with May:

May is a young woman of Anglo Spanish descent, who had recently been dismissed by her firm of solicitors based in the City of London. She had been referred to the Personality Disorder service after presenting to the Emergency Services with overwhelming thoughts of wanting to kill herself. She was diagnosed as having a Borderline Personality Disorder and offered treatment within the local Personality Disorder service. A major factor in her early history was her extremely cold and demanding parents. While she lacked for nothing materially, her memory of her childhood was of endless extra lessons and a stern father who was displeased if she slipped from being top of her class. During the introductory part of the treatment, she was in a group where Personality Disorder was being discussed. On hearing that Borderline Personality Disorder is the result of both genes and early experience the young woman burst into tears.

'So it is my parents' fault then. It hurts me to hear that. So why am I to blame? I am not a bad person but I am made to feel I am a bad person'

The above response illustrates the complexity of trying to work out the 'causes' of May's problems. In some ways it could be seen as the parents' 'fault' – due to both their genetic endowment and the environment they established for May as a child. Possibly the use of the word 'fault' makes things even more difficult in May's mind. May's parents bear some (but not all) responsibility for May's difficulties but they are not at 'fault'

– which has a moralistic ring to it. It is easy to see the progression of May's thinking – from 'fault' to 'blame' to 'badness'. [30]

With respect to Nina, while there are aspects to her history which contribute to her developing Borderline Personality Disorder, it is important to note that there is no single aspect which can be said to be the dominant contributing factor. Our personalities are the result of an interplay between the genes we inherit and the environment that we grow up in – we are the result of nature and nurture. In essence, no one cause has been identified.

Estimates for heritability of both normal and abnormal personality trait domains are usually around 50%.[31] A study has shown that Borderline Personality Disorder was considerably more frequent among the identical twins of borderline patients than they are in the general population.[32]

We've said earlier that personality is enduring. This is borne out by research. By school age, children's personality structure is similar to adults, and as early as age 3 years, personality traits are moderately stable and their stability increases across the lifespan until at least age 50. [33,34]

Regarding the environment: It seems intuitive that the individual's early childhood experience will have a bearing on how his personality develops. Research has shown that risk factors for the development of Personality Disorder include: childhood neglect or abuse (physical or sexual), early parental loss (due to death or divorce), and multiple caretakers as can happen in foster care. However not all children who have gone through this develop Borderline Personality Disorder. Moreover, some people who grow up in 'normal' families without any clear hardships in childhood go on to develop Borderline Personality Disorder. This fact is important to keep in mind as parents or other family members may have an unwarranted sense of guilt regarding why their loved one developed Borderline Personality Disorder.

Nina's sister is an identical twin, she grew up in the same household, she had similar friends and went to the same school, yet Claire did not develop Borderline Personality Disorder. This is clear evidence that there is no one set of conditions that inevitably leads someone to develop Personality Disorder. Current thinking is that although it is important to try to work out the influence of the environment or genetic factors on developing Borderline Personality Disorder, it is more important to work out the way in which the two interact. In Claire's case, she was also sexually assaulted as a child but did not go on to develop Borderline Personality Disorder. This illustrates the point that childhood sexual abuse is neither a sufficient, nor a necessary factor for the development of Borderline Personality Disorder.

Two evidence based psychological treatment approaches, Mentalization Based Treatment (MBT) and Transference Focused Psychotherapy

(TFP) have developed a way of understanding how early experience influences the child's personality.

Mentalization Based Treatment places emphasis on the child's attachment experience with the caregiver. In attachment theory, the development of a sense of self occurs in the context of how emotions are regulated within early relationships. It follows then that disorganisation of how attachment occurred leads to disorganisation of the sense one has of oneself.

Transference Focused Psychotherapy: In the case of Borderline Personality Disorder, the American psychiatrist and psychoanalyst, Otto Kernberg proposed that excessive feelings of aggression in the young child leads to an excessive splitting of positive and negative aspects of oneself and others. This results in the person with Borderline Personality Disorder being unable to have a realistic and balanced view, instead oscillating between extremes of good and bad. In Nina's case it is possible that being brought up by a mother who disregarded her emotional needs may have led to feelings of rage in her as a young child which she managed by compartmentalizing these difficult feelings to try to control them. This compartmentalizing could have taken the form of driving the rageful feeling underground namely into the unconscious, so that Nina was not aware of it. Does this all sound farfetched and fanciful? We all have an innate sense of what is fair – and that this sense of justice may be even stronger in us as children. If a child senses he is being treated unfairly by an all powerful adult what is he to do with the strength of that feeling? It seems to make sense that he has to hide it in some way – even from himself.

So What's More Important – My Genes or How I Was Brought Up?

The debate over whether nature or nurture is more important is redundant. Anyone who's been a parent or who has witnessed someone parenting can well see that a baby who is impossible to settle (is fretful, inconsolable, doesn't feed or sleep regularly) can evoke an exasperated response from the most loving person. In this way a child with a more challenging temperament may evoke a response from his parent that escalates the problem further – nature influences nurture.

This works both ways. Nature influences nurture, but nurture can in turn influence nature. A series of studies by a researcher, Kandel (on the marine snail *Aplasia*) showed that brain synaptic connections are strengthened and permanently altered through regulation of gene expression connected with learning from the environment.[35] This implies that the brain's hardwiring is influenced by the environment. Kandel suggests that psychotherapy may make similar neuroanatomical changes so that psychotherapy is a form of learning which produces alterations in gene expression and thus changes the way our synapses connect.

The implication of this is that psychotherapy can literally 'mess with your brain' and that undertaking a 'talking treatment' is a serious step, and not a 'light intervention' compared to taking medications or undergoing surgery. Psychotherapy can perhaps be seen as a form of 'virtual' brain surgery. Words, or interactions, if sufficiently emotionally significant can have as much effect over the brain as a pill or the scalpel.

Attachment: What's the Big Thing About It?

Why do you keep on asking me questions about my childhood and my relationship with my parents and extended family?

In this section we'll review key aspects of attachment theory as it is a useful way to think of personality, Personality Disorder, and generally just how we relate to others. Attachment styles are stable, leading to enduring strategies of regulating emotion and social contact. Just look at the attachment patterns described below and I think you'll appreciate just how it allows us all some understanding of how we, or our loved ones, relate to one another.

John Bowlby (1907–1990), a British psychoanalyst believed that attachment seeking is instinctive and a primary human motivation. Attachment theory refers to a person's characteristic ways of relating in intimate relationships to 'attachment figures'. These attachment figures may be one's parents, or romantic partners.[36] From birth, the infant's interactions with his primary caregivers establishes a base for personality development. These interactions mould subsequent close relationships, for example how much you expect to be accepted socially, or how you respond to rejection. Based on repeated interactions with significant others, the child creates a set of mental models of himself and others ("internal working models" or an inner template). These early attachment relations are crucial for being able to manage emotions and stress, control one's attention, to mentalize, and for the infant's sense of having some control over things and people around him (giving him his sense of self-agency).

<u>Studies on attachment in babies</u>

Attachment theory has undergone a significant amount of research – certainly more than other areas of psychodynamic thinking. This theory and research is helpful in identifying the patterns of attachment we have, not only as children, but in our adult lives as well.

A laboratory procedure, the Strange Situation, was used to study one year old infants' attachment behaviours.[37] The Strange Situation is a 20-minute drama in eight episodes. Mother and infant are introduced to a laboratory playroom, and then joined by an unfamiliar woman. While the stranger plays with the baby, the mother leaves and then returns. A second separation follows when the baby is completely alone. Finally, the stranger and then the mother return.

When briefly separated from their mother and left with a stranger in this unfamiliar setting, infants show certain behavioural patterns. Distinct attachment patterns have been identified, the main divide being between *secure* and *insecure* attachment patterns.

The *securely* attached baby plays happily while mother is present, regardless of whether the stranger is present or not. The baby becomes distressed when the mother leaves and seeks immediate contact with her on her return, becoming quickly calmed down. The baby treats his mother and the stranger differently.

Variations of *insecure* attachment are resistant/ambivalent, and avoidant.

The *resistant/ambivalent* baby is distressed when the mother leaves, seeks contact on her return but does not settle easily, simultaneously shows anger and resisting contact.

The *avoidant* baby ignores his mother and is indifferent to her play. He is little affected by his mother's presence and treats his mother and the stranger similarly. This infant is less anxious at separation, and may not seek contact with his mother on her return.

Studies on attachment in adults

Attachment has also been studied by asking adults about their attachments when they were children, using the Adult Attachment Interview.[38] In the interview, parents were asked open ended questions about their attachment relations in childhood and how these may have influenced their development. Three different attachment styles were identified: secure/autonomous, anxious/preoccupied and avoidant/dismissing. Many of the signs of insecure attachment resemble the symptoms of Personality Disorder.

In the *secure/autonomous style*, the adult is able to give a clear and coherent account of early attachment (even if they have not been satisfying).

In the *anxious/preoccupied* style the adult speaks of many conflicted memories about attachment but does not draw them into an organised consistent picture. This adult will show confusion, anger or fear in relation to the early attachment figures. This corresponds with a *hyperactivation* of the attachment system with increased proximity seeking, and translates into the individual being hypersensitive to signs of possible rejection or abandonment and to the increase of negative emotions. In contrast to dismissing individuals, preoccupied individuals are likely to have a lower threshold for perceiving threats around them. They are likely to be over dependent and care seeking. We can recognise these tendencies in Nina when she becomes anxious that Eddy will leave her. Individuals with a preoccupied style are vulnerable to developing borderline, histrionic, dependent or avoidant Personality Disorder. Studies have shown that 50–80% of Borderline Personality Disorder patients fit either the preoccupied or unresolved attachment styles.[39]

Adults with an *avoidant/dismissing* style will lack coherence in their stories, have few specific memories and either idealise or devalue early relationships. These adults are unable to remember much about attachment relations in childhood, In some, parents were idealised on a general level but influences of early attachment experiences on later development denied. Specific memories suggested episodes of rejection. These individuals *deactivate* the attachment system by not seeking closeness to others and trying to handle stress on their own. These individuals also tend to deny threats around them. They thus usually have a higher threshold for experiencing negative feelings or the need to attach to someone. They try to manage negative emotions on their own rather than involving others. These individuals try to inhibit negative emotions by regulating them in a way which is not interpersonal. The deactivation of the attachment system shown by dismissing individuals is associated with narcissistic, antisocial and paranoid Personality Disorders.

Further work has revealed a fourth pattern of disorganized attachment, which is often termed *unresolved/disorganized* for adults and *disoriented/disorganized* for infants.

The attachment styles from the infant Strange Situation and the Adult Attachment Interview correspond at a conceptual level. In addition, adult patterns were empirically correlated with infant patterns. So, for example, a dismissing parent tended to have an avoidant infant.[40]

Table 2 illustrates how the Infant Strange Situation, Adult Attachment Interview and DSM-5 categories relate to one another.

The above are examples of insecure attachment. So what is required for a secure attachment to form? The most important factor in developing a secure attachment is the presence of a primary caretaker who is sensitive to the infant's verbal and nonverbal cues and responds to them appropriately. 'Appropriately' means that the parent shows that he has an understanding of the infant's emotional world but marks it in a way that allows the infant to realise the feeling is not originating in the adult. Think of the last time you were in the park and a toddler fell off the swing – how the mother will pull all kinds of sorrowful faces when her beloved child is

Table 2: Links between the Infant Strange Situation, Adult Attachment Interview and DSM-5.

Infant Strange Situation	Adult Attachment Interview	DSM-5
Secure	Secure/Autonomous	
Resistant/Ambivalent	Anxious/Preoccupied	Borderline, Histrionic, Dependent or Avoidant Personality Disorder
Avoidant	Avoidant/Dismissing	Narcissistic, Antisocial or Paranoid Personality Disorder
Disorganised	Unresolved	Borderline Personality Disorder

wailing: in essence the parent is signifying to child: 'You are distraught. I realise that, look at my face, I am also showing distress. But the mother is signalling by the possibly comical look on her face: 'Can you see it is slightly different to yours.' The mother is suggesting to her distressed toddler – 'I am representing for you *your* emotion, not mine, and in doing it in this way I am helping you to have a mental representation of that dreadful feeling you are having, and see, it's not so bad, it's not so bad.' It is this *marked contingency* on the caring, but not overwhelmed parent's part, which is done a trillion times in the course of a loving parenting, which allows the baby to build a mental representation of their emotional states. It is this representation which someone with Borderline Personality Disorder lacks, and in some ways it is the role of therapy to help the individual build up this representation – so that they can start to accurately identify the inchoate feelings they are having. This points to the mammoth task in therapy – to address in the space of an hour's therapy session the gap of the trillion appropriate responses of the loving parent.

This brings us back to why the emphasis is on attachment in this book and in the minds of so many clinicians working with individuals at a psychological level. Individuals who grow up self reliant and stable have had parents who are supportive when called upon but also allow and encourage autonomy. The inheritance of mental health through family culture may be even more important than genetic inheritance. A final word to Bowlby, who concluded that to grow up mentally healthy, 'the infant and young child should experience a warm, intimate and continuous relationship with his mother (or permanent mother substitute) in which both find satisfaction and enjoyment.[41]

What implications does attachment theory have for treatment? There are several, the main one being that insecure attachment leads to an impaired internal state lexicon for the individual. Therapies therefore usefully include a component that allows patients to recognise, name and communicate their feelings. Specific evidence based treatments for Borderline Personality Disorder – notably Mentalization Based Treatment, Transference Focused Psychotherapy and Schema Focused Therapy are informed by attachment theory.[42]

Why Do You Keep on Asking Questions about My Present Family Set Up?

The context of the patient, specifically the social context in which he lives, is important to understand as it provides more understanding of the individual. It also helps identify whether the family system keeps the patient from needing to change. This may occur because the system has adapted in order to accommodate the patient's difficulties. This is often such an important factor that a particular psychological approach – systems-orientated or family therapy – specifically targets this.

We will meet Paul, Nina's brother later in the book. We'll discover that Paul has a Dependent Personality Disorder. An important question concerning Paul's dependency on his parents is how much they accommodate this aspect by allowing him to relate to them in this way. There is very little incentive for Paul to change his dependent ways. If Paul were in therapy the home situation would be an immediate threat to the treatment. Why should Paul do uncomfortable work in changing his dependency patterns if he is allowed to continue his dependent behaviour at home?

So How Does All This Link With Treatment?

The closest links are with 2 specific forms of treatment for Borderline Personality Disorder – Mentalization Based Treatment and Transference Focused Psychotherapy, both of which place emphasis on attachment.

Mentalization is the process by which we make sense of ourselves and each other through being able to identify what thoughts and feelings we, and others, are experiencing. The concept is rooted in attachment theory: our understanding of ourselves, and of others, depends on whether we had an experience as babies of being understood by caring and attentive adults. Individuals with Borderline Personality Disorder have a particular tendency to lose their ability to mentalize when under stress and it is the objective of Mentalization Based Treatment to increase the individual's ability to mentalize when stressed or, when it is not possible to mentalize 'live' in the stressful situation, at least restore this ability as soon as possible.

Within Transference Focused Psychotherapy, which uses as its premise how the individual represents himself or others, there is the recognition that these representations are derived from the attachment relationships with caregivers. Thus if the parent has been abusive to the individual when a child, the individual may grow up with an inner representation of himself as being a victim and of others as his persecutors. This inner representation may then play out in his relationship both to himself and to others.

Is My Personality Disorder Due to My Sexual Abuse?

This is an important question and one that professionals often get wrong. What is most important to remember is that the occurrence of sexual abuse does not equate with developing a mental illness or a Personality Disorder. Other factors, like the quality of the family environment and the nature of life events after the abuse also play an important part in the psychological effects on the individual concerned. About one third of sexually abused children are symptom free. However of those affected, the problems associated with sexual abuse occur on many levels – from emotional disorders (such as anxiety disorders, PTSD or Depression), to behaviour problems (such as aggressive behaviour, self-destructiveness or alcohol/ substance abuse) to social adjustment (such as teenage pregnancy or sexual problems).

There is often a history of sexual abuse in patients with a diagnosis of Borderline Personality Disorder but many patients with this diagnosis have not been sexually abused. So sexual abuse is neither necessary nor sufficient for Borderline Personality Disorder to develop.

Why Has it Taken So Long for Me to Get Help?

Problems here lie in the lack of knowledge both in the community and in professionals – both at primary level care (the family doctor) and in mental health services themselves. There may also be problems in the lack of clarity of pathways to care for these individuals to receive proper treatment.

At community level, the individual and their family may not recognise Personality Disorder or that the individual's symptoms need treatment. So they may not even seek help. Even when they do seek help with their family practitioner, the confusing way in which the individual presents to the doctor may lead to missing the diagnosis. For example, individuals may present saying they are feeling depressed and be misdiagnosed as having the type of depression which responds to treatment with antidepressant medication. Or these individuals may present with bodily complaints and physical symptoms when their problem is more linked to their mind. So there may be problems both in individuals not presenting themselves, and when they do, in the diagnosis being missed.

The problem does not stop here. Even if the diagnosis has been made, there has been a widespread belief in professionals that individuals with Personality Disorder cannot be successfully treated. This has led to a form of therapeutic nihilism where some psychiatrists actually decide to exclude patients with Personality Disorder from their list, in the belief that they can offer nothing to them. A factor which added to this attitude is the difficult way in which individuals with Personality Disorder interact – often making others dislike them (as shown in the study on the attitudes of British psychiatrists described above), and as can be seen in some of the interaction between Nina and Linda.

Nina's problems manifested at school, and also to the family medical practitioner. The fact that more definitive action wasn't taken either by the teacher or the family doctor, for example a referral to assess if psychological treatment was indicated, indicates the difficulty these professions face in dealing with sensitive issues, in this case an adolescent's development and possible self harm. Adolescence is a stormy emotional period for many already – how does one decide where 'healthy' storming ends and Personality Disorder begins? We'll come to this again when we think about the issue of 'emerging Personality Disorder'.

This means that the journey that individuals with Personality Disorder take before getting care is often tortuous, with many false trails.

Key Points

- Our personalities are developed through nature and nurture in more or less equal amounts.
- Neither nature or nurture lead to inevitable consequences – our lives are dynamic and we can make decisions or behave in a way which leads to change. This is a view which informs psychological treatment – we can effect change.
- Our ability to change is restricted as traits have developed due to our inherited temperament and early experiences. Restricted but not negligible – there is space for us to manoeuvre to actively change aspects of our personality.

- The different views of personality development – whether it mainly explained by a 'deficit' view (a lack or something missing in us) vs. a 'conflict' view (when we are torn between opposing options) informs the different therapeutic approaches.
- Sexual abuse is neither necessary nor sufficient for Borderline Personality Disorder to develop.
- There are many reasons why there may be a delay in getting help for Personality Disorder. These include a failure to recognise the problem (this may occur at the level of the person and family concerned, or at the level of actual contact with services). Even when the problem is accurately identified, the professional concerned may not have the appropriate stance or training to offer treatment, or the appropriate service to refer to.

CHAPTER 4

Stop Messing Around. What is Really the Matter With Me?

Nina's Story Part 4–Getting to Know Her More

After an extended period of assessment with the Personality Disorder service, Nina disappeared from view for several months. She did not respond to follow up letters. After 7 months she recontacted the Personality Disorder service requesting a further appointment and indicated that she wanted to engage in treatment. The Personality Disorder service was pleased to hear from her again and after due consideration, set up a meeting with her.

It emerged that there had been a significant development. Eddy had finally felt unable to cope with Nina's mood swings and had gone to live with his brother. He has kept in contact with Nina and was still supporting the children. Nina had predictably felt abandoned, had started drinking heavily and snorting cocaine again. Social services had become concerned about the children.

Nina is now saying to Linda: 'I've got to sort things out now – or I'm going to lose the kids.' Nina is even more worried than previously about Kate, whose behaviour is getting worse. She is truanting, has been very moody and angry at home, is hanging out with an older set of friends who are themselves troubled and have dropped out of school. She has also started head banging when feeling frustrated. Nina recognises this as reminiscent of how she was as a teenager.

The Psychological Formulation: How Can I Understand What Is Wrong With Me?

To respond to Nina's question, at the end of the assessment our psychological understanding of her problems, our formulation, is discussed with her.[43] The key parts of the formulation are that:

- Nina may have had some constitutional vulnerability as her mother may also have had personality traits which led to difficulties.

- It is likely that in her infancy, Nina's mental state was not adequately understood by her parents. Her early experiences of neglect and abuse have led to a disorganised attachment. This presently shows in how Nina sometimes avoids and keeps a distance from her loved ones, whereas at other times she rushes into intimate situations or is cloyingly close. Nina's problems seem understandable given her experience of parents who seem to have been uncaring and inattentive. However it is worthwhile remembering that problems can occur for the individual in even the most benign and loving of environments.
- From a Mentalization Based Treatment perspective, this disorganised attachment has also led to mentalizing difficulties so that Nina has difficulty in making sense of herself and others. An example of this is when Nina had felt Linda was criticising her when she discussed her diagnosis of Personality Disorder with her. Nina has such an overwhelming tendency to anticipate being blamed or having fault found with her, based on her early experience with a harsh and critical mother, that she felt she was being criticised by Linda. As the strength of this feeling was so powerful, she then felt it to be true so that for Nina her inner reality became *the* reality. Based on this belief she then incorrectly reads what Linda is thinking and feeling, ending up believing that Linda's intention is to blame and find fault with her. These mentalizing difficulties in turn contribute to Nina's problems in regulating her emotions, focusing her attention, and maintaining some self control.
- From a Transference Focused Psychotherapy perspective, Nina's early experiences also have led her to have very split views of herself and of others. For example, based on her early experience she at times experiences herself as a defective, worthless child relating to a contemptuous parent. Similarly she often experiences herself as an abused victim in relation to an attacking, cruel and persecutory parent. Not liking being on the receiving end, Nina will often suddenly turn the tables – so in the interaction with Linda she can move from being the defective one to suddenly feeling Linda is the defective worthless nurse whom she, Nina, holds in utter contempt. These very negative sets of roles may in fact hide the longing that Nina has for being a dependent, gratified child/patient in relation to a perfectly providing parent/nurse. These split views make it difficult for Nina to have a coherent sense of herself leading to the fragmented sense of her own identity, which has been felt to be at the very core of the difficulty of the person with Borderline Personality Disorder.

Is that all then?

No, good point. What is left out of this formulation is Nina's strengths and positive qualities. We could also describe Nina as a mother whose children adore her for her generosity, spontaneous shows of love, and fiery determination to seek what's best for them. As a partner to Eddy despite the ups and downs, she is capable of support and gentleness when he is feeling low. She recently supported him through a period when he was drinking very heavily. She is a loyal and affectionate daughter to her parents, in fact displaying more consideration and love for them, than they ever managed for her. Her friends say that although she has her moments when she can be unbearably quick to take offence and become hostile, she is also very loyal and has a warm sense of humour.

Patients in my service often say that health professionals do not acknowledge their positive attributes. This is an important point because the aim of working at the level of personality is not to change it completely. This is both impossible and would rob us of the uniqueness of each individual's qualities. Rather it is to recognise and modify certain aspects which are less useful. and to build on the positive qualities which the person already has.

The result of patients experiencing professionals as concentrating only on their negative qualities may account for why patients often view therapists as being overly critical. However another way of thinking about this is that clinicians, in their wish to help, may take the positive qualities as a given and focus on 'work to be done.'

Am I Too Defensive? What Do You Mean by 'Defence Mechanism'?

Freud's seminal work on defence mechanisms clarified that these are ways of coping that we all use to cope with life's anxieties. His daughter, Anna Freud developed this thinking further, contributing to an understanding that some defence mechanisms are more healthy, adaptive or mature than others. If we accept that we do in fact all use defence mechanisms, the hope would be that we use the more healthy, adaptive ones more of the time than the 'immature' defence mechanisms.

So when someone says 'Stop being so defensive' they probably are referring to something they detect in you which is maintaining some status quo, which may be indicating a defence mechanism. Whether they are being accurate in this perception is something you'll have to think about – without being too 'defensive'.

Iris, a woman in one of the groups in the Personality Disorder service was utterly dumbfounded when Rita, a fellow patient she was talking to, ran out of the room in tears. She said 'What's that about? I was just talking to her.' There was an uncomfortable silence. One patient said: Well it was quite aggressive what you did there.

Iris denied this: I was just talking to her – she's really sensitive –I couldn't have been aggressive – I was talking really quietly and reasonably.

Other members of the group also said that they'd experienced Iris as being quite aggressive. Iris continued to express surprise, saying she must have been misunderstood – she had been feeling quite calm throughout the group. 'If anything, it was Rita who was being aggressive – I'm the one who should have run out of the room – and now you're all ganging up against me'.

A way to understand the above interaction is that Iris is *splitting*; she is compartmentalizing any hostile feelings she has to such an extent that she has no awareness of these hostile feelings. When confronted with the contradiction between what she is aware of feeling and how she came across to other people, she shows a bland indifference. She could also be understood to be *projecting* any feelings of hostility she may have into Rita and then into the other members of the group. This interaction shows that we are usually unaware of the defence mechanisms we are using at any one time.

The following vignette is another illustration of defence mechanisms: A lawyer in his 40s fell in love with his attractive 25 year old secretary. He had been single for many years and longed to be in a relationship. He had invited her out for dinner on a couple of occasions and was hoping to develop a relationship with her. However after a few weeks she informed him that she had resumed a relationship with her ex-partner. The lawyer was distraught. He had thought she had developed feelings for him, and had been very moved that she had been bringing in his favourite coffee to work. He had thought everything about her was just what he wanted in a partner. On the evening of having been told that she had started seeing her ex-partner again, he bought a new album by her favourite singer. It was only on returning home that he realised that it could be inappropriate to give it to her. He started feeling tired at work and went to the family medical practitioner concerned he was developing chronic fatigue syndrome.

After a period of a few months, the lawyer recovered himself. He managed to control his feelings for the secretary and although still fond of her, he was able to restore their relationship to an office one. He channelled his energies into making better links with his daughter who he saw only occasionally and set up regular dinner outings with her. He remembered that one of his favourite authors had written a novel on the theme of an older man falling in love with a younger woman. He sought out the book and discovered himself chuckling with some sympathetic recognition at the travails of the suffering older protagonist in the novel as he battled with emotions of longing, impotence and envy.

One way of understanding this lawyer's behaviour is his use of defence mechanisms. Initially he used primitive defence mechanisms such as *denial* (that the age difference between them made it unlikely the young woman had a romantic interest in him), *distortion* (he interpreted what was in effect a thoughtful action – buying the coffee that he liked – into an idea that this was the woman signalling how thoughtful a partner she would be for him if they lived together. Indeed the first time she brought him the coffee he'd had an instant image of her pouring this coffee in his kitchen on the weekend – such was the strength of his wish-fulfilling needs. He also was *idealising* the woman by attributing perfect qualities to her rather than seeing her as a pleasant but extremely conventional person with limited shared interests. The buying of the album may be seen as a form of *acting out* in that he was acting on the fantasy that he could still give her the album in the way that a potential lover may give a gift – to avoid the painful feeling that in fact the relationship would never develop. He also started *somatising* by converting his emotional pain into physical symptoms and becoming preoccupied he may have chronic fatigue syndrome. All of these may be seen as primitive defence mechanisms.

However, to his credit, the lawyer was able to use more mature defence mechanisms several months later. He managed to *suppress* his feelings for the woman, allowing them both to resume an earlier respectful working relationship and he *sublimated* his longing for more closer ways of relating into trying to interact in a more meaningful way with his daughter. He became able to view himself with some gentle *humour* by identifying with the comically clumsy, but also touching attempts of the protagonist in the novel to develop a relationship with the younger woman that he is drawn to.

I've Heard Doctors Say I'm Just Manipulating Them – Is That True?

All of us have hopes or fantasies of what we would like to happen in our interactions. We usually go about trying to achieve our wishes without the other person ending up feeling manipulated. However in people with Personality Disorder, the interpersonal interactions are often fraught. The combination of the greater intensity of feelings, the split nature of these feelings, and the ability of people with Borderline Personality Disorder to get those around them to experience these feelings which they want to disown, may well contribute to others feeling that people with Personality Disorder are being manipulative. It is more useful to understand that what is occurring here is often an attempt by the person with Personality Disorder to manage their feelings rather than trying to get the better of others.

Why do I Have All These Other Problems – like Depression, Anxiety, Drinking and Eating Difficulties?

There are different reasons for this:

1. Criteria for Borderline Personality Disorder include emotional difficulties such as feeling angry, empty or having rapid changes in emotions. It is thus understandable that people with Borderline Personality Disorder experience feeling depressed or anxious as part of their Personality Disorder symptoms rather than necessarily having a separate condition such as clinical depression or Generalised Anxiety Disorder. Of course, if sufficient diagnostic criteria are met, it is possible that someone may have Borderline Personality Disorder and one of the other conditions such as clinical depression. My experience has been that this is usually not the case, although the majority of my patients have believed they have a depressive illness.
2. People will have different coping mechanisms for these emotional difficulties. These coping mechanisms may include using alcohol or drugs or eating abnormally.
3. These problems with depression, anxiety, alcohol, drugs or eating may become so prominent that they become separate psychiatric disorders in themselves with a different diagnostic label. So a patient with Borderline Personality Disorder may be diagnosed with a clinical depression and Alcohol Dependence Syndrome as well. Studies have shown that there is a higher prevalence of other psychiatric disorders in people with Personality Disorder than in those people without Personality Disorder.

What's the Difference Between Borderline Personality Disorder and Other Psychiatric Disorders?

If you get confused, so do a lot of professionals. It does point to the fact that it is at times difficult to make a clear psychiatric diagnosis. While there is good reason for the confusion, given that different psychiatric diagnoses have similarities, they can usually be distinguished by their differences. Of course it is possible for an individual to have two, or more, disorders.

So the confusion in diagnosis is understandable. If I feel anxious, is it a 'normal' amount of anxiety (we all feel anxious at times, and appropriately so). Or is it a specific type that merits a diagnosis on its own such as social anxiety. Or is it the kind of anxiety around people which is more characteristic of Borderline Personality Disorder. Or to complicate matters, does the anxiety take two forms – fulfilling criteria for both a specific social anxiety as well as the anxiety that may be part of the presentation of someone with Borderline Personality Disorder.

The following are indicators to help distinguish between the different conditions:

Anxiety Disorders Versus Borderline Personality Disorder

Examples of specific anxiety disorders are agoraphobia, social phobia, generalised anxiety disorder, Post Traumatic Stress Disorder (PTSD).

Anxiety is part of the presentation of someone with Borderline Personality Disorder. The clues suggesting that a specific type of anxiety disorder such as agoraphobia, social phobia or general anxiety disorder may be present include:

For *agoraphobia:* the anxiety occurs mainly in certain situations – crowds, public places, travelling away from home, and travelling alone. In contrast in Borderline Personality Disorder the anxiety is less specific to these situations – it is both more general in terms of the individual feeling anxious simply being out of the comfort of the safety of his home and more specific in terms of being more related to the emotional state of the individual. So at times when he is feeling more stable or positive, he has no problems in going out of his home.

For *social phobia:* The anxiety occurs due to a fear of being scrutinised by other people, usually leading to avoidance of social situations. They may be specific; only about public speaking or meeting with the opposite sex – or they may be more general, involving almost all social situations outside the family circle. It is usually associated with low self esteem and fear of criticism. The psychological and behavioural presentation is mainly due to anxiety. From this description you can see why there is confusion regarding social phobia and the social withdrawal that can occur in someone with Borderline Personality Disorder. The difference is that again in the person with Borderline Personality Disorder avoidance of people is more related to how they are feeling at the time. This means that their avoidance is less stable – they may be more willing to interact when they are feeling more positive. In someone with social phobia the social avoidance is the main issue and stable, in someone with Borderline Personality Disorder it is part of the issue – there are other issues too.

In *generalised anxiety disorder* the anxiety is 'free floating', so it is not restricted, or even mainly occurring, in any particular settings. There is a constant sense of apprehension and tension, with fidgeting and an inability to relax. There may be bodily feelings of anxiety such as feeling lightheaded, nauseous or sweaty. The person with Borderline Personality Disorder again has a wider 'palette' of symptoms that is less anxiety specific.

For ***Post Traumatic Stress Disorder*** **(PTSD):** This is often suggested as an alternative way of viewing Borderline Personality Disorder. Given that there has been childhood trauma in so many individuals with Borderline Personality Disorder (up to 70%), it has been suggested that Borderline Personality Disorder may be a variation of PTSD. This uncertainty about diagnosis is more driven by considering what caused the condition rather than thinking about how the two conditions actually show themselves in the individual -the presentation is usually quite different. Against this causal view of Borderline Personality Disorder is the fact that a significant number of individuals with the diagnosis of Borderline Personality Disorder (about 30%) have not had trauma in their childhood.

Another reason for viewing the two conditions as being different is that there is evidence for effective *different* treatments of them. Thus PTSD can be effectively treated with Cognitive Behavioural Therapy, while the treatment of Borderline Personality Disorder includes other forms of psychological treatment that are usually more exploratory than Cognitive Behavioural Therapy. There is even some evidence that treating borderline patients as victims of abuse usually made them worse.[44]

Having said all this, there still is an ongoing debate between the link with Borderline Personality Disorder and PTSD, best captured in the condition 'Complex PTSD'. Prolonged repeated trauma, such a repeated childhood sexual abuse, may lead to a more complex pattern of symptoms than in PTSD, hence the term Complex PTSD. This pattern of symptoms include dissociation (a loss of touch between one's thoughts, feelings and immediate surroundings) difficulty in controlling one's emotions, being impulsive, having many physical complaints which are more linked to one's state of mind, and difficulty in relationships. If you think back to what characterises Borderline Personality Disorder, you'll see why there is an overlap and confusion when thinking about these two conditions.

Mood (Affective) Disorders Versus Borderline Personality Disorder

Unsurprisingly the diagnoses of Borderline Personality Disorder and mood disorders are often confused.

Depression Versus Borderline Personality Disorder

People with Borderline Personality Disorder will often feel low in mood – essentially feeling that they are depressed. We may ask whether Borderline Personality Disorder is an atypical form of depression. To make it even more difficult to tell the difference, about 75% of Borderline Personality Disorder will have a major depressive disorder in their lifetime.

However the two conditions are different. This can be seen clinically, in the course of the different conditions and in the treatment. Clinically, people with Borderline Personality Disorder are different from those who have a depressive disorder in terms of how they are interpersonally and in their behaviour. Research has shown that Borderline Personality Disorder can be viewed as having sufficient of its own characteristics that it can be viewed as an entity on its own. Borderline Personality Disorder also has a different course to major depression. From a treatment point of view, the Borderline Personality Disorder's depression does not respond to antidepressants.[45]

Overall, this indicates that Borderline Personality Disorder is not simply a variation of, or closely related to, depression.

Bipolar Disorder Versus Borderline Personality Disorder

Bipolar Disorder and Borderline Personality Disorder are sometimes confused with one another both by professionals and patients.

Similarities Between the Two Disorders:

- Mood Changes: Bipolar disorder has extreme shifts in mood from depression to mania (a mood characterized by abnormal elation and energy, racing thoughts and speech, and a decreased need for sleep). Borderline Personality Disorder is also associated with mood changes – individuals can switch between feeling fine to feeling extremely distressed in a matter of minutes – or even seconds.
- Impulsive Behaviour: Both disorders cause people to act impulsively. These impulsive behaviours can include spending too much, risky sexual behaviours, reckless driving, binge eating, substance abuse and self injury.
- Drug and Alcohol Abuse: Individuals with these disorders may abuse alcohol or drugs as a way of coping with their symptoms.

Differences Between the Two Disorders:

- The length and intensity of the mood swings: The person with Bipolar Affective Disorder typically has the same mood for days or weeks at a time while the person with Borderline Personality Disorder experiences intense emotions that may last only hours – or even minutes.[46] The person with Borderline Personality Disorder will often say that they have many ups and downs in their emotions in the course of a single day – or more strikingly even within the course of an hour. One patient with Borderline Personality Disorder described it in the following way: 'It's like being on a roller coaster ride of emotions – the difference is this roller coaster goes on and on and you can't just get off it – it's exhausting.' The roller coaster image is also a useful one for capturing the sudden shifts in emotions in someone with Borderline Personality Disorder – the dips and lifts are precipitous and sudden and often as unpredictable.

- The cause for these mood shifts also vary. Borderline Personality Disorder mood shifts are usually a reaction to a stress in the person's life (such as an argument or being left alone), while Bipolar Affective Disorder shifts seem to occur out of nowhere or are not as clearly related to an environmental stress. What may be misleading is that the person with Borderline Personality Disorder experiences the change in mood as 'out of the blue.' This is more linked to the individual's lack of awareness regarding what may be setting him off rather than there being no internal or external stress.
- The types of emotions that people with these disorders experience differs. People with Borderline Personality Disorder may view themselves as fundamentally bad or unworthy and are more prone to feelings of loneliness, emptiness and a severe fear of abandonment. These particular feelings are not typical for Bipolar Affective Disorder whereas they are typical for Borderline Personality Disorder.
- Treatment: The most important part of Bipolar Affective Disorder treatment is medication, followed by psychotherapy. Borderline Personality Disorder treatment, on the other hand, focuses on psychotherapy, not medication. There are particular medications, classed as mood stabilisers, which have an evidence base for effective treatment of Bipolar Disorder. It seems intuitive that these medications would also be effective for the affective instability of Borderline Personality Disorder. Unfortunately there is at present no clear evidence from research that this has been the case and thus there is no clear evidence base for the use of mood stabilisers in Borderline Personality Disorder. There have been small studies claiming effectiveness of mood stabilisers but they are not authoritative. Some psychiatrists may advocate their use but there is no solid body of evidence which backs up this practice.

There are two further conditions to consider – Cyclothymia and Dysthymia.

Cyclothymia is a persistent instability of mood with many periods of mild depression and mild elation but which have never been severe enough to be diagnosed as either a depressive disorder or a bipolar affective disorder.

Dysthymia is a longstanding low mood which is not severe enough to meet criteria for a depressive disorder. Individuals with this condition describe feeling tired and depressed for most of the time (often for months at a time), everything feels an effort and nothing feels enjoyable.

One can see that someone with Borderline Personality Disorder may have some of the presentation of cyclothymia and dysthymia. Again the palette of symptoms in Borderline Personality Disorder is broader, and in Borderline Personality Disorder the feelings of being low or elated are more understandable in the context of the individual's life and its goings on, while in cyclothymia and dysthymia the mood disturbance is usually not related to life events.

Schizophrenia Versus Borderline Personality Disorder

The term 'borderline' has roots in both psychotherapy and psychiatry. With regards to psychotherapy, individuals with Borderline Personality Disorder were regarded as being on the border of being neurotic (and thus treatable from a psychoanalytic point of view) or psychotic (and therefore untreatable from a psychoanalytic point of view).

However it is the psychiatric view which concerns us in this section. Psychiatrists identified patients we would now understand to have Borderline Personality Disorder as having a tendency to go into 'borderline schizophrenia' states of mind. However in terms of the difference in the symptoms, the lack of familial association and difference in course and treatment of the two conditions, it is now clear that Borderline Personality Disorder is a separate entity, and not a variation of schizophrenia.

Given the above, it is not surprising that there is often an underlying anxiety in people with Borderline Personality Disorder – a secret fear that they are 'mad.' 'Madness' is often thought about in society in a similar way to how psychiatrists would think about psychosis – a loss of contact with reality. The clearest example of psychosis is someone who is suffering from the full-blown symptoms of schizophrenia although it's important to keep in mind that the majority of patients with this diagnosis are very treatable. This loss of contact with reality can take various forms. The most important forms are:

Thought interference: the individual in some ways experiences thoughts in an alien way – they may feel that they have a thought which has been inserted inside their mind and which is not theirs or they may feel that their thoughts are being broadcast so that others have access to their most intimate thoughts.

Passivity: the individual believes that in some way someone else can control their thoughts, emotions or behaviour.

Auditory hallucinations: individuals may experience hearing voices or sounds when there is in fact no one around.

Delusions: the patient often has fixed, unshakeable persecutory beliefs such as a belief that there is a plot to harm them.

One can imagine someone with Borderline Personality Disorder having some of the above beliefs. Someone with Borderline Personality Disorder may well believe that their feelings are being influenced by those around them or that at times others are aware of what they are thinking. It is also not uncommon that someone with Borderline Personality Disorder may feel quite 'paranoid' and believe that everyone is against them. What distinguishes schizophrenia from Borderline Personality Disorder is that in the latter the beliefs are less bizarre and more understandable within the context of, and influenced by, relationships. They also are less fixed – there is usually more room for doubt about some belief in someone with Borderline Personality Disorder than in someone with Schizophrenia. But again this is time specific – someone with Borderline Personality Disorder is quite capable of having a very fixed idea about something, particularly at a time when they are stressed. However when the level of stress diminishes they are able to be more flexible in their thinking and able to entertain the notion that the fixed view they had is not the only view to be had. In other words, they are more able to 'mentalize'.

For example, we can see that when Nina argues with Eddy she can develop quite extreme views. 'I know that you hate me and that you're scheming to leave me and take the children and leave me alone in this house'. What makes this more of a Borderline Personality Disorder picture is that there is a clearer reason for Nina developing this view (Nina and Eddy had been rowing for a few days), there is no extended conspiracy theory, and it only lasts while Nina is very stressed. In this case, a day after the outburst by Nina, she had received a call from social housing telling her that Eddy was making enquiries about moving in with the family again, and Nina's paranoid thoughts lessened. The picture more typical for someone with schizophrenia would be a less understandable reason for the suspicious thinking, sometimes a more elaborate belief system (for example Eddy being part of a wider conspiracy of people scheming to get at her), and a longer period of the psychotic belief.

A particular issue concerns hearing voices. The public, as well as psychiatrists place much importance on voices as an indicator of psychosis.

The thinking would go: if Personality Disorder is not a psychotic illness (as opposed to schizophrenia) then someone with Borderline Personality Disorder cannot experience true auditory hallucinations, they cannot experience hearing a voice (when there is in fact no voice to be heard) as though it is coming from the outside through one's eardrum. The problem is that patients with Borderline Personality Disorder frequently report the experience of having a true auditory hallucination. Does this mean that they have a psychotic illness?

My own view is that what is important is whether being out of touch with reality is the enduring position. This would be the case in someone with schizophrenia who presents with auditory hallucinations and who is not treated with medications. This is however not the case in Borderline Personality Disorder. The person with Borderline Personality Disorder may experience hearing voices or feel persecuted at times when they are feeling more stressed but this is not the de facto or default position – it is more a temporary (albeit recurring – because the lives of people with Borderline Personality Disorder are stressful) phenomenon.

Why Do I hear Voices – Does it Mean I'm mad?

We've covered this before – but let's just have another go – it's clearly an important question.

DSM-5 describes as one of the criteria for the diagnosis of Borderline Personality Disorder 'Transient, stress-related paranoid ideation or severe dissociative symptoms.' Thus it allows for individuals to experience very paranoid or suspicious thoughts.

The hearing of voices may be due to severe dissociation. Dissociation is the experience when there is a disconnect between mental processes, emotions and the external world. As part of this, patients may describe hearing voices which are as real as when someone is in fact speaking to them, but the person from whom the voice seems to emanate is not present. This is what psychiatrists would term an *auditory hallucination*. Thus an individual with Borderline Personality Disorder may become extremely paranoid or say he is hearing voices. I would still not say this person is 'mad' in the sense of having an enduring psychotic illness. The distinction between the two conditions lies in the duration of the symptoms. An enduring psychotic illness is just that – the psychotic symptoms go on for a long time. This is different for the individual with Borderline Personality Disorder – who has psychotic symptoms for a shorter period of time. In my clinical work I use this difference in time period as the main way of distinguishing between the two conditions and no longer try to distinguish if the voices are truly hallucinatory ('the noise is coming through my ears from outside') or pseudo hallucinatory ('the voices are in my head') at a point in time.

Why Do I Harm Myself?

This is an act that is incomprehensible to most people. When one speaks to people who do self harm though, it becomes more understandable as a means (albeit not a healthy one) of coping with stress. Clearly it must serve some function if the individual uses this behaviour. There are different ways to understand this. Below is a list which is neither mutually exclusive, nor exhaustive.

1. As an attack on oneself. Harming oneself may seem odd to the onlooker – how on earth can someone subject this to oneself? A way of understanding it is that the individual who self harms is punishing an aspect of himself which he hates and which he disowns so strongly that he is no longer fully aware in his mind or his emotions that he is actually doing harm to his own body. This relates to the point we made about splitting earlier in the book.
2. As an attack on the other. While the self harmer is doing harm to himself, he may also derive some gain from the torment this act may inflict on others who care for him. Thinking of the self harm as an attack on oneself or the other underlines the aggressive nature of the act of self harm, something which can be missed.
3. To experience an emotion. Some individuals say that they feel so numb and blocked off from their emotions that cutting is a way of getting back in touch with emotions.
4. To stop thinking. The act of self harm may serve the function of temporarily stopping painful thoughts.

Clearly the act of self harm is distressing for the person doing so. It is also distressing for those around the person – both their loved ones and the professionals working with them. However, the aggressive nature of self harm should not be lost sight of – after all it is an assault, though the fact that it is one's own body may mask the aggression. How others react may be a response to this aggression. This may explain at times the response to individuals who self harm being one of dismissal or anger. Relatives or friends may then feel guilty about their lack of sympathy. It's important to keep in mind that this response is not easy to control nor is the person necessarily even aware of this negative response at the time.

One patient said: 'When I arrived at A&E after I'd cut myself, the nurses and doctors were really cold and unwelcoming. Nothing that they said to me directly– but I overheard one of them saying before they saw me: 'That girl's back here again – she's cut again – I've got this patient in cardiac failure and I now I have to deal with this patient doing these things purposely to herself.' When they did get to see me they were so cold and clinical. They didn't seem at all interested in me as person or why I'd cut myself again. I never want to go back to A&E again – you get patched up but at what cost?'

Looking at this situation one could sympathise for everyone involved. Clearly most of our sympathy lies with the distressed individual – but it's possible that the frustration of the A&E staff is also about the realisation of the limits of what they can do in their present capacity to really help the distressed person they are attending to.

What is Repetition Compulsion?

When I read the psychiatrist's assessment on me, I read 'repetition compulsion' – what does this mean – like I'm on repeat mode or something? And why 'compulsion' – does it mean I can't get out of repeat mode?

This is a term that Freud used when thinking about the repetitive patterns he noted in the patients he was seeing. If you think about it, we all have aspects of our lives where we keep on getting into the similar difficult situation – often with the same unsatisfactory outcome. There are different ways of understanding this. One way is that we keep on getting ourselves into the same situation in the hope that things will turn out differently this time. However the way that we have got used to thinking and feeling in these situations kicks off in the same way as though we have a set template. Given that these tried and tested patterns may not have worked in the past, it is unlikely they will work again in the future – unless we fundamentally change something.

So the repetition is the trying, yet again, of old patterns. The compulsion is, yet again, getting into the situation because we so desperately hope that this time around the situation will be different.

There are many examples we could probably think of which illustrate this in our daily lives. We probably all know friends who keep on getting themselves into relationships with people where it's unlikely to be successful for whatever reason, such as always choosing a partner who is already in another relationship.

The Treatment Contract: What is it and Do I Need To Agree to it?

You keep on going on about what you'll expect of me in the treatment and what I can expect of you and you call it the *treatment contract*. So is this some kind of legal thing or what?

The context to this question is that Nina is initially angry at being told that she needs to agree to the contract that outlines a way of working together and specifies what her responsibilities are, before the treatment will start. She feels that it is being imposed on her and is too paternalistic – for example it outlines that it is her responsibility that she comes to therapy regularly and consistently, even when she doesn't feel like it. She also needs to undertake to reduce and eventually stop her self harm *during* the time she is in treatment rather than allowing her to set this objective for some distant time in the future.

Different treatment approaches and different clinicians use the contract to varying degrees. A contract serves to clarify how the service and patient can work together and tries to define the respective responsibilities of both patient and therapist. It helps to identify quickly if there is some deviation from the agreements, so that this can be attended to as a priority. It also allows an opportunity to focus on understanding what led to the deviation. Given that there will always be some ambivalence in anyone in therapy about changing themselves, and that this ambivalence often shows through testing the treatment set up (also called the 'framework of treatment') the contract serves as a useful tool to highlight any breaks to the frame.

For example, any patient needs to agree to come on time and regularly to the sessions. This seems such an obvious way of doing therapy that it seems almost silly to specify it. But just imagine three months ahead, when the therapy really starts to 'bite', it will be very tempting for the patient to engage in avoidance tactics; such as missing sessions or coming in late. But it is exactly at the times the therapy is starting to bite that the most valuable therapy can occur . Why is the therapy biting? What is happening which is so disturbing? In exploring this we stand a real chance of understanding something important about the individual. By the individual staying at home (although it may be more comfortable for her in the short term) we lose that opportunity to understand something of value.

Give the above, hopefully it's clear that the contract is not a legal document. After all there is no law legislating the individual undertakes therapy. The contract is a clinical document which spells out an agreed way of working to check that neither patient nor therapist are losing their way – this is highly complex work after all. It also allows a conversation to occur when there is a straying from the contract and it prioritises and specifies what to initially discuss, focussing on the aspect of the contract which is being broken.

There is an example of the therapy contract we use in my service in the appendix to give you some idea of what is useful to agree on at the outset of treatment. If you (or a family member) are considering a psychotherapy treatment, how ready are you to undertake a contract like this?

Nina is now more committed to starting therapy. As part of this renewed commitment she is able to work out her aims in coming for therapy and also to commit to an understanding of how she and the Personality Disorder service will work together – the contract.

At first Nina said that what she wants to get out of therapy is for Eddy and her children to be more understanding of her difficulties and to make less demands on her. It required some time for Nina to accept that as she was the person in treatment, it would be more helpful to think of what she may want to change in herself rather than expecting change in those around her. She felt she wanted to stop her destructive behaviours (by which she means her cutting herself and taking overdoses), to get a better sense of herself – what she wants out of life, to stop having these sudden changes in mood, and to be a better mother to her children. She would also like to have a better relationship with Eddy, but she was uncertain if this is possible. The feedback to Nina was that these aims seemed important but that it was first necessary to break them into smaller more feasible steps.

Why Must I Stop Using Street Drugs?

It makes no sense that you say I need to stop using street drugs to get treatment for my Personality Disorder. That's part of my problem – so it's a catch 22 – and I'll never get treatment then.

This is an important point. Many individuals with Borderline Personality Disorder use recreational drugs or alcohol in a harmful way. The emphasis is on *in a harmful way*. If the use of the drugs leads to harm or potential harm for the individual in some significant way – such as causing health problems, placing them in vulnerable situations, or leading them to do very destructive things – then this is a clearly an important factor in their treatment.

The first issue is to establish the priority. If someone is dependent on drugs or alcohol then this will take up all their thinking and energy and they won't have enough space to do psychological work – either to take in the new experience or to process it. This will also be the case if they are using drugs to the extent that, even if they are not dependent, it is harming them in some significant way.

Here are some examples:

Stanley is a mixed race man in his mid twenties who started the introductory part of the treatment programme. He was a heavy cannabis user and continued to use while in the group. It was difficult to work out if his very passive silence in the group, followed by rambling and barely intelligible monologues, was due to his social isolation over many years, or due to the cannabis. He continued to use cannabis very heavily and would return each week saying he had no memory of the previous session. He lasted 4 sessions and then disengaged from the programme. While his personality was thought to have contributed to his difficulty in using the programme, his clinicians felt that his ongoing heavy use of cannabis had contributed to his non-engagement. 'Why should I expose myself to doing psychological work which is embarrassing and exposing when I have this warm bath of cannabis I can sink into in my flat?' The cannabis also helped to ablate his memory of the sessions week to week.

Diane is a woman in her 40s who has a longstanding problem with alcohol, not helped by her occupation as a bartender. She started the programme and continued in it for five months. On one occasion she came to the session intoxicated and was asked to leave until she had sobered up. The sessions were filled with her accounts of the risky situations she put herself into when intoxicated, and also with her complaints with how unfairly her employers were treating her. In all this she also showed some ability to discuss and process some painful aspects of the abusive relationship that she was in with a married man. However Diane would drink after these sessions and return to the next appointment at exactly the same point where she had started the previous session. It became clearer in the course of the treatment that Diane had been dishonest regarding the level of her ongoing alcohol use and that she met criteria for alcohol dependence. Diane felt unwilling to address this. The treating team began to understand that Diane was unwilling to address her alcohol dependence even though it was the most prominent issue for her and causing her so many problems in her life. The decision was made to discharge her with the invitation to return if she sorted out the alcohol problem.

Cleo was a young British woman who was alcohol dependent. She had also had an extremely abusive childhood and presented as someone whose difficulties were so acute and understandable that both she and the treating team were keen to start treatment. The sticking point was the alcohol dependence and Cleo's wishing to continue using alcohol. Despite their reluctance, the team discharged Cleo, saying that she needed to sort out the alcohol dependence before starting treatment. A year later Cleo presented to the Personality Disorder service again, having had her alcohol dependence successfully treated.

The above examples point to what may be a function of the drug use (to escape reality – which is the opposite of the very reason for coming to get therapy), and of the problems of ongoing use while in therapy such as difficulty taking in new information and difficulty in coping with unwanted feelings that come up in the course of therapy. The end result is that these difficult feelings are ablated rather than processed.

These examples also point to a balance that needs to be reached. Many people with Borderline Personality Disorder use alcohol and drugs excessively, so clearly it cannot be a reason to refuse them treatment – but at what point is the offer of treatment not useful because the alcohol or drug use is getting so dangerous or so much in the way? This point may be when extreme harmful use or dependence is present.

Responsibility: What's the Big Deal About It?

Ok so there is some sense in what you're saying about the contract – but why do you keep on going about responsibility? It's getting boring.

The basis of a therapy that is trying to do something as ambitious such as changing aspects of your personality is that this has to be something you are willing and able to do. How willing (you may at times be quite unwilling!) and how able (it's really difficult) may wax and wane. But finally the decision to change, and the ongoing struggle to change, is *your* responsibility. Your therapist has a responsibility to provide the setting that gives you the best chance to change – you'll see I've said *chance* – as there is no guarantee. Therapy is hard graft and that is what makes it different to taking a medication which may work in a more passive way - from a psychological perspective anyway.

Experience in my service is that the main distinction between those patients who have benefitted from treatment and those who have not, has been their ability to take some responsibility for themselves and how they used the treatment. This is a significant point – because if it's correct then it is not the type of diagnosis or how bad someone's early experience was, or how genetically loaded they are, or even how severe someone's presentation is, that is the determining factor of whether they benefit from treatment. The determining factor is how much responsibility they can take for really engaging in their treatment. Of course the above factors may all influence the ability of the individual to take on responsibility. Because to take on responsibility the individual has to have some sense that what they do does have some effect – that they have some agency.

The following example is my most haunting patient in terms of reminding me how difficult it may be for someone to have a sense of agency in their lives.

Kay was a 53 year old woman who was six months into her treatment and was making very little progress. She blamed this on the other patients in the group who she felt ganged up against her and also on the staff who she also felt were fundamentally unsupportive of her, including in not siding with her in her continuing fights with the other patients in her group. In all her ongoing, simmering resentment there were pockets of time when she was able to make the most moving contact with fellow patients or her therapist and her longing to be a good mother and wife shone through.

A watershed moment came at six months into the treatment when she had an argument with a fellow patient. This patient told her that she was too paranoid to be a good mother. This accusation hit Kay very hard and she became obsessed with getting an apology from the patient and in turn fixated on the therapeutic team for not extracting an apology from the patient she was angry with. All attempts to think about the actual interaction, in which Kay had been quite provocative, or why the 'accusation' was as disturbing to Kay as it was, were refused by Kay. This situation continued for 2 months, with Kay being unwilling to think about anything other than getting patients and staff 'on side' or receiving an apology. She continued to feel persecuted by patients and staff. In essence Kay felt unable to accept any responsibility either for her role in the dispute or for thinking she contributed at all to how hurt she felt – it was all either the patients' or staff 'fault.' Kay finally refused to continue coming to the group as she felt unable to trust the other patients without an apology. Individual sessions were offered to her but after 8 months of these Kay finally stopped coming to these as well as she felt the service was not seeing things from her perspective by not siding with her.

So we may think Kay had a responsibility for how she viewed her role in interactions and how she used therapy but felt unable to assume this responsibility, and this led to her dropping out of treatment. While accepting that Kay had at least some responsibility for the poor outcome, what helped the clinical team to not blame her, was their knowledge of her early history.[47] When a little girl, her father would demand an answer of her – 'Is it yes or is it no, come on tell me, tell me now'. Kay would desperately think of what to answer – yet knew that whether she answered 'yes' or 'no' a blow awaited her. It becomes clear in Kay's case just why it was so difficult for her to take on a sense of responsibility – her earlier experience had left her with a sense that whatever she did made no difference to the outcome – she was not raised to have a sense of her own agency. And without a sense of agency why should she feel responsible?

The whole question of finding something 'boring' is a very interesting one and its meaning would be explored in therapy. Boredom is – contrary to what one may expect – a fascinating emotion that is often a catch phrase for far more complex and varied emotions, including anger.

Kate is 16 – Could She Have Borderline Personality Disorder?

Kate is 16, so by convention, as the diagnosis of Personality Disorder is not made before the age of 18, Kate does not have the formal diagnosis of Personality Disorder. Clearly this is an arbitrary cut off point and Kate may (and in fact does have) aspects of her personality which would contribute to a diagnosis of Borderline Personality Disorder. This is consistent with the finding that the main aspects of our personality (for example whether we are extravert or introvert) are laid down early in childhood.

There are numerous reasons why there has been a reluctance to make the diagnosis of Personality Disorder before reaching the age of 18. These include the potentially stigmatising impact of receiving this diagnosis and the difficulty of being clear that the diagnosis is in fact Borderline Personality Disorder as opposed to the stormy period some adolescents experience at this age as part of normal personality development. While there has been concern that there is greater instability of this diagnosis at this early stage, there has been considerable evidence that the diagnostic criteria for Borderline Personality Disorder (and other Personality Disorders) are as valid, reliable and stable before age 18 as after age 18.[48]

Given that there is a high prevalence of Borderline Personality Disorder in teenagers (around 1 to 3% which is similar to adults), that it has a large impact on their lives, and that this is a period in which the traits show considerable flexibility and malleability, there is an argument for early intervention in emerging Borderline Personality Disorder.[49]

Consistent with this, The National Institute for Health and Care Excellence (NICE) recommends that young people with a diagnosis of

Borderline Personality Disorder, or symptoms and behaviour that suggest it, should have access to the full range of treatments and services recommended by NICE for adults, but within the Child and Adolescent Mental Health Service.[50]

We'll see what happens to Kate and whether it served a useful function to not have made a diagnosis too early.

Commentary

As psychological treatment needs the active participation of the patient for any change to occur, it does need some motivation on the part of the individual. Understandably this motivation may be variable – we all have good intentions and manage to carry them out with mixed success – but some intrinsic motivation in the individual is necessary.

The person entering treatment needs to believe that any change that will occur will be because of changes that he/she needs to make rather than depending on those around her to change. This is a point often misunderstood by the patient in question, his family or referrer and leads to frustration that psychological services are inaccessible, 'ivory tower' or simply turn patients away. Although some ambivalence to change is inevitable, for the treatment to have some chance of success there has to be some internal wish on the individual's part to really want to change. This wish in itself needs to be at least sizeable enough to attempt to weather the inevitable storms that good therapy will arouse. These storms are inevitable because it is disturbing to be challenged about the usual patterns in which we think, respond emotionally and behave.

Key Points

- Borderline Personality Disorder is a very 'busy' disorder, so there may be a number of accompanying problems including feeling depressed or anxious, misusing drugs or alcohol or having eating problems. More usually these are accompaniments of Borderline Personality Disorder but at times they will merit a separate psychiatric diagnosis.
- When thinking about one's personality, it's important to identify not only the problematic points that are leading one to seek treatment but to also acknowledge the positive qualities. At times something may be a positive quality which becomes problematic if too accentuated. Thus being considerate about the needs of others is fine and good until it

becomes so overriding that you lose the ability to think of what may be good for yourself and so to stand up for yourself.
- There are different reason why people with Borderline Personality Disorder harm themselves but the aggressive nature of the act should be kept in mind.
- Having a treatment contract which specifies the respective responsibilities of the person undergoing treatment and of the treatment provider is useful as it provides a framework and some rules for what will be a long and complex undertaking. Think of exploring a foreign country with many opportunities for misunderstandings and getting lost. The treatment contract serves as a guide and memorandum of understanding before negotiating this thorny terrain.
- Individuals with Personality Disorder may be experienced as being manipulative. There are however other ways of understanding this. One perspective is that individuals with Personality Disorder have less flexibility in their interactions and may negotiate a social interaction in a more clumsy or intrusive manner than someone without interpersonal difficulties. Another way to understand this is that the uncomfortable feelings, (which may include feeling manipulated), result from ways that the person with Personality Disorder is trying to manage his own feelings.
- While by convention the diagnosis of Personality Disorder is not made under the age of 18, there is frequently a sense among clinicians working with adolescents that the teenager may have an 'emerging Personality Disorder.'

CHAPTER 5

What is Wrong With the Others? Different Types of Personality Disorder

Nina's Story Part 5–Why Pick on Me?

Nina has completed the assessment, agreed to the contract and has been recommended for treatment. Before the treatment starts she attends a preparatory group which readies her for entering treatment. Some of the discussion in this group usefully illustrates some points regarding Personality Disorder. We join some of this discussion and will think of its relevance to understanding Personality Disorder.

Nina is in a session with her preparatory group. There are seven other patients present, and two facilitators. It is one of the lighter moments. Nina is talking about one of her friends, Jessica.

Nina: We got to the party really late because Jessica spent ages getting ready – deciding what dress to wear, doing her makeup. Of course when we get there, Jessica becomes the life and soul of the party. She's outrageous – started flirting with one of the men at the party even though his girlfriend was there. Eventually this girlfriend couldn't take it any longer and had a flaming row with Jessica and we had to leave the party. I'm the one coming for treatment but Jessica seemed madder than me on Saturday. So why do I have Personality Disorder and she doesn't?

Meeting Some Other Patients

Neville's Story

Sitting in the group is a man called Neville. He is 42 year old White British man. He has struggled to attend this group. When he does attend he is mainly silent and withdrawn, making little eye contact or communication. Neville has now not spoken since the group started, other than saying his name when people were introducing themselves to the new patient who had just joined the group. The facilitator in the group tries to bring him in.

'Neville, I'm aware that you've been rather quiet and I wonder if it would be ok to bring you in a bit?'

Neville looks uncomfortably at the floor but remains silent

Then, after a long pause he says: Nothing to say really.

Therapist: There was quite a bit of talk earlier about how to manage things when you're fighting with family. I wonder if you have any thoughts on it?

Neville: No, not really.

There is an uncomfortable silence and the therapist decides to not pursue this and the group moves elsewhere in their discussion.

Possible reasons for Neville's way of being and interacting will be discussed later.

Paul's Story

Nina is talking about her brother Paul. Paul is 30, four years younger than her. His parents are away visiting a sick relative for a week. Paul is living with them and they felt concerned how he would cope and asked Nina if she could keep an eye on him.

Nina is saying: Paul's been alone at my parents' home for two days now but he'd driving me a bit mad really. He phoned me last night to ask which motor car insurance company he should use. I mean I know it helps to talk this through with someone but he'd been on the phone about this for an hour the day before. And he's been asking Eddy too. Then he asks me last night, after talking through all the options – can I tell him which insurance company to go with – he can't decide. He just can't seem to make any decisions himself – he's always been like this. You should have seen what he was like when he started going out with Helen (his former wife – they now are divorced and live apart). At the time he also fancied a girl called Naomi. So he would ask me which one should he go with – if I was him who would I choose?'

Like I said, the parents have only been gone for two days – but he's been calling me all the time – what cycle should he put the washing machine on if he's washing his cotton shirt – how long should he microwave the broccoli for? I think he's just feeling really anxious that my parents aren't around – he even hinted whether he could come and stay with me and I ignored that. The flat is small enough already without having Paul over as well. I mean compared to him and Jessica I'm wondering who's more mad – but I'm the one coming for treatment!

Gregory's Story

Gregory is a 34 year old patient in the group. He is a strikingly good looking British man of mixed Anglo Cypriot descent. He works as a male model. He is talking bitterly about his partner and his work. I can't stand the way Peter gets all friendly with the other guys at work. When we go out for a drink they're all over him and I'm pretty sure he's angling to get into bed with one of them – I mean I've suspected this for the last 8 months. I've got no proof but I think that's just because he covers his tracks so well. He's always takes his mobile into the bathroom with him – why should he do that if he didn't want to check his texts or text someone?

Gregory talks about work: I know that agency doesn't really look hard enough for assignments for me. It's from that time when they booked Ulrich for that Rome shoot when they should have booked me. I've never forgotten that. I'll never forgive that agency for that. I mean look at me – and look at Ulrich – why should they have given that assignment to him? It's just because they've got it in for me. Because I stand up for what's my rights. I don't know why else they do these things against me – but they do – and they're not the only agency. I'm sure all these agencies have talked about me and put me on some blacklist.

Description of Specific Personality Disorders

'Extra content' There are several specific Personality Disorders described in ICD10 and DSM-5. These descriptions appear in Table 3, along with case examples of each specific Personality Disorder.

A note on diagnostic criteria: these are included for reference in case the reader wants more information on a specific Personality Disorder. The reader is invited to skip the section on diagnostic criteria as they are 'extra content'. A word of caution is that the reader should take care in using these diagnostic criteria to either make a self diagnosis or a diagnosis of others. They may give clues to how the issues may be labelled but the diagnosis should only be formally made by a professional with some experience in Personality Disorder.

Table 3: Classification of Personality Disorder in DSM-5 and ICD10.

DSM-5	ICD-10
'The Odd' (Cluster A)	
PARANOID	PARANOID
SCHIZOID	SCHIZOID
SCHIZOTYPAL	-
'The Dramatic (Cluster B)	
ANTISOCIAL	DISSOCIAL
-	**EMOTIONALLY UNSTABLE:** a) impulsive type
BORDERLINE	b) borderline type
HISTRIONIC	HISTRIONIC
NARCISSISTIC	-
'The Anxious' (Cluster C)	
AVOIDANT	ANXIOUS
DEPENDENT	DEPENDENT
OBSESSIVE-COMPULSIVE	ANANKASTIC

Paranoid Personality Disorder

ICD 10	DSM-5
F60.0 Paranoid Personality Disorder A. The general criteria of Personality Disorder (F60) must be met. B. At least four of the following must be present: 1. Excessive sensitivity to setbacks and rebuffs. 2. Tendency to bear grudges persistently, e.g. unforgiveness of insults, injuries or slights.	**301.0 Paranoid Personality Disorder** A pervasive distrust and suspiciousness of others such that their motives are interpreted as malevolent, beginning by early adulthood and present in a variety of contexts, as indicated by four (or more) of the following: 1. suspects, without sufficient basis, that others are exploiting, harming, or deceiving him or her. 2. is preoccupied with unjustified doubts about the loyalty or trustworthiness of friends or associates.

ICD 10	DSM-5
3. Suspiciousness and a pervasive tendency to distort experience by misconstruing the neutral or friendly actions of others as hostile or contemptuous. 4. A combative and tenacious sense of personal rights out of keeping with the actual situation. 5. Recurrent suspicions, without justification, regarding sexual fidelity of spouse or sexual partner. 6. Persistent self-referential attitude, associated particularly with excessive self-importance. 7. Preoccupation with unsubstantiated "conspiratorial" explanations of events around the subject or in the world at large.	3. is reluctant to confide in others because of unwarranted fear that the information will be used maliciously against him or her. 4. reads hidden demeaning or threatening meanings into benign remarks or events. 5. persistently bears grudges (i.e., is unforgiving of insults, injuries, or slights). 6. perceives attacks on his or her character or reputation that are not apparent to others and is quick to react angrily or to counter-attack. 7. has recurrent suspicions, without justification, regarding fidelity of spouse or sexual partner.

Case Illustration of Paranoid Personality Disorder: Gregory's Story continued *'Don't trust anyone – or they'll get one over you'*

Gregory is the male model we discussed above. He is a patient at the Personality Disorder service. He nearly dropped out after only 4 weeks. He had suspected that staff and patients were in some way against him; it was difficult to understand why he thought this but he muttered darkly about some conspiracy. He fell out in particular with a member of the staff who he felt 'cut him off' in one of the first groups he attended. The staff member had apologised to Gregory for interrupting him, explaining he had wanted to bring in another member of the group who had not yet spoken. Gregory hangs onto his grievance, feeling it unacceptable that he had been slighted. This was particularly painful to him as he regarded himself as 'a man of 34 who has seen a thing or two' and had a clear sense that his opinions were worth hearing.

On reviewing Gregory's history it seemed he was replicating his previous experiences – he had always thought people were not to be trusted, that in some way they were against him. He has few friends as he has little ability to 'give and take' in his social interactions and had been inclined to take offence easily. Gregory's arresting good looks had resulted in a promising career as a model but he gets hired less and less as people find him too difficult to work with. He has had a couple of relationships which had both ended because he had worn down his partners with his ongoing accusations that that they were having affairs with his fellow models.

Schizoid Personality Disorder

ICD10	DSM-5
F60.1 Schizoid Personality Disorder A. The general criteria of Personality Disorder (F60) must be met. B. At least four of the following criteria must be present: 1. Few, if any, activities provide pleasure. 2. Displays emotional coldness, detachment, or flattened affectivity. 3. Limited capacity to express warm, tender feelings for others as well as anger. 4. Appears indifferent to either praise or criticism. 5. Little interest in having sexual experiences with another person (taking into account age). 6. Almost always chooses solitary activities. 7. Excessive preoccupation with fantasy and introspection. 8. Neither desires, nor has, any close friends or confiding relationships (or only one). 9. Marked insensitivity to prevailing social norms and conventions; if these are not followed this is unintentional.	**301.20 Schizoid Personality Disorder** A pervasive pattern of detachment from social relationships and a restricted range of expression of emotions in interpersonal settings, beginning by early adulthood and present in a variety of contexts, as indicated by four (or more) of the following: 1. neither desires nor enjoys close relationships, including being part of a family 2. almost always chooses solitary activities 3. has little, if any, interest in having sexual experiences with another person 4. takes pleasure in few, if any, activities 5. lacks close friends or confidants other than first-degree relatives 6. appears indifferent to the praise or criticism of others 7. shows emotional coldness, detachment, or flattened affect

Case Illustration of Schizoid Personality Disorder: Frank's Story
The cold fish

Frank is a 28 year old man who is unemployed and lives with his elderly mother. He had attended the Personality Disorder service at the insistence of his mother who was concerned that her son spent all his life in his room and did not seem interested in having a girlfriend or any form of social life. He spent time instead making elaborate drawings with a ball point pen about a science fiction television series from the 60s which he meticulously filed away but did not show anyone. When Frank's relatives teased or cajoled Frank for his solitary occupation, Frank would be unaffected, returning to his room with a cup of tea.

Frank did not really see any reason for coming to the assessment at the Personality Disorder Service. The staff member assessing him struggled to establish any rapport with him, Frank was not unfriendly but he seemed cut off as though he was relating through a glass wall. He showed little emotion throughout the meeting. Frank ended the meeting 10 minutes early, saying he 'was okay thanks' and wanted to get back to his room.

Schizotypal Personality Disorder

ICD10	DSM-5
Schizotypal disorder is listed with the Schizophrenia and delusional disorders block	**301.22 Schizotypal Personality Disorder** A pervasive pattern of social and interpersonal deficits marked by acute discomfort with, and reduced capacity for, close relationships as well as by cognitive or perceptual distortions and eccentricities of behaviour, beginning by early adulthood and present in a variety of contexts, as indicated by five (or more) of the following: 1. ideas of reference (excluding delusions of reference) 2. odd beliefs or magical thinking that influences behaviour and is inconsistent with subcultural norms (e.g., superstitiousness, belief in clairvoyance, telepathy, or "sixth sense"; in children and adolescents, bizarre fantasies or preoccupations) 3. unusual perceptual experiences, including bodily illusions 4. odd thinking and speech (e.g., vague, circumstantial, metaphorical, overelaborate, or stereotyped) 5. suspiciousness or paranoid ideation 6. inappropriate or constricted affect 7. behaviour or appearance that is odd, eccentric, or peculiar 8. lack of close friends or confidants other than first-degree relatives 9. excessive social anxiety that does not diminish with familiarity and tends to be associated with paranoid fears rather than negative judgments about self

Case Illustration of Schizotypal Personality Disorder: Tom's Story
The odd man

Tom is a 26 year old unemployed man living in sheltered accommodation. He mainly keeps to himself as he has a nagging suspicion that people will harm him in some way, but doesn't have a clear idea about this. He has a belief that there is a special force in communication with him through some sixth sense and particularly at dusk feels a tingling in his skin which he attributes to this communication. He is not absolutely sure that this is the case.

He sees his elderly father but has no friends. People tend to avoid him, finding his thinking difficult to follow because it seems so idiosyncratic. They also find they don't really warm to him and also avoid him because his clothing attracts attention for its oddness.

Histrionic Personality Disorder

ICD10	DSM-5
F60.4 Histrionic Personality Disorder A. The general criteria of Personality Disorder (F60) must be met. B. At least four of the following must be present: 1. Self-dramatization, theatricality, or exaggerated expression of emotions. 2. Suggestibility easily influenced by others or by circumstances. 3. Shallow and labile affectivity. 4. Continually seeks excitement and activities in which the subject is the centre of attention. 5. Inappropriately seductive in appearance or behaviour. 6. Overly concerned with physical attractiveness.	**301.50 Histrionic Personality Disorder** A pervasive pattern of excessive emotionality and attention seeking, beginning by early adulthood and present in a variety of contexts, as indicated by five (or more) of the following: 1. is uncomfortable in situations in which he or she is not the centre of attention 2. interaction with others is often characterized by inappropriate sexually seductive or provocative behaviour 3. displays rapidly shifting and shallow expression of emotions 4. consistently uses physical appearance to draw attention to self 5. has a style of speech that is excessively impressionistic and lacking in detail 6. shows self-dramatization, theatricality, and exaggerated expression of emotion 7. is suggestible (i.e., easily influenced by others or circumstances)

Case Illustration of Histrionic Personality Disorder: Jessica's Story *The drama queen*

Jessica is a friend of Nina's as described above. She works in TV as a producer's assistant. Although they've been friends since childhood, Nina finds Jessica hard work – she is sometimes exciting to be around and sometimes exasperating. At parties Jessica attracts a bevy of people around her with her swooping statements and giddy emotions. As Nina knows her well, she is aware how much time she spends on looking attractive, and is no longer outraged at how flirtatious she can be with other women's partners. She also has a weary knowledge that the opinions Jessica makes with such force at any one time will change by the next party.

Dissocial (Antisocial) Personality Disorder

ICD10	DSM-5
F60.2 Dissocial Personality Disorder A. The general criteria of Personality Disorder (F60) must be met. B. At least three of the following must be present:	**301.7 Antisocial Personality Disorder** There is a pervasive pattern of disregard for and violation of the rights of others, occurring since age 15 years, as indicated by three (or more) of the following:
(1) Callous unconcern for the feelings of others. (2) Gross and persistent attitude of irresponsibility and disregard for social norms, rules, and obligations. (3) Incapacity to maintain enduring relationships, though having no difficulty to establish them. (4) Very low tolerance to frustration and a low threshold for discharge of aggression, including violence. (5) Incapacity to experience guilt, or to profit from adverse experience, particularly punishment. (6) Marked proneness to blame others, or to offer plausible rationalizations for the behaviour bringing the subject into conflict with society.	1. failure to conform to social norms with respect to lawful behaviours, as indicated by repeatedly performing acts that are grounds for arrest 2. deceitfulness, as indicated by repeated lying, use of aliases, or conning others for personal profit or pleasure 3. impulsivity or failure to plan ahead 4. irritability and aggressiveness, as indicated by repeated physical fights or assaults 5. reckless disregard for safety of self or others 6. consistent irresponsibility, as indicated by repeated failure to sustain consistent work behaviour or honour financial obligations 7. lack of remorse, as indicated by being indifferent to or rationalizing having hurt, mistreated, or stolen from another

Case Illustration of Antisocial Personality Disorder: Jason's Story
Part 1 *I have smacked a few people – I know that's not great – but then they shouldn't wind me up*

Jason is a 31 year old British man who is a patient at the same Personality Disorder service that Nina attends. His problem is anger. He admits he has a very short fuse and gets furious at any sense that he is being slighted. He has often been violent in the past and has severely beaten up several people. Although he professes to regret these events, this seems more regret that he was caught out rather than any real sense of any damage he has done to anyone else. His expressed regret seems perfunctory and superficial. On being asked regarding his last assault he said 'yeah, I smashed a glass into his face and I shouldn't have done it I know – but if he hadn't spoken to me like that I wouldn't have done it.' He has also had numerous skirmishes with the law for theft, and he has been banned from driving due to repeated traffic offences. Repeatedly cautioned or jailed for these offences, these sentences deter him very little and he continues his destructive path.

He has a remarkable ability to explain away any of his misadventures – they always seem to be due to force of circumstance or due to someone else's influence – but never due to him. The explanations are very convincing though. It is in getting to know him for a longer time that this pattern emerges.

He has been in a number of short term relationships – his last girlfriend leaving him after he had seriously assaulted her when she had found evidence of him having an affair. When asked about this in his assessment, he had responded 'Yeah I know I slapped her around a bit but she asked for it – going on and on about me seeing someone else. She knows I've got a temper on me – she should have just backed off and seen she was winding me up and would get a smack. She wasn't too bright – you know?'

Case Illustration of Antisocial Personality Disorder: Ronald's Story Part 1

Ronald is a 27 year old man who is also attending the service. Similarly to Jason, his problem has also been characterised by angry outbursts. There are many similarities with Jason, including a disregard for social rules, a chilling callousness regarding how others feel, and a seeming inability to learn from previous bad experiences. However there are subtle but significant differences between them.

While both have been responsible for violently beating up other men, Ronald's lack of regret is more chilling. In fact his regret seems entirely because he was caught out rather than any real sense of any damage he has done to someone else. He has also been a more problematic member in the service. While both were at times provocative with other patients and also with staff, Ronald's baiting was more sustained and effective. Indeed he seemed to have a talent for seeking out other's vulnerabilities and using this to upset them. At one point in a meeting, Nina had been tentatively discussing her suspicion that her partner Eddy was interested in an ex partner of his. Sensing that she may be feeling insecure in competition with a younger unattached young woman, Ronald had embarked on a tale of how he knew of a friend who'd dumped a previous partner for the more obvious attractions of a younger woman. Nina had become visibly more upset and Ronald seemed to be getting some excitement out of her increasing agitation.

Anankastic (Perfectionist) Personality Disorder

ICD10	DSM-5
F60.5 Anankastic Personality Disorder	**301.4 Obsessive - Compulsive Disorder**
Note: Often referred to as obsessive-compulsive Personality Disorder. A. The general criteria of Personality Disorder (F60) must be met. B. At least four of the following must be present: 1. Feelings of excessive doubt and caution. 2. Preoccupation with details, rules, lists, order, organization or schedule. 3. Perfectionism that interferes with task completion. 4. Excessive conscientiousness and scrupulousness. 5. Undue preoccupation with productivity to the exclusion of pleasure and interpersonal relationships. 6. Excessive pedantry and adherence to social conventions. 7. Rigidity and stubbornness. 8. Unreasonable insistence that others submit to exactly his or her way of doing things, or unreasonable reluctance to allow others to do things.	A pervasive pattern of preoccupation with orderliness, perfectionism, and mental and interpersonal control—at the expense of flexibility, openness, and efficiency—beginning by early adulthood and present in a variety of contexts, as indicated by four (or more) of the following: 1. is preoccupied with details, rules, lists, order, organization, or schedules to the extent that the major point of the activity is lost 2. shows perfectionism that interferes with task completion (e.g.is unable to complete a project because his or her own overly strict standards are not met) 3. is excessively devoted to work and productivity to the exclusion of leisure activities and friendships (not accounted for by obvious economic necessity) 4. is overconscientious, scrupulous, and inflexible about matters of morality, ethics, or values (not accounted for by cultural or religious identification)

ICD10	DSM-5
	5. is unable to discard worn-out or worthless objects even when they have no sentimental value
	6. is reluctant to delegate tasks or to work with others unless they submit to exactly his or her way of doing things
	7. adopts a miserly spending style toward both self and others; money is viewed as something to be hoarded for future catastrophes
	8. shows rigidity and stubbornness

Case Illustration of Anankastic (Perfectionist) Personality Disorder: Linda's Story Part 1 *'I'd like to re-recheck that again please – I like the job to be perfect'*

Linda is Nina's nurse at the Personality Disorder service. She enjoys her job but struggles with various aspects of it. She is a stickler for rules – following the various regulations regarding documentation of notes and data entry meticulously. She also sets a very high standard for her work, making her reports very lengthy and detailed. In fact she is so meticulous and sets such a high standard that she often leaves the office late to complete her work. Part of the reason for the excessive detail is that she often doubts her clinical judgement and is thus very cautious. Linda is aware of these perfectionist tendencies and tries to curb them – aided by her team who tease her regarding her obsessive attention to detail. She is liked by Nina and the other patients and is well regarded by her team.

Anxious (Avoidant) Personality Disorder

ICD10	DSM-5
F60.6 Anxious (Avoidant) Personality Disorder A. The general criteria of Personality Disorder (F60) must be met. B. At least four of the following must be present:	**301.82 Avoidant Personality Disorder** A pervasive pattern of social inhibition, feelings of inadequacy, and hypersensitivity to negative evaluation, beginning by early adulthood and present in a variety of contexts, as indicated by four (or more) of the following:
1. Persistent and pervasive feelings of tension and apprehension.	1. avoids occupational activities that involve significant interpersonal contact, because of fears of criticism, disapproval, or rejection

ICD10	DSM-5
2. Belief that oneself is socially inept, personally unappealing, or inferior to others. 3. Excessive preoccupation about being criticized or rejected in social situations. 4. Unwillingness to get involved with people unless certain of being liked. 5. Restrictions in lifestyle because of need of security. 6. Avoidance of social or occupational activities that involve significant interpersonal contact, because of fear of criticism, disapproval or rejection.	2. is unwilling to get involved with people unless certain of being liked 3. shows restraint within intimate relationships because of the fear of being shamed or ridiculed 4. is preoccupied with being criticized or rejected in social situations. 5. is inhibited in new interpersonal situations because of feelings of inadequacy 6. views self as socially inept, personally unappealing, or inferior to others 7. is unusually reluctant to take personal risks or to engage in any new activities because they may prove embarrassing

Case illustration of Anxious (Avoidant) Personality Disorder: Neville's Story Part 2 *Ooh I'd rather not if you don't mind*

Neville is a 47 year old white British man born in Nottingham whose family moved to London when he was 4. He came to the attention of services in his early thirties because his family were increasingly concerned that he was isolating himself, barely leaving his bedroom after having dropped out of an electrical engineering course and having done a number of unskilled jobs since. He described feeling very uncomfortable in company, feeling that he had nothing to contribute to the conversation, that he was boring and unattractive and in his words 'a drag to be around. When I'm around I seem to suck the oxygen from the conversation – they're probably thinking who's he anyway, why doesn't he just disappear?'

He has one close friend who he's known since school and meets up with sometimes. Although he feels lonely and would like to meet a partner, he is reluctant to do anything about it because he feels he won't be liked, and more likely, will be found wanting.

As above, Neville is in treatment in the Personality Disorder Service. Neville's withdrawn way of interacting in the group is explored further in an individual session with the therapist in the Personality Disorder service. Neville says he really has to force himself to come to the group. He feels so comfortable in his house and the thought of being in the group makes him very anxious. In the meeting with his therapist he says 'They'll just think I'm weird anyway and I've got nothing to say anyway and if I do say something it's so boring that it's not worth saying really. I'm not a cool guy

– I don't even need to open my mouth for people to think I'm someone you don't really want to spend time with – that it would be a bit boring. You're probably wishing you'd been allocated a different patient as well'.

Neville continues: I'm sure that when I talk, people are thinking what I'm saying is stupid or boring and that it's a bit of a waste of time listening to me. I never say it right anyway. I really like Nina – but she doesn't really know I exist – and nothing I say would really change that – I'm just not that attractive am I? But at least she's nice – not like some of the others in the therapy group. I'm sure that they're just sitting there thinking that what I say is rubbish and I'm sure they wish I wasn't in the group. That's why I'm quiet in the group. I'm glad that it's a rule in this service that patients can't socialise outside the programme; I'd never get invited if patients got together for a meal or to go out for a drink. But even if I had been invited I wouldn't go because I wouldn't enjoy it and I'd be feeling nervous all the time that people were wishing they hadn't invited me. So I wish I could just stay at home really – but then I get lonely just being by myself, even if it's so comfortable'.

Dependent Personality Disorder

ICD10	DSM-5
F60.7 Dependent Personality Disorder	**301.6 Dependent Personality Disorder**
A. The general criteria of Personality Disorder (F60) must be met. B. At least four of the following must be present: 1. Encouraging or allowing others to make most of one's important life decisions. 2. Subordination of one's own needs to those of others on whom one is dependent, and undue compliance with their wishes. 3. Unwillingness to make even reasonable demands on the people one depends on. 4. Feeling uncomfortable or helpless when alone, because of exaggerated fears of inability to care for oneself.	A pervasive and excessive need to be taken care of that leads to submissive and clinging behaviour and fears of separation, beginning by early adulthood and present in a variety of contexts, as indicated by five (or more) of the following: 1. has difficulty making everyday decisions without an excessive amount of advice and reassurance from others 2. needs others to assume responsibility for most major areas of his or her life 3. has difficulty expressing disagreement with others because of fear of loss of support or approval. Note: Do not include realistic fears of retribution.

ICD10	DSM-5
5. Preoccupation with fears of being left to take care of oneself. 6. Limited capacity to make everyday decisions without an excessive amount of advice and reassurance from others.	4. has difficulty initiating projects or doing things on his or her own (because of a lack of self-confidence in judgment or abilities rather than a lack of motivation or energy) 5. goes to excessive lengths to obtain nurturance and support from others, to the point of volunteering to do things that are unpleasant 6. feels uncomfortable or helpless when alone because of exaggerated fears of being unable to care for himself or herself 7. urgently seeks another relationship as a source of care and support when a close relationship ends 8. is unrealistically preoccupied with fears of being left to take care of himself or herself

Case Illustration of Dependent Personality Disorder: Paul's Story Continued *I don't know – what do you think I should do?*

Nina's brother Paul is a clerk in his father's business and moved back to living with his parents after his marriage failed 3 years ago. He had met Helen, his former wife, at school and they had been going out since. Helen still cares for Paul but finally felt unable to continue in the relationship. She'd explained to Nina 'I don't know – Paul just can't make any decisions for himself – he wanted me to decide whether he should stay working for your father or retrain. But it's not only on the big things he wants help to decide. He would phone me to ask if he should top up his mobile phone or wait a bit – small things like that. And when we went to see a film I was never sure if he did want to see it or if he was just going because I wanted to see it. After all these years it just got too much – how much he was expecting of me – I feel awful because I still love him in a way – I just wish he'd grow up and think for himself for once.'

Nina and her family are worried about Paul, who seems to be obsessed with his parents' health and they are worried what will happen to him when they pass away. He is unhappy when they go on holiday abroad as he doesn't like running the house on his own and has said, only half jokingly, that the next time they go away they can invite him along.

Narcissistic Personality Disorder

ICD10	DSM-5
This diagnosis is not listed in ICD10	**301.81 Narcissistic Personality Disorder** A pervasive pattern of grandiosity (in fantasy or behaviour), need for admiration, and lack of empathy, beginning by early adulthood and present in a variety of contexts, as indicated by five (or more) of the following: 1. Has a grandiose sense of self-importance (e.g., exaggerates achievements and talents, expects to be recognized as superior without commensurate achievements). 2. Is preoccupied with fantasies of unlimited success, power, brilliance, beauty, or ideal love. 3. Believes that he or she is "special" and unique and can only be understood by, or should associate with, other special or high-status people (or institutions). 4. Requires excessive admiration. 5. Has a sense of entitlement, i.e., unreasonable expectations of especially favorable treatment or automatic compliance with his or her expectations. 6. Is interpersonally exploitative, i.e., takes advantage of others to achieve his or her own ends. 7. Lacks empathy: is unwilling to recognize or identify with the feelings and needs of others. 8. Is often envious of others or believes that others are envious of him or her. 9. Shows arrogant, haughty behaviours or attitudes.

Case Illustration of Narcissistic Personality Disorder: Damian's Story

I'm special, oh so special, so special so special me
Why oh why do all the others not just simply agree?

Damian is a 43 year old White British man. He trained as a solicitor and interned in the City but has since been working in a modest local law firm. He feels that it has been a disappointment in life that he was not kept on by the prestigious firm where he trained as he feels that he belongs there, being briefed with cases worth millions of pounds rather than the hum drum of 'Mundane people with their ordinary little lives.

Filled with boring disputes, divorces and suburban wives.'

This is a ditty that he hums to himself while smiling to his clients. He has become isolated from a professional perspective, spurning the company of his present colleagues who he regards as boring and as petty as his clients. He has also lost contact with his former colleagues who he believes have glittering lives and wives, which makes him feel vastly inferior.

In the therapy group Damian is quiet for extended periods. He is the least popular member of the group. When he does talk it is to offer advice to other members of the group but this is given in a rather patronising manner and usually misses the emotional point. His other favoured topic is the kind of work he will do when he 'gets back to work in the City', which will involve razor sharp negotiations in cases worth millions of pounds. He is single and has been so for several years, waiting for the right partner to come along who will be a good enough match for him in terms of her attractiveness, intelligence, education and income.

Damian is a patient in the programme. But not all individuals with a Personality Disorder are receiving a treatment. A case in point is Nina's mother, Cressida. Reading about her also may give us some understanding of how Nina's difficulties may have developed as they did.

Case Illustration of Narcissistic Personality Disorder: Cressida's Story

Nina's mother, Cressida has always felt that she deserves more recognition than she receives and feels in some way cheated and underappreciated. A talented piano player in childhood, she had not made the grade as a concert performer to her immense chagrin and she took up teaching instead. She rose through the ranks and is now Head of English at a reputable girls secondary school. However she is disappointed that she has been passed over as deputy head of the school. She regards only the head teacher as her real equal and tends to avoid the staff tea room. She is not popular among her colleagues, who experience her as rather arrogant and distant. She has ongoing dreams of being appointed deputy head of her school although there is no real prospect of this.

She has also been working on an unfinished novel for the last 13 years and grimly reads the short list for the Booker prize each year as this is where she believes her novel should be placed. She has also turned down invitations to join her local book reading club believing it too parochial. Although she is struggling to finish her novel, and has been eyeing a workshop run annually on 'How to finally finish that novel' she feels she cannot attend as she'd feel too exposed discussing her work and would feel diminished as the workshop leaders would probably be younger than her and have successfully published novels.

She has an underlying sense that her children have not lived up to her expectations. She very much wanted Nina to follow in her footsteps and be a school teacher and thinks her interest in teaching English to foreigners is misguided and beneath her station. She considers that Nina's interest in this is rather perverse and at times wonders if she specifically does this to deny her a mother's satisfaction in seeing her daughter achieving the status of a 'proper' teacher.

Cressida regards her two most important relationships as her husband and her head teacher. Richard, her husband has been her most loyal admirer, still disbelieving that this attractive and intelligent woman had chosen him as a partner. Cressida is acutely aware of how her head teacher relates to her and is constantly positioning herself to gain her good will; she feels immensely pleased if she detects approval and similarly bereft if she feels this approval is withheld.

Commentary

The concept of narcissism is a very complex one. This complexity is added to by:

1. The long history of divergent ways of understanding the term and the condition.
2. The term is also used in common language in a very dismissive and disparaging way.

Divergent Views

While there are divergent views, a useful way to understanding the problem is of an individual whose early experience has led him to have a very low sense of himself and who constantly needs approval from others to allow him to feel alright about himself. This may be more or less obvious in different individuals, who deal with this poor sense of self and need for approval in different ways.

The profile of the person with problems of narcissism, which has been described in the DSM-5, is the more *thick skinned* rather than the more *thin skinned*, more clearly vulnerable type.[51] The thick skinned or *oblivious narcissist* tends to be more arrogant and aggressive, appears to have little awareness of the reactions of others, and is more clearly self absorbed.[52]

The thin skinned narcissist is inhibited, shy, even self-effacing, is highly sensitive to the reaction of others, and tends to direct attention more towards others than towards self.[53] The point though is that the underlying psychological problem for both 'types' of narcissism is the same – a low sense of self – which is more vigorously denied in the thick skinned narcissist. A careful understanding of the thick skinned narcissist will reveal underlying similarities with the thin skinned narcissist.

Misuse in Common Language

A way to possibly take the sting out of the term *narcissism* is to consider that we are all prone to narcissistic difficulties. If we consider that the defences we adopt due to these difficulties are there to protect us from feeling vulnerable or exposed, and then apply this to the individual with more extreme narcissistic difficulties, it could give us some understanding for the individual. We shouldn't underestimate the difficulty of being able to take this understanding position though. So when Nina is experiencing her mother being contemptuous of her cake making ability, she may have some understanding that this is due to Cressida's sense of competitiveness, and envy that Nina is making more of an attachment with her own children than she herself had been able to with Nina. However it may be very difficult for Nina to hold on to this understanding while Cressida is being so rude.

What's In a Name – Is It a Disorder?

Linda has traits of an Anankastic (perfectionist) Personality Disorder but does not meet formal criteria for the diagnosis as the impact of her perfectionism is not quite severe enough. Indeed, her manager values having a team member who adheres to the organisation's rules without having to be chased.

Linda's case illustrates that the personality traits that some individuals have are often valuable and it is only when they become too pronounced and start impacting negatively on the individual's life or on those around them that it becomes a disorder. So one can see that having some of the traits of being histrionic – being self-dramatising, seeking to be the centre of attention, being seductive in appearance or behaviour – are ingredients of what may help to be a successful actor.

The distinction between disease, illness and sickness is often debated. A simple way to think about this is to consider how the condition affects the individual concerned at different levels: that disease indicates some pathology, illness the individual's subjective experience and sickness the social consequences of the condition. A medical way of viewing this may be the condition of diabetes. Someone who is diabetic has a faulty processing of their glucose (disease), they may at times feel unwell when their blood glucose levels are too high (illness), and may miss an important meeting at work and be regarded as a less dependable employee and be passed over for promotion (sickness – social consequences).

Diagnosis is a key part of a medical assessment. It is important because if an underlying cause can be found then this may help determine how to treat the condition effectively.

However this level of understanding about the cause of disorders, and therefore of its treatment, is not always present in general medicine and is usually even lower in psychiatry. There is recognition of this in the classification system within ICD10 and DSM-5 where conditions are described more as *disorders* than *diagnoses*. ICD10 describes *disorders* as implying 'the existence of a clinically recognisable set of symptoms or behaviour associated in most cases with distress and with interference with personal functions.'

Therefore using the term *diagnosis* when referring to Personality Disorder is not strictly accurate. The condition may be more accurately be understood as a *disorder*. Understandably clinicians in the field would avoid the clumsiness (and greater acceptance of limits to our knowledge) of calling this a 'disorder of Personality Disorder.'

Who Gets the Diagnosis?

Paul's Dependence

Paul may have a dependent Personality Disorder but has never presented to the services and never been diagnosed as such. This illustrates that there may be many individuals in society who may meet criteria for the diagnosis of a Personality Disorder but who never present themselves and are thus never formally diagnosed. It also shows that family or partners take on roles which adapt for particular personality configurations. This adaptation may then hide the level of difficulty the individual is having. Paul's parents put up with his excessive dependence (although they grumble a bit) and in this way Paul feels reasonably comfortable and does not have to confront any problems resulting from his personality.

If we did some crystal ball gazing we would find that in 20 years time Paul will be referred to a psychotherapy service and be diagnosed as having a Dependent Personality Disorder. The question arises: if the general criteria for diagnosis of Personality Disorder is that it is early onset and enduring, is this the correct diagnosis? Surely this should have been made earlier? As stated above, Paul has not presented to services before and a reason for this is that he always had someone to look after him – first his wife, then his parents. It is only on the death of his mother (his father had died 13 years previously of an unexpected heart attack) with whom he had continued to live, that the level of Paul's dependency emerged. Until that time there had always been a system to buttress Paul's personality so that the level of his disorder was not apparent to himself or others.

If we did some further crystal ball gazing on Paul regarding his progress in therapy; we will learn that although he stayed for the duration, Paul benefitted very little from the treatment and remained very dependent on social services for his needs. Given that our personalities are difficult to change, it may have been useful for Paul to have been assessed and offered treatment at an earlier age. Personality Disorder is no different to other medical conditions regarding the usefulness of getting an accurate diagnosis to enable appropriate treatment to occur.

So why do I have Personality Disorder and she doesn't?

I know a lot of people who I think have a Personality Disorder and they're not in treatment

There are many people in the community (estimates are 6–10%) who have Personality Disorder who do not come into contact with psychotherapy services and thus do not 'gain' a diagnosis. There may be different reasons for this, including individuals or their families not seeing their personality difficulties as something requiring treatment, or not finding services accessible, or when individuals do present to general services they do not get referred onto mental health services. This may be due to individual values or due to cultural aspects; some ethnic groups may express their psychological difficulties through physical complaints more easily than talking about their relationship difficulties.

I tick all the boxes- am I a Superpoly Personality Disorder and Really Messed Up?

Depending on the mood you're in, you may well feel a number of the Personality Disorder diagnoses apply to you. This indicates a number of things: assessment of Personality Disorder will be influenced by the state you are in at the time; we are thinking of aspects of personality – it would be more surprising if you felt many of the criteria had absolutely no relevance to you. I know that on days when nothing seems to be going right for me I often think I have quite a few Personality Disorders. It is the age of onset, the pervasiveness, the enduring nature of it and how much of an impact it is having on your life – the general criteria for Personality Disorder – which will tip (albeit arbitrarily) what may be a set of personality traits you have, to being considered to have a 'personality disorder.'

Key Points

- If you've gone through the criteria for Personality Disorder and think you have a number of them– relax! In all likelihood you don't – the studies of prevalence of Personality Disorder indicate there's a greater than 10:1 chance you don't. The concern that you meet the criteria for a Personality Disorder is likely to be more a reflection that you may be feeling particularly anxious or self critical at the present time.
- Not everyone with a Personality Disorder is in treatment – you may wish they were.
- Take these diagnostic criteria with some healthy scepticism – less certainty exists than they imply. However this is not to say that we should just discard these classifications. They are of some clinical use. However their limitations should be understood and diagnoses should be made, and received, with caution.

PART TWO

What is the Treatment?

CHAPTER 6

The Treatment

Nina's Story Part 6–Treating Nina

Nina has now completed the preparatory group and joined the treatment group. We join her at various points.

The following exchange occurs in a one to one session with her therapist.

Week 3: 'Don't Let Me Waste Your Time' a Prickly Encounter

Nina: I can't stand Allie (another patient who is in the same treatment group as Nina) – she's such a hypocrite – she has the nerve to lecture me about how to bring up my own kids.

The therapist clarifies Nina is referring to an exchange that happened in the group the previous week. Nina had been complaining about social services being on her back again about the children. Nina had become very angry one afternoon at the children and started shouting at them. A concerned neighbour had asked the police to investigate. When the police visited they found nothing to concern them, but they had contacted social services, who had in turn visited the home. Allie, a fellow patient in the group had said it really upset her when she saw parents shouting at their children. Nina had taken offence and had stormed out of the group. She is now complaining about Allie.

> Linda: You were very upset by what Allie said.
> Nina: Of course I was!
> Linda: What did she say again?
> Nina: Something like it really upsets her when she sees parents shouting at kids.
> Linda: You felt that she was criticising you?
> Nina: Of course she was! What else could she have been doing – why did she have to say that?
> Linda: Well I don't know, I wasn't in the group. Do you think it's possible she was thinking about the children – and getting worried about them?

Nina: Well that's the same as criticising me isn't it?
Linda: Again I'm not sure – it's possible that it's more an expression of concern about the children. Do you-
Nina: (interrupts) – Right that's it – you're taking her side. Do you also have a problem with my parenting skills? Do you want to get onto social services – don't let me stop you – I can leave the meeting now and you can get onto the phone – I don't want to waste your time – you've been wasting mine anyway – I want another therapist.

Nina storms out. Linda collects her notes. This is the third time Nina has stormed out from one of their sessions over the last 3 weeks. Linda realises she is now feeling shaky and very upset herself and wonders why.

Week 4 Should I Admit Her to Hospital?

Nina continues to struggle. Social services remain involved. Eddy is also becoming increasingly concerned about the children's welfare and wants them to come and stay with him, even if temporarily. Nina sees this as evidence that Eddy wants a permanent split and has a raging row with him. She becomes intoxicated, and cuts her wrists, and then phones Eddy to inform him she is feeling suicidal. Eddy phones the hospital and an ambulance takes Nina to the Emergency Services. She is assessed by a junior psychiatrist who seeks advice from the consultant. The junior psychiatrist says that he has assessed a patient with Borderline Personality Disorder who has cut her wrist superficially, and is saying she still feels she may harm herself if she is sent home. The junior psychiatrist asks his senior: Should I admit this patient to hospital?

Between weeks 4 and 12 Nina continues with her treatment. She has problems with her attendance at times but seems to have on the whole engaged in her treatment.

Week 12 Give Me the Pills Please

Nina is seen 3 months after the start of her treatment at the Personality Disorder service to review her progress. Nina is finding the therapy difficult. In fact she is feeling worse than when she started. She believes she is more depressed. The psychiatrist in the Personality Disorder Service assesses her but does not make a diagnosis of clinical depression. Nina is outraged. 'How can you say I'm not depressed? My mood is really low. I want to be put onto antidepressants – or any medication that makes me feel better. I want them prescribed as soon as possible – I'm feeling dreadful. Are you going to write them up for me or not? If you don't I'll ask my doctor to write them up or get them off the internet. I've already told my family doctor I'm depressed and he said he can't understand why I'm not on antidepressants and that he'd discuss it with you.' She breaks off, glaring at the psychiatrist.

Evidence Based Psychological Treatments

As described earlier, it is useful to think of someone's personality along the lines of how they usually think, feel, behave and how they relate to others. In the prickly encounter that Nina has just had with Linda, there is evidence of a particular pattern in which she thinks, feels, acts and relates to others that impacts negatively either on her or others around her. The treatment approach to this differs with various therapies having different emphases – as shown in Table 5.

The treatments with the strongest evidence base for Borderline Personality Disorder, demonstrated through randomised controlled trials are Mentalization Based Treatment (MBT), Transference Focused Psychotherapy (TFP), Schema Focused Therapy (SFT), Dialectical Behavioural Therapy (DBT) and Cognitive Analytic Treatment (CAT).

Given the high prevalence of Personality Disorder and its impact on society it is remarkable and disappointing that there is little evidence for the treatment of other Personality Disorders as diagnosed by ICD10 or DSM-5, although there is a little evidence for the treatment of Antisocial Personality Disorder and Avoidant Personality Disorder with Cognitive Behavioural Therapy.

Common Characteristics of Psychological Treatments

The evidence based treatments above share common characteristics. As shown in Table 4 these include:[54,55]

So if you want to judge your own Personality Disorder service, you could measure it alongside these criteria to see how it matches up.

Extra Content: Brief Descriptions of the Different Evidence Based Treatments for Borderline Personality Disorder

There are more similarities than differences between the evidence based treatments for Borderline Personality Disorder.[56] There is also no clear evidence base for the superiority of one treatment over another. Therefore the reader should not get too focused on selecting one particular treatment.

Table 4: Common Characteristics of Evidence Based Treatments for Borderline Personality Disorder.

A primary clinician who works with the patient	Assesses day to day and overall progress, including risk.
An agreed upon, well structured treatment	Objectives of treatment and roles of patient and therapist are defined, including limits of roles and guidelines on crisis management
An emphasis on collaboration	
A clear focus of work	
Connecting acts and feelings to behaviour	Therapist refuses to see things as inexplicable, constantly trying to link thoughts and feelings to behaviour
Patient is active in the treatment	Patients need to know that their progress depends on how active they are in controlling their thoughts, feelings and behaviour and their very future
Therapist is active in the treatment	The therapist is active in the treatment rather than passive or laissez-faire. The therapist monitors the patient's safety, confronts silences and avoidance
Therapist works in a structured and supported environment	Therapist is able to share thoughts and feelings of working with complex individuals with colleagues and receives supervision in his work
Makes sense to both the clinician and patient	The therapeutic approach is coherent and understandable
Are relatively long-term	Treatment usually lasts between 1 to 2 years
Link in well with other services	Easy access to emergency services and medical review

This short overview will attempt to give some sense of the main aspects and approaches of the different treatments by applying them to Nina. It is written so that you have information about the type of therapy which is being offered and also in case there is choice (less likely in public sector – where the more severe forms of personality disorder will be treated). While I've tried to unpack some of the terms, it hasn't always been possible to do so. If you do read this section, I suggest you go for its overall sense rather than getting too preoccupied with detail. A second way to read this section is to appreciate how the different proponents, as they develop their theory and approach, start to overlap. Just as Freud sharpened his understanding and technique based on what actually happens with the patient, so have the methods below developed from the clinical treatment of the individual with Borderline Personality Disorder.

The treatments with the strongest evidence base, demonstrated through randomised controlled trials are shown in Table 5:

Mentalization Based Treatment

Theoretical Background

Mentalization Based Treatment has been adapted from psychodynamic therapy mainly by two psychoanalysts in London – Peter Fonagy, a psychologist, and Anthony Bateman, a psychiatrist.[57] It draws particularly on developmental and attachment theory.

Drawing from developmental theory, Peter Fonagy suggests that the ability to mentalize (namely to understand the behaviour of others in terms of their thoughts feelings, and intention) does not just occur constitutionally. Instead the ability to mentalize is a developmental achievement. For this development to occur depends on having had a secure attachment. And for a secure attachment to occur depends on having one's experiences appropriately mirrored in childhood.

It is thought that patients with Borderline Personality Disorder have an insecure attachment, leading to deficits in mentalizing . These deficits lead to problems in regulating one's emotions, attention and self control.

Key Concepts

Borderline Personality Disorder is due to a greater tendency to lose the ability to mentalize particularly in the context of attachment.

Mentalizing: is the process of making sense of ourselves and each other. It is both implicit (conveyed but unspoken) and explicit (conveyed by what we say or by our actions). It is thought about in social terms – what we think may be going on in the mind of the other person when we are interacting with them.

Essentially we are mentalizing all the time – think of the last time you had coffee with a friend. What probably happened (if you were mentalizing that is) is that you were in touch with what you were thinking and feeling, and also in touch with what your friend's thoughts and feelings. Lets imagine you were feeling quite good, but were aware that your friend may be

Table 5: Evidence based Treatments for Borderline Personality Disorder.

	Mentalization Based Treatment (MBT)	Transference Focused Psychotherapy (TFP)	Schema Focused Therapy (SFT)	Dialectical Behavioural Therapy (DBT)	Cognitive Analytic Treatment (CAT)
Theoretical background	Psychoanalytic • Development theory • Attachment theory Cognitive	Psychoanalytic • Object relations • Drive theory	Cognitive Behavioural Therapy (CBT)	Cognitive Behavioural Therapy Dialectical theory	Psychoanalytic Cognitive
Key concepts	Mentalizing Deficits in mentalizing Self structure	Identity diffusion, Aggression Object relations Primitive defence mechanisms	Schemas Coping strategies Schema modes	Emotion dysregulation Invalidating environment	Self states Reciprocal roles and procedures
Mechanisms of change	Increased mentalization	Increased integration of concept of self	Change in maladaptive schemas	Learning new behaviour Synthesising opposing ideas	Change in reciprocal procedures
Treatment goals	Increase the ability to mentalize within an attached relationship Improved relationship to self and others	Integration of identity Improved relationship to self and others	Identify and modify schema	Emotion regulation Distress tolerance Interpersonal effectiveness Control over behaviour	Recognise and revise unhelpful patterns

Patient therapist relationship	Collaborative Therapist not assume an expert stance Exploration of relationship	Therapist neutrality Exploration of relationship	Collaborative Reparenting	Dialectical relationship – acceptance and change	Non collusive
Techniques	Enhancing mentalizing (including about the transference) Keeping patient's mentalizing deficits in mind	Clarification Confrontation Interpretation (within the Transference)	Identifying schemas Guided discovery	Problem solving Validation Skills training Affect control Mindfulness	Description (writing letter to patient) Identifying roles patient adopts and expects
Framework	Group and individual 2–5x week 18 months Outpatient/day hospital	Individual 2x week 1 year Outpatient	Individual 1–2x week 1 year	Group and individual 2x week 1 year Inpatient/Outpatient	Individual 1x week 6 months Outpatient

struggling in a close relationship. You listened to what she wanted to tell you but you didn't go into much detail about feeling great yourself. Instead you helped her think about what was upsetting her, whether she was taking things too hard. This is all good mentalizing – being in touch with you own thoughts and that of your friend. So we all mentalize, and can do it effortlessly most of the time. However we all lose this ability at times when we feel under some kind of stress. People with Borderline Personality Disorder are prone to lose the ability to mentalize very quickly. This loss of mentalizing ability is particularly present in interacting with others, particularly when attached to them.

Treatment of Borderline Personality Disorder thus focuses on the capacity to mentalize. Recovery of mentalizing helps the individual to regulate his thoughts and feelings, helping him to both manage himself and his relationships better. The cognitive and behavioural changes which occur due to better mentalizing occur almost as a positive side effect.

Deficits in mentalizing: the treatment particularly picks up this. Three specific deficits in mentalizing are described by the rather technical terms 'psychic equivalence' 'teleological thinking' and 'pretend mode' and these have been described earlier in the book (page 17) as:

1. Psychic equivalence mode: Mode of thinking in which reality is equated with mental states. This is where the person believes that what he is thinking or feeling is unequivocally the truth and the only way to view the situation – his view is the 'truth' and no other perspectives are possible.
2. Teleological mode: When there is an overemphasis on the physical rather than the mental – thus experience is only felt to be valid when there is some physical 'proof' of it. This may be expressed by someone saying 'You say you are acting in my best interest and care. I feel I can only really believe it if you give me a hug.'
3. Pretend mode: When the person's thoughts and feelings lose touch with each other, and with reality. This may result in intellectualising or speaking in a meaningless way.

Self structure: this describes the individual's sense of himself. A child who cannot develop a representation of her own experience through being appropriately mirrored (namely marked mirroring, where the parent mirrors the child in a way which, while contingent, is sufficiently distinct for the child to realise the emotion is not actually the parent's) internalizes the image of the parent as her self representation. The problem is that as this is not actually the child's experience but that of the care giver, the child has a *alien* part to herself now, leading to a sense of incoherence about herself. The individual with this incoherent sense of herself constantly tries to get rid of this alien part into those around her. This pattern is similar to the concept of *projective identification* (this term is defined in the glossary).

Mechanisms of change: This occurs through increased mentalization. The increased ability to accurately identify what is going on in one's own mental state and that of others is of fundamental importance in negotiating our way through the world.

Treatment Goals

The main task is to increase mentalizing. This entails encouraging a curiosity about the way mental states motivate and explain the actions of oneself and others.

The main understanding of Borderline Personality Disorder in Mentalization Based Treatment terms is the loss of mentalizing in the context of attachment. Therefore it is Mentalization Based Treatment's explicit goal to improve the patient's ability to 'mentalize' *within* at attached relationship, in this case with the therapist. This points to the conundrum in therapy which Mentalization Based Treatment attempts to address: to keep the focus on mentalizing while at the same time activating attachment. Remember we said that the ability to mentalize can be decreased in the context of feeling attached. Mentalization Based Treatment is saying we know 'love is blind' but lets see how much you can keep mentalizing in this context of being in love/attached. The 'love is blind' state can also be used for therapeutic advantage – we all know how, when we are in love, we are more open and less guarded. In the same way, when the patient is in an attached state, his defences may drop a little and he may be more open to rewiring established (but unhelpful) neural pathways.

Patient Therapist Relationship

The therapist is not the expert: Instead he shows an ability to realise that there can be no certainty of what goes on in the mind of the other (in this case the patient) and that he is curious to work out what this is. This is not at all to say the therapist does not have expertise (he has to, to hold onto this stance in the face of the demands of the patient!) just that he does not have some god given privilege on the contents of the mind of the other.

Exploration of relationship: this is used to increase the patient's ability to mentalize. For example the therapist may say: 'I'm not sure but I seem to have upset you – can we just go back a bit to understand a bit better what was happening in the session?'

Collaborative: both have responsibility to understand mental processes.

Techniques

Enhancing mentalizing: unusually for a manualized treatment, there is a permissiveness of techniques allowed in MBT, with the rider that whatever the approach taken, it needs to be with the aim of increasing mentalizing ability.

The therapist works in a way which lives out the mentalizing approach. Thus the therapist shows:[58]

- Humility – deriving from the sense of not knowing. While the focus is on the thoughts and feelings of his patient, the therapist can never be absolutely sure what is going on. This is what is meant by the therapist not taking an 'expert stance'.
- An active interest in the viewpoints of others and a real willingness to accept different perspectives.
- Openness in admitting failures in his own mentalizing (given that we all have problems in mentalizing at times).
- A particular way of working with the transference – 'mentalizing the transference'. In the Mentalization Based Treatment approach the aim of interpretation is not specifically to improve insight. Instead 'mentalizing the transference' aims to encourage patients to think about the relationship they are in with the therapist with the aim of focusing their attention on another mind (the therapist's) to contrast how they see themselves or others with the perception of the therapist.

Keeping the patient's mentalizing deficits in mind: The therapist is fine tuned into detecting when the patient stops mentalizing and then rewinds back to the point when this deficit occurred to explore the patient's thoughts and feelings at that point.

Framework: The treatment is delivered as individual and group therapy, twice weekly or as part of daily attendance at a day hospital.

Relationship to Other Treatments

Mentalization Based Treatment is closest in approach to Transference Focused Psychotherapy in terms of its origins in psychodynamic thinking, also being influenced by theories of internal objects and understanding of projective identification.

Mentalization Based Treatment differs from Transference Focused Psychotherapy in the following ways:

- In its focused attention on increasing the patient's ability to mentalize.
- in its approach to the transference. The Mentalization Based Treatment therapist is more open about what may have been non mentalizing on his part than is the case in Transference Focused Psychotherapy.
- in its reluctance to describe more complex mental states.

How Mentalization Based Treatment would be applied to Nina

Nina shows two aspects which are common in individuals with Borderline Personality Disorder.

1. She has an insecure way of attaching to others. This can be seen in the very long time Nina requires to develop some trust in the Personality Disorder Service.
2. Her ability to mentalize is lost particularly easily when she becomes attached to someone. Thus at the times when Nina felt particularly close to her therapist Linda, she also often became more suspicious of her.

The treatment would therefore emphasise:

1. Working in a way that allows a more secure attachment to develop.
2. Helping her regain her ability to mentalize when it is lost with people she is close to.

Transference Focused Psychotherapy

Theoretical Background

Transference Focused Psychotherapy is form of psychodynamic therapy developed by the American psychoanalyst and psychiatrist, Otto Kernberg.[59]

It is based on his theory of *object relations*, which describes opposing representations/ways of seeing oneself and of others. The object relations view emphasizes how someone with Borderline Personality Disorder perceives events in a way which is strongly influenced by internal representations of himself and of others, and by the very strong affects which link these representations.

Drives represent for human behaviour the equivalent of what instincts constitute for animals. The *drive theory* originates from Freud's dual-drive theory of libido and aggression – Freud believed that as humans we have an instinct for love and life but also an instinct for aggression and death. These positive and negative tendencies may also be reflected in different object relations, for example a positive one of being perfectly looked after by a perfect carer and a negative one of a child being abused or neglected by a cruel carer.

Key Concepts

Otto Kernberg has developed a psychoanalytic categorisation of personality structure which he refers to as *Borderline Personality Organization*. This categorization does not equate to the DSM-5 diagnosis of Borderline Personality Disorder. Instead the Borderline Personality Organization includes a number of specific Personality Disorders, including, Borderline, Narcissistic and Antisocial Personality Disorder. Borderline Personality Organisation is due to:[60]

1. *Identity diffusion:* Transference Focused Psychotherapy sees this as the core of Borderline Personality Disorder. It views this as the individual lacking a sense of continuity of his experience of himself and of others. This lack of continuity results from an inner world which is split and polarized. In this inner world others are likely to be experienced as being either persecutory or idealised as rescuers.[61]
2. *Aggression:* The identify diffusion is due to the individual having an excess of aggressive internalised object relations over idealised ones. In order to protect the idealised part of the self and others from this excessive aggression, the individual has to use the defence mechanisms described below.
3. *Objects relation dyads:* this rather technical term means that ways of representing oneself and other people are linked to specific feelings/affects. For example, Nina often represented herself as a vulnerable child in relation to an uncaring dismissive parent and thus unsurprisingly, the emotion she felt in this self image was of fear, hurt and being unloved.
4. *Primitive defence mechanisms:* these include projective identification (see annexure for definition), omnipotence, devaluation, denial and idealisation.

Mechanisms of Change

Change occurs with the integration of opposing internal representations. This is achieved by having the contradictory parts of the individual uncovered and painstakingly worked through in the therapy. This moves the individual with Borderline Personality Disorder from his one-dimensional, polarised representations of himself and others into a more complex whole. This move to a more complex whole provides a sense of coherence and continuity in the individual's experience of himself and of others.

Treatment Goals

The objective is to integrate the patient's contradictory representations, allowing for the integration of split off aspects of personality. The treatment focus is on the therapy relationship.

Patient Therapist Relationship

The therapist maintains a *neutrality* in the face of the opposing views the patient has both of himself and of the therapist. This does not mean that the therapist is cold or indifferent to the individual's struggle, more that he observes the patient's conflicting views and communicates this to the patient. In this way the patient becomes more aware of these contrary views in order that he can try to integrate them.

Techniques

The therapist constantly keeps in mind the relationship the patient has to him by focusing on the transference to him. In Nina's case, is she relating to him as a vulnerable child would to an uncaring parent?
Transference Focused Psychotherapy relies on:

Clarification: of what is on the patient's mind.
Confrontation: the therapist tactfully drawing attention to the patient's inconsistencies or contradictions.
Interpretation: is more focused on the present rather than the past than in standard psychoanalysis.

Framework It is delivered as twice weekly individual therapy

Relationship to Other Treatments

Transference Focused Psychotherapy is closest in approach to Mentalization Based Treatment. A key difference is in how the transference is worked with in the treatment. In Transference Focused Psychotherapy there is a specific focus on the dyads which may be operating at the time – both the negative ones and positive ones.

How Transference Focused Psychotherapy Would Be Applied to Nina

Nina shows particular aspects which are common in individuals with Borderline Personality Disorder. She has problems with strong feelings of aggression. She has difficulty with having a joined up or integrated sense of herself. Instead she has very divided extreme views of herself and of others which shift rapidly from one view to the other. So at times Nina's view of herself would be as a defenceless child, but at times she would suddenly adopt the very role she felt at the mercy of, namely of an uncaring all powerful adult. These sudden changes would not only confuse Nina but all those around her. And the underlying emotion in all of this was anger and aggression. There were probably a number of other emotions present as well – even, confusingly of love. In this case we may understand that having a negative emotion of anger was protective for Nina. It helped her to not be in touch with feelings of love and longing, a far more dangerous sentiment for her than that of anger.

The treatment would therefore emphasise working in a way which identifies the different extreme views she has of herself and others and helping her to bring them together. This would enable her to have more of a joined up sense of herself. Similarly to MBT, it focuses on the therapeutic relationship, as the patient's usual way of relating inevitably surfaces in the course of treatment.

Schema Focused Therapy

Theoretical Background

Schema Focused Therapy was developed by Jeffrey Young as an extension of Aaron Beck's original cognitive behavioural therapy model to treat individuals with personality problems.[62] These extensions included:

1. Increasing the duration of treatment.
2. Spending more time exploring the childhood experience of patients.
3. Emphasising the therapeutic relationship more.[63]

Young also drew more heavily on analytic concepts of attachment and object relations.[64]

Key Concepts

Schemas are enduring themes that develop during our childhood and persist into adulthood in a dysfunctional way. Young described schemas, coping strategies (schema processes) and schema modes.

Schemas are deep underlying thoughts. These are are enduring features or *traits* of personality – our systems of perceiving and organising new information. Young identified 18 Early Maladaptive Schemas, examples of which are *abandonment* and *vulnerability to harm*.

Coping strategies maintain the schemas and prevent new learning. These manoeuvres (also called 'schema processes') include:

1. Maintenance or surrendering to the schema – thinking or behaving in a way which directly reinforces the schema, thus giving in to the schema and accepting the resulting negative consequences as being unavoidable.
2. Avoidance – avoiding triggers that may activate the schema.
3. Compensation – overcompensating behaviours or thoughts, which are so extreme that they may reinforce schemas, often acting as though the opposite was true.

Schema modes are *states* rather than permanent traits, temporarily dominating the individual's personality. These modes are made up of clusters of schemas and coping strategies, The schema modes which are essential for Borderline Personality Disorder are:

1. The abandoned child.
2. The angry child.
3. The punitive parent.
4. The detached protector mode.

These modes are seen as coping mechanisms. A fifth mode, the healthy parent mode, contains the healthy part of the patient. Schema Focused Therapy emphasises the role of these dysfunctional schemas and the processes that inflexibly maintain them.

Individuals are encouraged to explore the role that these core beliefs played in helping them to adapt to adverse circumstances in the past and to assess if they are appropriate for adapting to their present circumstances.

The aim is to make contact with the abused and abandoned child to help correct the dysfunctional schemas, to enable the person to learn new schemas and thus take on the more healthy adult part.

Mechanisms of Change

This occurs through relearning, resulting in changes in maladaptive schemas.

Treatment Goals

The objective is to identify and modify dysfunctional schema composed of the patient's memories, feelings and thoughts.

Patient Therapist Relationship

There is an emphasis on collaboration as the therapeutic alliance is an important tool for modifying schemas. It may involve elements of reparenting (providing what an individual needed but didn't get from their parents).

Techniques

Besides using techniques used in standard Cognitive Behavioural Therapy, specific techniques like 'limited reparenting' and 'empathic confrontation' (validating the defensive schemas while at the same time confronting the necessity for change) are also used. Interventions focus on identifying and modifying three core manifestations of maladaptive schemas:

1. Problems with self functioning (linked to difficulties with identity).
2. Affect dysregulation.
3. Problems in interpersonal relationships.

Framework It is delivered as individual therapy once or twice a week.

Relationship to Other Treatments

Schema Focused Therapy is based on Cognitive Behavioural Therapy, but draws on psychoanalytic thinking (particularly attachment and object relationships).

How Schema Focused Therapy would be applied to Nina

Nina shows particular aspects or schema modes which are common in individual with Borderline Personality Disorder. She often feels like an abandoned child, or an angry child, or may become a punitive parent. She also can go into the detached protector mode. For example she can suddenly switch from being needy and vulnerable to saying 'That's ok, I don't need you or anyone else, I can manage myself thank you very much.' Of course she can't at that point, but she assumes the role that she can.

The treatment would therefore emphasise identifying and modifying these schema modes.

Dialectical Behavioural Therapy (DBT)

Theoretical Background

Dialectical Behavioural Therapy was developed by Dr Marsha Linehan based on work with chronically suicidal women.[65]

Its roots are revealed in its name: both cognitive behavioural therapy and the principle of dialectics. As part of its dialectical approach, it draws on principles of Zen philosophy.

Its cognitive behavioural roots are shown in its emphasis on collaboration in the treatment, education, and the use of standard cognitive and behavioural treatment strategies.

The dialectic for the patient and therapist is the need for both acceptance and change. 'Dialectics' refers to the process of synthesis of opposing ideas, which people with Borderline Personality Disorder struggle to do.

Zen principles underline the strong need for patients to develop an attitude of greater acceptance of a reality that is often painful. Other key Zen principles and practices which inform Dialectical Behavioural Therapy are being mindful to the present moment, seeing things as they are in reality, and accepting this reality without judgement.

Key Concepts

Borderline Personality Disorder is primarily a dysfunction of emotional regulation resulting in part from an invalidating environment. As in the theoretical background described above, the main concepts are based on Cognitive Behavioural Therapy and the dialectic of acceptance versus change.

Dialectical Behavioural Therapy is a biosocial model, holding that Borderline Personality Disorder results from the interaction between the person (who has a dysfunction in regulating his emotions) with an invalidating environment. While this invalidating environment may have occurred in the individual's childhood, its legacy continues. The individual who has an intense emotional response in turn elicits invalidation of his experience by others who cannot understand the degree of this intensity. The experience of being persistently invalidated in turn leads to increased emotional dysregulation.

Mechanisms of Change

These occur through learning new behaviours in areas of mindfulness (being aware without being judgemental), interpersonal effectiveness, emotion regulation, distress tolerance, and self management, developing a greater acceptance of reality, and synthesising opposing ideas.

Treatment Goals

Treatment focuses on emotional regulation, distress tolerance and interpersonal effectiveness.

The primary goal is stabilization by helping patients to gain control over their behaviour.

Patient Therapist Relationship

The therapist relationship to the patient is that of maintaining a balance between acceptance (through being nurturing and compassionate) and a steady expectation that the patient changes. The therapist thus accepts the patient as he is, while persistently pushing for him to change. The therapist also thinks in a dialectic way. This allows him to not become polarised, instead seeing the value of opposing points of view and being able to synthesise them.

Techniques

The treatment consists of the dialectical of two core strategies: to validate (accept) and problem solve (change). This consists of using supportive techniques balanced with directive, problem solving techniques based mainly on behaviour therapy.

Framework

Treatment is delivered as individual therapy, and group skills training. Telephone calls between sessions are used for coaching, crisis intervention and opportunities for repairing the therapeutic alliance.

Relationship to Other Treatments

Dialectical Behavioural Therapy is a modification of Cognitive Behavioural Therapy (CBT) and is firmly rooted in the principles of Cognitive Behavioural Therapy.

How Dialectical Behavioural Therapy would be applied to Nina

Nina shows particular characteristics that are common in individual with Borderline Personality Disorder. Specifically Nina has shown numerous problems with regulating her thoughts, emotions, behaviour and relationships.

The treatment would therefore emphasise ways of increasing her ability to regulate all of the above through both accepting what she is experiencing, validating her experience of how poorly she feels about herself while maintaining some pressure on the need to change. This would involve problem solving strategies with her, such as working towards applying for jobs.

Cognitive Analytic Treatment (CAT)

Theoretical Background

Cognitive Analytic Treatment was developed by a medical doctor, Anthony Ryle. It is an integration of psychoanalytic (particularly drawing on object relations theory), cognitive psychology and therapy, and social formation.[66]

Key Concepts

Borderline Personality Disorder is maintained by 3 factors:

1. 'Self states' which are unstable and dissociated (where different ways of experiencing oneself are quite divorced from one another). The individual seeks another to reciprocate his role. Nina, in the role of a needy child has an expectation based on her early experience of being responded to by a neglectful parent.
2. When the individual cannot find someone to reciprocate this role, the person with Borderline Personality Disorder will move onto another self state. We can see how Nina's episode of impulsively agreeing to go with the stranger and finally having sex with him is an example of this. Not having the response she wants in her needy state (Eddy not being around to soothe her), she moves into a state of being cut off. In this cut off state the reciprocal roles are of having no responsibility, in response to no demands being placed on her. In this state she can have an impersonal and risky sexual encounter.
3. Due to this switching between different self states there is an absence of a central self observing and self managing capacity.

Reciprocal role procedure: In relationships, the individual attempts to find or elicit an appropriate response from another – a reciprocal role. Reciprocal role procedures develop from early parent-child interactions.

These roles and the procedures to maintain them are the building blocks of the self.

Mechanisms of Change

These include making clear the reciprocal roles the patient has, what he does to maintain them and working out strategies to change these.

Treatment Goals

To aid integration and mobilise the individual's capacity for self reflection and self control. The treatment aims to clarify reciprocal roles and procedures with the aim of changing these patterns.

Patient Therapist Relationship

Noncollusive – the therapist resists pressures to collude with the role allocated to him by the patient. Thus Nina may be in the role of a needy child whose needs are unmet by the therapist who is cast in the role of a contemptuous and neglectful parental figure.

Techniques

Techniques focus on helping the patient to reformulate, recognise and revise the roles and patterns of behaviour he gets into.

1. Reformulate: this involves an accurate description (*not* interpretation as in psychoanalysis) of the target problems and target problem procedures (such as the self maintaining nature of sequences) and thus the nature of change required. Reformulation includes writing a letter to the patient, a summary description of the target problems, and identifying the repertoire of reciprocal roles.
2. Recognise: ways this occurs includes through self observation and diary keeping.
3. Revise: including 'exits' or ways of breaking out of known problem procedures.

Framework

This is a weekly therapy either in an individual or group setting.

Relationship to Other Treatments

While influenced by psychoanalytic theory, the Cognitive Analytic Treatment model does not contain the unconscious, nor understand unconscious conflict as central to the understanding of psychological phenomena.

How Cognitive Analytic Treatment would be applied to Nina

Nina shows particular characteristics which are common in individuals with Borderline Personality Disorder, particularly taking on the role of a vulnerable, needy child and expecting that others are in the role of an uncaring adult, and then acting in ways that perpetuate this. By being very needy and demanding she may elicit a weary exasperated response from those around her 'Oh Nina, here we go again.'

The treatment would therefore emphasise identifying when she gets into this role and working with her to develop a different way of behaving which doesn't perpetuate this role.

What About Psychoanalysis?

You mention the above treatments – but you don't list psychoanalysis – should I not do it?

The answer (like most of life) is not straightforward. Psychoanalysis is resource intensive – for the patient and the therapist. It means going for individual treatment sessions 5 (or at minimum 4) times a week. So it is not easy for most individuals to either commit that time or get access to such intensive treatment. Most practitioners would also suggest that if the individual has moderate to severe Borderline Personality Disorder, then that person is better placed in a Personality Disorder service where there is a structured programme provided by a team, rather than by a solo practitioner, which is the usual setting for a psychoanalytic treatment. The contribution of psychoanalysis has been in forming the bedrock from which modified evidence based treatments have developed, in particular Mentalization Based Treatment and Transference Focused Psychotherapy. The characteristics of psychoanalysis however, including the lower activity of the therapist, the less structured approach and its patient-led quality all make it less suitable for treating individuals with more severe Borderline Personality Disorder.[67]

Which Treatment Should I Choose?

Although this seems a very difficult question to answer, there are theoretical and practical reasons why it may not require endless agonising. Reasons for this include:

- Theoretically, the above treatments have all been shown to be effective but there is no convincing evidence that one 'brand' is better than another. It has been said in jest that the main key to success for anyone wanting to start a new treatment for Personality Disorder is to use a 3 letter acronym (hence MBT, TFP, DBT, SFT, CAT).

- The above treatments in fact share many common features (as described above, such as a structured approach, an emphasis on consistency, being consistent with a particular theory of the mind) and we do not know enough about what is the active ingredient of a specific treatment. In other words, we cannot identify the particular component of any treatment method that makes it beneficial.
- The actual relationship that the therapist has with the patient is critically important – and how that relationship develops, is of course not determined by the brand of therapy.
- On a practical level, in your area you may not have access to all of the different forms of therapy.

Who Should I Go To When I Seek Treatment for Borderline Personality Disorder?

This depends on the stage that you are at:

If you are at acute risk of harming yourself, then psychiatric services are the most appropriate – you have to be alive to receive psychological treatment! It's also important that you are in a settled enough state to be able to make use of psychological treatment. Of course it is very helpful to receive acute psychiatric care which is psychologically informed. For example it is helpful if the psychiatrist keeps in mind the distress and meaning of the suicide attempt while assessing the patient for risk. However this psychologically informed psychiatric assessment should not be confused with taking part in a psychological treatment which is attempting to make deep psychological change.

If you are not at acute risk of harming yourself and you are seeking psychological treatment, then the severity of your difficulties would determine which is the appropriate treatment. For example if you are at constant risk of harming yourself, or needing to use emergency services very often because you are feeling mentally unwell, then a specialist Personality Disorder service may be appropriate. If on the other hand you are managing to function reasonably well and are managing to hold down a job, or studying, then you may be able to see a psychotherapist working as a solo practitioner. It's difficult to make these judgements yourself and in most countries, the first port of call is your family medical practitioner, who can help you decide where to go next. There is some emerging evidence suggesting that individuals who have greater complexity, such as having more than one Personality Disorder, may need specialist Personality Disorder treatment.[68]

How do I Actually Choose My Therapist?

If you are in the position of having to select a therapist, the following questions may be helpful.

Relevant Questions When Choosing a Therapist

Regarding the therapist:

- Duration and intensity of his training?
- What is his training organisation?
- What is his work experience?
- What qualifications does he have?
- Personal characteristics of the therapist – such as gender, age, ethnicity

Regarding the treatment model:

- What is the treatment method?
- Is it psychodynamic or cognitive or some other approach?
- What is its evidence base?
- What are its objectives and how does this fit with my problems?

Practical arrangements:

- Would the offered time and venue suit you? Ensure that being able to attend the sessions is practically viable for you to give yourself the best chance of sticking to the treatment.
- What is the cost – can I afford it for the proposed duration of the therapy?
- What is the proposed frequency of sessions? For addressing aspects of personality this should be at least once a week.
- What is the planned duration? For addressing aspects of personality this should be at least one year. If the duration is open ended, will there be a review date?
- What is the procedure if there is an emergency? What happens if I feel at risk of harming myself?
- What happens when the therapist is away? Who is to be contacted in an emergency?

A final word about choosing a therapist: I appreciate that it may be difficult for the reader to weigh up the above information, for example regarding the intensity of the therapist's training. But it is important for the prospective patient to have confidence in the knowledge that the therapist is registered with a reputable organisation. After all we often take a great deal of care in choosing which school to entrust in educating our children – it seems to make sense to take the same care in entrusting someone else with the intimacies of our mind.

You do have the critical say in two crucial areas – you are the best person to decide on: the therapist and the practical arrangements.

Regarding the choice of therapist: *trust your instinct* – do you feel you can work with this person? Does the therapist seem to be someone you may be able to trust and discuss some very personal matters? If so, this is an important issue. The question of the therapist's age, gender, ethnicity may be less critical – it is the human encounter with another person who has sufficient interest, expertise, and ability to form a relationship with you that is the important aspect.

Regarding the practical arrangements: Once you make that critical decision to start therapy, you should not drop out lightly. That is why it is so important to make sure that the practical arrangements are suitable – will you really be able to get to the therapy at 5 o'clock? Or will it be difficult to leave work on time, so that you'll either end up being frequently late, or arriving so preoccupied about the possibility of having been late, that you are unable to use the session for other issues. Is the cost manageable or will you feel the need to stop the treatment prematurely due to its unaffordability? Is it really feasible to travel for an hour and a half each way to therapy?

The above section is mainly concerned with someone seeking treatment in the private sector. Within the public sector there may be less ability to make specific choices.

Should I Go for Group or Individual Therapy?

It is difficult to make a firm recommendation on this. It depends on many factors – your personality, what the issues are that are causing the most problem, what level of treatment you need, your preferences, and the reasons for these preferences. If you need treatment within a Personality Disorder service, the balance of individual or group treatment is less relevant than the overall coherence of the treatment delivered.

Individuals often feel very reluctant to enter a group treatment as they anticipate it will be too exposing to discuss very personal, sensitive issues attached to a lot of hurt or shame or anger. This needs to be balanced with the experience of many patients who feel a great sense of relief at hearing the experience of others with similar problems. I have often heard patients say in a group 'That's exactly how I feel – I'm so relieved to hear you say that – now I don't feel I'm the only person also feeling that.' It is often easier for individuals in treatment to hear something painful but true from a fellow patient than from a professional.

The following is a selection of quotes from patients who have found the group format useful:

- 'No disrespect to you professionals – but you can't really understand me the same way as someone can who's gone through the same experiences as I have.'
- 'When I talk to you therapists, I can't really trust you – its far easier to trust that another patient understands what I'm saying.'
- 'Before I felt I was the only one who had these problems. It's so good to come in and realise other people also feel the same.'
- 'When the group said they were worried about me last week when I didn't come in – I suddenly realised I have an impact on other people. You may not believe this – I've never thought that before.'

Patients will often question being put in a group with other people with relationship problems. This is eloquently captured in a patient asking me: 'Let me get this right. I have relationship problems. So you want to put me into a group of people who also have relationship problems, who are the same as me when it comes to getting upset or having arguments. What's the point of that? They're the last kind of people I should be mixing with.' From the patient's perspective these initial concerns are entirely understandable. However it is the dynamics which get set off between patients in the groups that allow the greatest opportunities for understanding the individual. Following this line of thinking, it is just as useful for a patient to have someone in the group that they dislike as having someone they like – as both the liking and the disliking allow an opportunity for understanding something about the individual. Our buttons for liking or disliking someone get pushed for reasons that have become hardwired and are linked to our earlier experience. Like dreams, they thus serve as a highway to understanding key aspects of ourselves – working out reasons why we like or dislike someone is a route into understanding what makes us tick. How we relate to others is a clue to what is happening in our minds.

Case Scenario

In a group therapy meeting Nina was describing how she had once become so angry in a restaurant at the poor service she was receiving that she had thrown her dishes onto the floor. Felicity, another patient in the group, had responded by saying she had no interest in this story, 'it left her cold.' In her manner she clearly showed a distaste for Nina. Felicity continued 'I would never act like this – I just don't understand this behaviour.' After some work had been done to address how Nina felt about this rather sharp response the group went on to explore the psychological meaning of this response. It emerged that in fact Felicity had similar feelings of aggression as Nina experienced. However in Felicity's case she was so worried about the destructive consequences of showing this aggression that she had made a pact with herself to not show it to others. Felicity was able for the first time to both identify her aggressive feelings more openly and also how terrified she was of what may happen if she let these feelings surface more openly. Nina had very effectively pushed Felicity's buttons, allowing Felicity to understand herself better through exploring this interaction in the group.

Are Hospital Admissions Helpful for People With Borderline Personality Disorder?

Psychiatrists have previously resisted admitting patients with Borderline Personality Disorder to psychiatric hospital. Psychiatrists often felt that there was no effective treatment for these patients and that the admissions were often unhelpful to the patient, or even seemed to make things worse. However views on this are now less fixed.

A study has shown that brief time-limited admissions to hospital may benefit some Personality Disorder patients in crisis. In a Randomised Control Trial (RCT) on 100 psychiatric emergency cases allocated to community or hospital based services, patients with Personality Disorder (50% of the patient group) showed greater improvement in depressive symptoms and social functioning when referred to the hospital based service.[69]

Individuals with Borderline Personality Disorder are primed to be highly responsive to stress. Unfortunately these responses are usually inappropriate. They thus often improve when they leave highly stressful situations.[70] This may explain why a patient with Borderline Personality Disorder may have been acutely stressed or suicidal but will rapidly settle on the ward once in a low stress environment. This sudden change may sometimes perplex staff, who may think 'Was he just putting it on?' This is a good illustration that individuals with Personality Disorder may leave other people with a feeling of having manipulated them or the situation, when it may be more accurately understood as a rather clumsy and unsuccessful way of the individual managing his stress.

It seems sensible though, that admissions to hospital are made only if absolutely necessary for the patient's well being or safety and that it is brief. Indeed plans for discharge should be made even when the individual is being admitted, with the aim of reintegrating the individual back into his life in the community as soon as possible. There are a number of reasons for this. They include the risk of the patient becoming dependent on the ward and being less able to manage in the community independently, or of the impulsive behaviour escalating in a busy ward with other acutely ill psychiatric patients. In addition, it may be difficult to mount a coherent response to challenging behaviour given the ability of the patient to split both fellow patients and staff.

Do Health Workers Cry? An Illustration of the Countertransference

Why did Linda feel so bad when Nina stormed out of the session? The answer to this is complex. Linda had had an upsetting argument with her partner that morning. So she had started the meeting with Nina in a vulnerable state. But something also happened in the encounter with Nina. Nina had managed to pass on some of her 'bad vibes.' At the end of the encounter, Linda believed she'd got something wrong and felt incompetent. This was in fact exactly what Nina had been feeling, a feeling that she understandably did not want to experience and which she managed to get Linda to experience on her behalf, leaving Nina to feel better. This is what is meant by the *countertransference* – the feeling which the clinician has towards the patient. It may reflect a response to the patient, or may reflect a problem that the clinician brings into the encounter, or both as in this present example.

The interaction with Nina described above gives some sense of the kind of defence mechanisms she uses. Some of Linda's feeling of being good for nothing was not initially her own but 'passed on' from Nina who was feeling that emotion (for further explanation see the glossary entry on *projective identification.*)

There are a number of points we can make about the countertransference in this example.

- It underlines the importance of therapists having their own therapy so that they can better understand whether the feelings that they experience are what they are bringing into the encounter or what the patient is bringing into the encounter.
- It points to the need for supervision for clinicians working with patients so that their responses to the feelings that patients invoke in them can be identified. Sometimes the clinician involved may be unaware of the response being invoked.
- If in fact Linda is not helped to process this countertransference, this may lead to her 'acting out' (replacing a painful thought with an action). An example of such acting out would be if Linda had become hostile and rejecting to Nina in response to believing she'd got something

wrong and feeling good for nothing. An opposite response may have been for Linda to counteract any feelings of hostility she had by going to the extreme other end – by showering Nina with increasing amounts of warmth and concern. This could be understood as *reaction formation*. Possibly you've also resorted to this when responding to an odious relative with more warmth than you genuinely feel.

- It shows how the countertransference can be a useful clinical tool, allowing an insight into the patient's inner world. In this case, if Linda had not had her own issues, when she detected feeling she'd got something wrong and thought she was good for nothing, she may then have realised in the moment that in fact this is what Nina is feeling and her next step would be informed by an awareness of this. She could then attend to Nina's feeling of wretchedness rather than her own.

What do You Mean I Don't Have Depression and You Won't Give Me Pills?

Many individuals with Borderline Personality Disorder will feel low in mood as part of the condition and believe they are depressed. However the low mood which meets the criteria for a psychiatric diagnosis of depression often holds a different quality to that of the low mood which is a part of Borderline Personality Disorder. An important distinction is that the low mood which is part of Borderline Personality Disorder *does not respond to antidepressants* or other medications.

Therefore when psychiatrists do not make a diagnosis of depression in someone with Borderline Personality Disorder they are merely applying a set of diagnostic criteria as doctors. In the same way a fasting blood sugar of 126 mg/dL or higher on two separate tests indicates you have diabetes.[71] However this is often understood by the patient as in some say discounting the low mood they are experiencing and that not giving medication is not respecting or believing this low mood. In some way patients often experience this as almost a 'moral' judgement by the psychiatrist that 'your depression is not really a depression and its either depression-lite or a fake.'

In my view it is about making the correct assessment as a doctor and using the correct treatment based on this diagnosis. Of course it is possible, and does occur, that someone with Borderline Personality Disorder does also have a clinical depression and in this case antidepressants are indicated. The important point is that if there is not a clinical depression then the individual needs to realise that the important work lies in therapy rather than relying on medications.

What About Medication for Borderline Personality Disorder?

There is no robust evidence for the use of medications to treat Borderline Personality Disorder. The NICE guidelines recommend avoiding the use of medications for Borderline Personality Disorder or individual symptoms. It is estimated that 75% of Borderline Personality Disorder patients had received too much medication (polypharmacy).[72]

Given the lack of certainty regarding the benefit of medication, if a psychiatrist was prescribing medications for me as a patient with Borderline Personality Disorder I would want to ask the psychiatrist why he is taking this approach. I'm not saying it's wrong in all cases. But in many cases it is, so it's worth being very clear about its use.

Regarding my own clinical practice, as there is no robust evidence for the use of medications to treat Borderline Personality Disorder, I am reluctant to use them. If I am thinking of using medication, I would want to check myself to see if there is some l reason why I am thinking in this way. Am I responding to some pressure that I am not aware of? If I did use medication, I would make sure the patient knew we were doing a 'trial of treatment', agree on what symptoms we were trying to target and agree that the duration is for 6 weeks and that if there is no change after that period of time that the treatment would be stopped. This clarity of agreement is useful before starting what is in truth a 'trial of one' therapy.

Key Points

- There is an evidence base for psychological treatment of Personality Disorder, most clearly for Borderline Personality Disorder.
- The 5 types of psychological treatment that have been shown to be effective for treating the Borderline Personality Disorder should be treatments of preference, but there is little sound evidence for choosing one of these treatments above another.
- There is no clear evidence base for medications treatment of Personality Disorder.
- There may be a role for brief planned hospital admissions for patients with Personality Disorder.
- Feeling low in mood and depressed may be part of the picture of Borderline Personality Disorder but may not mean the presence of what a psychiatrist would diagnose as clinical depression – although the occurrence together of both Borderline Personality Disorder and clinical depression is possible.

CHAPTER 7

Moving Life Forward

An underlying aim in psychotherapy is to increase the individual's success and satisfaction in the key areas Freud outlined – love, work and play.

It is important that the individual does not just focus on the therapy to the extent of losing touch with his life outside therapy. Instead the individual will benefit most from therapy by trying out new ways of relating while in treatment. For example, a patient on the programme was very reluctant to spend any time socialising although he felt desperate about how isolated he felt holed up in his flat all day. Part of this patient's work in the treatment programme was to set himself goals of arranging regular social activities – and then to explore in treatment the stress that these situations caused him, and how to understand and respond to this stress.

Nina's Story Part 7–Love, Work and Play

As part of the therapy at the Personality Disorder service, these areas of love, work and play are considered carefully with Nina.

Love and Important Relationships

It was clear that Nina and Eddy had very little time to themselves with all the demands of their young children. Nina's twin sister Claire agreed to look after the children once a month. Nina and Eddy have only taken up this opportunity once so far – it wasn't an entirely successful evening out and they felt awkward without the children around them. Nina said to Linda the following day.

'It's been such a long time that Eddy and I did something together alone. I felt really nervous. But he also said he was felt awkward and we made a joke about us being on a date again and that was nice – just bringing back memories. I looked at him and he was laughing in that funny way of his –his nose wrinkles like this – and I remembered that first time I met him when he laughed just like that and I remember I'd thought 'I really fancy him'. I'd forgotten that.'

Work

Nina had been interested in languages and is encouraged to volunteer to teach in the English language course that her borough runs for minority ethnic groups. She is initially keen, but nervous. After much delay, she teaches for one hour a week. She is excited at having made a start and feels highly enthusiastic for a couple of months. However after an exchange with the course coordinator (who she experienced as unduly critical after she arrived late for a class), she has now stopped going. She is being encouraged to reconsider this.

Play

There is a local young mother's group set up by the council. Nina feels too intimidated to join this. However there are a couple of mothers attending this group who she now meets casually at the local cafe and she is pleased that she is slowly widening her social circle – although she still feels very anxious when socialising.

Nina had also enjoyed singing when a child and had been part of the school choir. She is being encouraged by the Personality Disorder service to make contact with the local singing group in her community arts centre, though she feels too reticent to do so at present.

What about Other Forms of Treatment?

Nina asks Linda one day: 'There's a traditional Chinese medicine doctor opening on the high street and he's advertising that he can heal relationship problems so I've been thinking of going there as well.' She looks pleadingly at Linda. 'I suppose you're going to say I can't go to other therapists now aren't you?'

How Can I Progress In Love, Work And Play When I Haven't Loved, Worked or Played For Years?

Patients in my service often ask this question. They continue 'I don't have a partner, I haven't worked for many years, I haven't any hobbies or social activities – it's all very well saying I should progress in 'love, work and play' but I haven't done these things for years now – so what can I do?

This situation affects many people. Having a partner, having work or being socially engaged is important but it is important to bear in mind that this doesn't happen quickly or easily. The small steps towards these are very important – both in terms of the psychological shift necessary to make the 'small step' and because of the large change in how one can feel about oneself that can result as a result of the 'small step'.

Torvik, a patient who was undergoing treatment in the Personality Disorder service had previously been involved at a supervisory level in a retail store but had not been working for over 10 years. Although he wanted to get back into work, he felt affronted at the thought that a first step may be working as a volunteer in a charity shop. He said 'After my experience why should I work for no pay – and I certainly am not going to be supervised by some upstart with less experience or who may be younger than me.' After many months of hesitation, Torvik did start volunteer work and found that the gains of being back in an environment where he had a function outweighed his injured sense of pride at being supervised by someone he continued to regard as being less skilled than he was.

Commentary

What is the role of complementary and alternative therapies? If the overall objective of therapy is to allow the individual to have a more fulfilled life in love, work and play, then treatments which can be applied within this approach, can be pragmatically included.

As well as medication and talking therapies, some people use complementary and alternative therapies to deal with, and reduce the difficulties and 'symptoms' associated with Personality Disorder diagnoses. Regarding complementary and alternative therapies:

- There is no strong evidence base for its use.
- It is not curative.
- Some individuals do find it helpful.

Based on the above it is reasonable for the person concerned to assess on an individual basis whether they want to use it or not. A way of thinking whether it would be useful is to consider that treatments which diminish arousal such as yoga or mindfulness based practice may be preferable to activities which may increase tension or interpersonal strain, such as some religious cults.

As a precaution, the person should always talk to their doctor or psychiatrist, as well as to the qualified complementary or alternative therapist about their treatment and any possible interactions with the alternative treatment.

If used, it is important to ensure that it is within the individual's resources and also that it genuinely does compliment and not replace or jeopardise the psychological treatment. After all there is solid evidence that the psychological treatment can be curative. There is a necessary level of arousal and anxiety required for the therapy to be effective and lead to change in the individual. There is also the need to process new thoughts or emotions or experiences. There is thus a qualitative difference between, for example meditation on the weekend to provide a structure and period of well being, as against meditation immediately after a psychotherapy session which may serve the function of destroying the work of that session. The use of meditation immediately after a session may then be seen as direct competition, or at least diversion, as opposed to being complimentary.

The psychological treatment should occur from one service. The risk of the individual getting psychological treatment from different services at the same time is that he may take certain emotions to one service and different emotions to the other. Given that the whole aim of psychotherapy is to help the individual to join up the disparate, often conflicting parts of himself, it makes sense that he is helped to do this by structuring the treatment so that he has to bring in the different parts of himself to the same place.

A list of complementary and alternative treatments with a brief outline of each and details of more information may be found at: http://www.emergenceplus.org.uk/therapy-guide/124-personality-disorder-and-alternative-therapies2.html

Nina's Story

In Nina's case, the timing and reasoning for her wish to go to the traditional Chinese medicine doctor was explored. It emerged that Nina was becoming disillusioned with the treatment at the Personality Disorder service as she and Eddy were still getting on so badly. The Personality Disorder service felt that in this case Nina would see the Chinese medicine doctor as a replacement for the psychological treatment so she was recommended to stay with the psychological treatment for the present time, so that the reason for her disillusionment could be better understood rather than allowing herself to be diverted into another treatment. Nina was unhappy with this recommendation but after a couple of weeks did not seem interested in pursuing the Chinese medicine doctor.

Key Points

- Whatever steps the person can take to improve their lives in the areas of love, work and play should be considered and actively planned. We are after all talking about changes to aspects of personality – a very broad task.
- There is at present insufficient evidence to make any specific recommendation regarding alternative treatments to psychotherapy.
- However other treatments which address similar objectives as psychotherapy may be helpful by increasing the ability to cope with stressful situations, or increasing the ability to reflect.
- If in a therapy already, it is better to involve the therapist in any thinking about other treatments to ensure that adding another treatment is complementary and not a diversion.
- Expect to have setbacks – acknowledge that what may seem a small thing – ringing up a friend you've lost touch with – can be a very big thing emotionally.
- Take small steps at a time.
- Appreciate any small gains made.

CHAPTER 8

What Can Family and Friends Do?

This chapter is directly addressed to friends and family of someone with a Personality Disorder. It has relevance to the individual with Personality Disorder as it gives a view on what may be more helpful responses from those around them even if this response may not be the one he wishes for or expects at the time. It also has relevance to the health professional in guiding families in how to set up a framework and boundaries in relating to their loved one. It is this aspect which families need the most help with and which is the most valuable skill they need.

Nina's Story Part 8–With a Little Help From My Friends

Nina is now twelve months into treatment. After a difficult starting period, things have improved. She is more able to identify the destructive patterns that she gets into regarding her thoughts, feelings and actions. Social services are no longer expressing concern about the welfare of the children. She has even started evening classes to complete her training to be a teacher for adults with English as a second language. But most exciting of all for her, she and Eddy have been trying to restart their relationship.

The relationship went reasonably well for the first few months. But now Nina has requested a meeting with the Personality Disorder service to meet with her and Eddy as they are struggling again, and Eddy is considering moving out.

> Nina, Eddy and Linda are 10 minutes into the meeting and the atmosphere is tense.
> Eddy: 'I can't take it anymore – Nina's just too difficult for me – I wanted it to work – I care for her and there's the kids to think of. At first it was okay when I moved back in – the kids were happy I was back – Nina was good too – busy as she'd started her new course and I thought that was really good and was telling her to go for it and she was really excited about it too. But then

it started all over again – the arguments and Nina's moods. One minute she's happy and the next she's feeling really upset or angry or just goes silent and goes into her room – and then I think what have I done – or is she going to cut herself now? Honestly I don't know what she's going to do next – I feel I've got to walk on eggshells around her – she's that sensitive. And sometimes she can't stand it when I go off with my friends. Don't get me wrong, I really like being with her – well most of the time – but sometimes she wants me around 24/7. And she's all over the place – one minute she wants to be a teacher – then just a housewife – then suddenly she tells me she wants to be a nurse. She fell out with the course instructor at the language course– she thought he was criticising her all the time. When I said I thought he wasn't just being critical Nina felt I wasn't supporting her enough – that I was also being critical. And then she started cutting herself again and I just can't take it. I've told her I'm going to leave a lot of times before but now I'm going to do it.'

Nina complains that Eddy underestimates how difficult it all is for her – and that he doesn't support her enough and spends more time out of the house than with her. The precipitant to the present crisis was when Eddy wanted to go to a friend's birthday party for the weekend. Nina had wanted him to stay with her and the children and had threatened to harm herself if he did go. Eddy had finally stayed but fumed over the weekend. Nina had then concluded that he no longer loved her and had cut herself.

Commentary

Nina's presentation is very much in keeping with the difficulties she experiences as someone with Borderline Personality Disorder. If we again consider Nina's personality according to how she thinks, feels, behaves and relates to others we can realise the following. In her thinking she is having difficulties with her sense of self – who she is. She has become somewhat paranoid, feeling easily criticised and put upon. Regarding her emotions, Eddy describes her moods as being dramatically changeable within the course of minutes at times. She is frequently angry and is complaining of a feeling of emptiness. Her behaviour is impulsive and at times destructive. So it is not surprising that she is having difficulty in her relationships, which are often stormy. She can't stand being on her own and has said she'll harm herself whenever she feels abandoned in some way – which is very often.

While all these factors show that Nina meets criteria for a diagnosis of Borderline Personality Disorder, it is the way in which she thinks, her mental processes, which are really important to understand. So, from a mentalizing perspective (for more on mentalizing see the section on Mentalization Based Treatment in Ch 6) she shows the following problems in her thinking:

Psychic equivalence thinking: During arguments about Eddy being out of the house, Nina sometimes accuses Eddy of seeing other women. When Eddy denies this, Nina responds by saying 'I know you are, because I just feel it.' Nina is confusing the strength of the feeling she is having as giving her access to what is 'truth.' Another example of psychic equivalence thinking is in the black and white quality of her thoughts, as in: 'you never think of me and the kids – you always want to spend time away from me- I think I'm better off dead than in this sham relationship.'

Pretend mode thinking: In some periods when Nina and Eddy have been having very difficult fights, Nina has seemed untroubled, even serene. In the treatment sessions Nina has been talking about more trivial things. We could understand in these examples that Nina is out of touch with the more troubled thoughts and feelings she is having, that she is in 'pretend mode.'

There have been useful guidelines for families with members who have Borderline Personality Disorder.[73,74] Recommendations drawn from these guidelines apply to Nina and Eddy's situation.

Drawing from the above guidelines, the approach taken in this book is to

- Be realistic, go slow.
- Look after the system/family environment.
- Look after the person with Borderline Personality Disorder.
- Look after yourself.

Although we've divided the section up in this way, it's more a way of structuring our thinking – given that we're dealing with personality and thus the essence of relationships. There is no clear line between looking after the family, the person with Borderline Personality Disorder and yourself!

Be Realistic, Go Slow

The most important principle is to allow time for improvement to occur – to go slow, to be patient and not get carried away or place unrealistic expectations on the person with Borderline Personality Disorder – or yourself – for that matter.

Changing aspects of our personality is very difficult for any of us. How often have you said (or at least thought) in the middle of an argument when someone is being critical of you: 'Well that's just who I am – take it or leave it.' So changing aspects of personality for an individual with Borderline Personality Disorder may be even more difficult given the greater background of stress and the less adaptive way the person with Borderline

Personality Disorder may respond to this. It makes sense therefore not to set up the individual to fail.

Conversely the person with Borderline Personality Disorder may get alarmed when they start to improve if they feel that their family and friends will support them less. As a result the person with Borderline Personality Disorder may start getting worse again. A slow but steady approach to change may be less alarming for the person with Borderline Personality Disorder.

What you can do:

- Allow the person and yourself to go slow – 'I think this is a good thing to aim for. Lets keep in mind this is difficult though and there may be ups and downs along the way.'
- Plan small steps.
- Anticipate there will be problems – that it will be 2 steps forward and 1 step back.
- Set realistic goals, start on one goal at a time.
- Lower expectations (including your own!).
- Be sensitive that your loved one may feel 'cut down' when being encouraged to break down longer term objectives into smaller ones.
- Think short, medium and long term. Thus the plan to return to work may be a very long term one and a short term aim may involve getting the person used to a routine of attending appointments and keeping more regular hours. Similarly the plan to do a university course may be a long term one and the individual may more usefully set a shorter term objective to complete a short course at a local learning centre.
- Recognise progress which has been made – small practical steps may be of huge emotional importance.

In Nina's case, both she and Eddy are advised to appreciate that change is difficult, and that at times of stress we all resort to familiar patterns of relating. Nina is advised to consider dropping one of her college courses and to be less ambitious about completing in one year. Both are advised to lower their expectations a little – to recognise that Nina may be improving but that she cannot take on too much.

Looking After the System/Family Environment

Given that people with Borderline Personality Disorder respond to stress with difficulty, it is useful to reduce stress in the family environment as much as possible.

Given that the core of the problem is personal and interpersonal (as the person with Borderline Personality Disorder feels easily hurt or rejected in interactions), this is a key issue to manage well.

In cases where the individual is living alone or very socially isolated, the aim is then to work out ways to increase the persons' social interactions and social life.

Given that a problem for the person with Borderline Personality Disorder is impulsivity and a sense of chaos in their lives, it is useful to establish some routine.

What you can do:

- Keep things calm: try to plan in some routine events such as a family meal on a set day of the week.
- Try to respond to the unexpected (there will probably be a lot of these) in a calm way.
- Maintain family routines: try to ensure there are times when family can do normal things with one another.
- Keep contact with wider family and friends. At times families with a member with Borderline Personality Disorder may become so focused on the problems in the house, that they may isolate themselves. However if there are people you can trust, whose judgement you value, allowing them to be aware of the problem and having their perspective on the situation can help. They may allow you to realise that there is sometimes a limit to what you can achieve. They may also help by pointing out something you've missed.
- Find time to talk: keep lines open to one another, talk about the little mundane things as well as the big things.
- Act in a joined up way: try to work out a coherent way of responding. Individuals with Borderline Personality Disorder often get very different responses from those around them. The problem is that the different responses can lead to more confusion for the individual, who already has a pre-existing confusion about what they really want. Having a joined up way of responding will require some discussion between family members and a willingness to compromise if very different views are held regarding the way forward. Involving a professional may be useful for bringing in an independent point of view.

In Nina's case, Eddy raises a problem in that he and Claire respond differently at times to Nina when she threatens to harm herself. He has been trying to not immediately give in to Nina when she uses self harm as a threat. Claire on the other hand readily accedes to Nina when she makes these threats. Claire and Eddy are advised to try to work out a joined up approach so that Nina gets some consistency in response to her threats. It was also agreed that the response of family needed to be consistent with that of the health service.

Looking After the Person with Borderline Personality Disorder

Dealing with Difficult Interactions

Individuals with Borderline Personality Disorder struggle to define a sense of themselves. They may become very suspicious or have sudden changes in mood. They can be very angry, do impulsive things, may self harm, hold extreme views of those they're close to (either they're wonderful or are absolutely terrible) and often are afraid their partner will abandon them.

All of this often leads to very difficult interactions with the individual with Borderline Personality Disorder, who may become very critical of you and say hurtful things. The difficulty then is that this behaviour does not generate empathy or sympathy. Essentially you have to help the individual to keep on being able to think effectively while not becoming too defensive yourself – this means you have to keep thinking effectively yourself – not easy when under attack!

What you can do:

- Try to keep calm and open minded about what the person is saying. 'I think you may have a point there – can we discuss it further?'
- Accept the emotion that the person is feeling. Take their feelings seriously even if you can't agree with their view of a situation or understand why they are so upset.
- Ask questions that open up the topic. 'I'm sorry I embarrassed you. Can you tell me what was happening for you at that time? I may have missed something' is clearly a better way of responding and keeping things open than 'I'm sorry I embarrassed you but you have to admit I have a point – maybe you're a bit too sensitive?'
- Try to identify the emotion they are expressing. However it's also important to acknowledge that the individual may not know what emotion he is feeling. After all this is the specific difficulty in someone who has Borderline Personality Disorder. At these times it may be better not to keep on digging for something which is difficult to uncover. It may make the other person even more anxious and unable to identify more clearly what he is feeling. Sometimes what may be most important for

the individual is just to have acknowledgement of the upset or hurt feelings he has.
- Ask more questions to clarify the issues and look for what triggered the reaction. Say things like 'I'm not following this, can you explain more?' It will have to be genuine curiosity though – not a courtroom procedure to catch the other person out.
- Check that you have understood what is being said. 'Can I just clarify this – when I was in the kitchen on Tuesday evening and you overheard me on phone speaking to my friend, you thought that...'. Or you can check if you have understood something; ' So what may have happened is that when I said that you seem to be overstretching yourself you felt that I was saying 'you're a bit pathetic if you can't cope with that' and that is why you then decided to....does that sound right?'
- Accept if some criticism seems accurate 'I think that's right – I think I did come across as being very severe then. I'm sorry I did do that.' If you can be less defensive this allows the other person to be more willing to be less defensive as well.
- Keeping calm and open-minded does not mean you have to just accept whatever is being said, particularly if it is inaccurate. At times it may be necessary to point out that you have a different view of a sequence of events for example. However it's better to approach the discussion trying to understand the other person's point of view, why they may be so upset, rather than getting into a legalistic battle about whose point of view is 'better' or 'true'.
- If you feel the situation is just too heated for anything useful to occur then be prepared to 'pause'. Its important to do this in a way which the person can tolerate and which doesn't seem dismissive. So you may say something like: 'it seems difficult for us to think clearly at present because we're so upset. This is so important, I'd like us to discuss it with cooler heads so we can do it justice. Let's take a break. Can we think about when we can set up to discuss this again?'

In Nina's Case

Nina identifies particular responses from Eddy that incense her, such as feeling that he is overly critical. The two of them think about it and reach the conclusion that both of them may play some role in this. Nina acknowledges she is hypersensitive to feeling criticised. Eddy in turn accepts that at times he does take on a hectoring tone with Nina. Both undertake to be mindful of these patterns that they have of interacting and negotiate how they will raise this if they realise that they have fallen into this way of interacting again. They agree that it is particularly important to begin negotiations before the atmosphere gets too heated. They also agree that it's better to hear each other out rather than getting into an argument at each little point.

Setting out Responsibilities and Limits

A key problem for individuals with Borderline Personality Disorder is that they often lack a sense of agency in the world, or put more simply, that they find it hard to believe that they are able to achieve the outcome that they had intended.

This links with John Bowlby's theory of attachment. John Bowlby was a British psychoanalyst who believed that the baby will develop certain expectations of the world based on his experience of the responses he received from his early care givers. For example, if the baby is unsettled and hungry and his mother responds with appropriate attentiveness and feeds him, the baby develops a sense of making an action (crying, being fretful or signalling he has a need) and getting an appropriate response. He develops a sense of agency in the world – that he can do something that leads to an outcome he wants. Contrast this with another baby who is in the same position of being unsettled and hungry. If this baby gets an ignoring or an angry response, then he has a diminished sense of the impact that he has on others. With this diminished sense of agency comes a diminished sense of responsibility – why should I take on responsibility for this when it's never going to work anyway? The problem with this stance is that it can lead to individuals being very passive in the way they lead their lives. In its more extreme form this can lead to the person being completely maintained by family or services. For the individual to regain a fuller sense of their lives with respect to love, work and play, they need to be helped to regain a greater sense of their own responsibility.

Family members may feel so sympathetic to the struggles of the person with Borderline Personality Disorder that they may feel it is harsh to expect them to take responsibility. The problem with this is then a perpetuation of the problem of not taking on responsibility. Also we're all human – having someone in the house who takes on no responsibility inevitably builds up resentment in others. So it is far better to address the issue in a planned way rather than letting the resentment erupt during an argument.

Family members may also not set responsibilities very clearly. The problem then is that the person concerned may not know what is expected of them. Also it will be difficult to establish if the expected task was done. Thus a mother may say to her daughter with Borderline Personality Disorder 'I would like us to have a fairer share of household duties. I shall expect that the washing in the kitchen is done by the time I get back at 6 so I can prepare dinner' This may be clearer than saying 'I want the house to be tidy by this evening'.

As with setting up responsibilities, family members may also struggle with establishing consequences if responsibilities are not met. Again they may feel they are being too harsh and so either do not set them up or do not follow through on them. Alternatively a consequence may be set up in the heat of an argument which is not implementable. The problem then is that the consequence becomes an empty threat and the person with Borderline Personality Disorder will not be motivated by this experience into taking on more responsibility.

What you can do:

- State clearly what you see as the responsibility of the person with Borderline Personality Disorder.
- State clearly what your expectations are, explaining why.
- Identify small steps rather than issuing an ultimatum.
- Organise a discussion to agree an approach to the problem rather than threatening something during an argument that you cannot follow up on.
- Ensure that any consequence of your expectations not being met are feasible to carry out.
- If you're trying to sort something out when you're feeling angry and frustrated – don't. Instead organise a time to discuss things when both of you are more calm.

There are numerous examples of how families of patients in my service have not been able to assert what is a reasonable expectation of the person in treatment. Not all these examples are dramatic. In fact most are of the common routine practicalities of living – the daily rub of our lives. Below are some examples from my service of family situations of patients who were being assessed for treatment.

The 66 year old mother of a patient who was being assessed continued working beyond retirement age in order to financially support her 38 year old son, who lived with her and did not work. The son would text her to bring him a Coke from the kitchen to his bedroom and she would dutifully comply.

A married man in full time employment had taken over all the family shopping, house chores and cooking. He also did all the school runs to collect the children. His wife, who was the person being assessed, worked part time and took to her bed on all her off days as she felt depressed on days she was not at work.

The partner of a patient who was being assessed, informed us that he did all the practical tasks for his partner, including running his household (they lived separately). The partner ended up paying all the bills, ensuring there was food in his 'lover's' house, and even ensuring he remembered to attend his hospital appointments. I've put the word 'lover' in inverted commas because they had not in fact had sex for over 10 years. Even though the partner longed for this, the patient being assessed did not feel inclined as he felt too tired and unattractive. The partner put up with this because he did not want to be 'too demanding'.

Yet each of these individuals being assessed for possible treatment said they wanted to get on with their lives. They said they wanted to be more independent and productive. In each of these cases it was agreed that although the person being assessed professed wanting to be more responsible for their lives, they had not managed to for many years, and had very little push to change as their loved ones had accommodated them. Given this, it was recommended in each case that role expectations in the home situation would need to be revised before treatment could be considered as the home situation worked against the objectives of therapy – of gaining a greater sense of agency in one's life.

Allow the Person to Learn From the Consequences of their Actions

Constantly protecting the person from the consequences of their actions allows them to avoid facing reality or their own responsibility. This is a difficult ask for family members who may, as a result of following through on this, have to witness their loved one struggling with the consequences of their behaviour. However any other approach, while in the short term seemingly protective, also robs the person of the chance of growing up (which is after all the aim of them being in treatment) or of leading a normal life, whether in treatment or not.

What you can do:

- Carefully choose what issues you want to focus on.
- Plan ahead and think of likely scenarios.
- Think of the ways in which your resolve may be tested.
- It may be useful to have someone act as a sounding board to help you to check that you are sticking to a plan without being too inflexible.

Abusive Treatment and Threats

The individual with Borderline Personality Disorder may well become very abusive or threatening as part of their habitual manner of responding to stress. They may well have received positive reinforcement for this behaviour in the past. This could have been by getting their way, by family members backing down, or even by eliciting an aggressive response back. Similarly with self harm, this behaviour may be seen as one which is poorly adaptive and which needs to be challenged directly in a way which does not escalate the situation further.

What you can do:

- Say that you will not accept abusive behaviour.
- You will walk away if the person does not stop it.
- You will try to work out later with the individual what led to the outburst.

Self Destructive Acts or Threats of Self Harm

Family members may feel uncertain how to address self harm as the person with Borderline Personality Disorder may reject any questions about this problem, or may make you feel you're invading their privacy. However self harm does need to be addressed. At the most fundamental level it is for the individual's safety. At a psychological level, it is a way of preventing the individual from walling off different parts of himself. The self harm can be seen as a way of communicating and a pattern of expressing a feeling or thought – and wanting to change personality is about changing some of these patterns to more adaptive ways. Therefore while it may be painful for the individual concerned to have to discuss the self harm, and the underlying issues which contribute to the self harm, it is part of what the individual needs to go through to start joining up the different parts of himself.

The mere fact of asking about it does not instil the idea of self harm into the individual. Therefore enquiring about self harm does not in itself create the problem – or if it seems to, then this needs understanding as you are expressing concern about someone you love. If we agree that deliberate self harm can be seen as a form of communication, it does seem unfair if the individual who has self harmed then refuses to talk about it. It is the equivalent of someone saying something provocative in a conversation and then saying 'I don't want to talk about it'.

What you can do:

- Ask in a straightforward way if you are concerned your loved one is self harming.
- Be gentle but insistent if the individual tries to put you off and you remain uncertain or worried.
- Be prepared to say to the person with Borderline Personality Disorder that you cannot carry the burden of this worry yourself and that you will speak to others in the family and also will be willing to seek advice from a professional.

Looking After Yourself

Communication with Professionals

As a family member you have the potential of knowing the person really well, having their concern at heart. But there are also limits to what you can see, given how involved you are, and to how much responsibility you can bear. Contact with a professional can also help to increase understanding and support for you too.

A question of privacy and autonomy: at times it may be very difficult for family members to get the balance right between respecting someone's privacy and taking a caring response. For example, someone with Borderline Personality Disorder may say 'It's my life, you have no right to ask me that. I need my privacy'. Or they may say 'Ok I will discuss it with you but I don't want you to talk to anyone else about it.' This clearly leaves the family member in a dilemma. However a way to think about this is that if there is an unhealthy situation (if a person is self harming) and it is leaving either the person or someone else involved in an unhealthy and risky position, then this situation needs to be addressed and professionals need to be involved.

What you can do:

If the person is not in contact with health services, it may be the time to seek help in the following cases:

- If you feel your loved one is having problems related to their personality which is having a significant impact on their lives.
- If you feel that your loved one is at risk, for example through self harm.
- If you feel things in the household or relationship are very problematic and you cannot cope.

Do hospital admissions help?

It depends – there may be a role for a short admission with a clear discharge plan from the time of admission. Lengthy admissions where there are no plans for the patient to re-enter their normal life are unhelpful. Often the kinds of problems the individual has outside get repeated in the ward and the individual may develop very dependent relationships with staff on the ward, losing the practical skills required to cope with normal life.

What do you do if approached by work or school or other agencies (for example housing or social services) regarding problems related to your loved one?

The issue of confidentiality is important and it is really best to check with your loved one before you say too much. This approach also helps your loved one to feel included. It is very useful though to hear if there are concerns at these places so that you develop a better understanding.

Link in with Others and Get Informed

In a similar way that patients are relieved and helped by opportunities to hear about and share experiences related to their difficulty; 'I thought I was the only one who thought like that – it's such a relief to hear you say that – that's how I feel at times', family members can also be helped by sharing their experiences with others.

Borderline Personality Disorder is a complex problem that has attracted a lot of attention so there is a range of useful information now available on the internet. Useful sites are listed in the annexure.

What you can do:

- Ask your local service if there are any groups for families of persons with Borderline Personality Disorder.
- Go online for information you may find helpful (see annexure and below).

Continuing to Lead Your Own Life

You can best support your loved one if you aren't burnt out yourself, so it's important that you also maintain your own life and interests. Having your own life and interests has a number of advantages. It can help you set boundaries if the individual with Borderline Personality Disorder is making a lot of demands on you. It sets an example. This requires some resolve as you may feel guilty about this – and if you do feel very guilty, this would be a point of interest to explore with a therapist. The point is that we probably all would have areas worth exploring if we were inclined to enter into therapy. And the point of this is that there is not necessarily such a divide between someone who is called a 'patient' and someone who is not – we all could do with some help.

What you can do:

- Give yourself a break, don't allow your life to be subsumed by your loved one's difficulties.
- Continue planning and sorting out your own life.
- Continue planning and thinking about the rest of the family and your friends, thus maintaining important relationships.

As part of addressing this chapter to family and friends of the individual with Personality Disorder, I'm aware that there is the danger of seeming to scapegoat the individual with Personality Disorder. Suffice to say that there is a whole discipline of systemic psychotherapy which clearly conceptualises many (not all) problems as being best understood by the way families and friends have grown accustomed to interacting with each other. As described earlier, Personality Disorder can be thought of as problems arising from the self and interpersonally. Problems arise in the self within a social context. All of this means it makes no sense to identify one person as the source of all problems, and therefore the source of all required change.

Key Points

- The role of family is critical and can play a large part in either helping the person to change or conversely in keeping the person stuck in the same position. So the family can be a force either for, or against, change.
- Go slow.
- Try to keep things stable.
- Be prepared to set limits and to stick to them.
- Try to find out more about Personality Disorder.
- Don't take on all the responsibility.
    - some responsibility does, and should, reside in the individual with the Personality Disorder. Approaching the loved one with this expectation is finally helpful for this person.

- some responsibility also resides in the health service.
- given the above 2 points, try to establish a working alliance between the 'patient', health service and yourself (not always easy to achieve, or to maintain).
• Given the important role you can play, look after yourself so that you are in a fit state to play this role.

CHAPTER 9

What Happens in Therapy

The following chapter outlines Nina's progress in treatment. It aims to show how a person with Borderline Personality Disorder struggles in their own lives and how this struggle is reflected in their therapy. It also attempts to show what actually happens in therapy within a group setting, in individual therapy and in the minds of clinicians working psychotherapeutically.

Nina's Story Part 9–The Long and Winding Road

Nina and Eddy were at home one evening. They had enjoyed a good evening – they tasted its sweetness for its rarity. Eddy had finished a big job in his work as an electrician and had just been paid. To celebrate he'd bought some wine glasses that he and Nina had spotted in the high street. He'd bought Chinese takeaway food, which the family loved. The family had broken into laughter when little Natasha had bravely tried using the chopsticks and dropped the spring rolls plop into the sweet and sour sauce. 'Why can't it always be like this' Nina had mused looking at the children and man she knew she loved so much.

Later, the children happily in bed, Nina and Eddy were settling down to watch some television with the remains of their bottle of wine. It was a moment of peace and enjoyment of one another's company. They held hands in silent companionship.

Then Eddy received a text. He read it and went a bit quiet. Nina was curious and asked who the text was from. Eddy just muttered 'Someone from work' and continued watching the TV. Somehow the mood of the evening shifted and they became stiff with one another.

When they went to bed they didn't kiss and make love as had been in the air earlier in the evening. When Eddy started snoring, Nina went to look at the text message. She knew the password to Eddy's phone. The message read: Hi Eddy – in town next week.– wld love meet up. R u free Noleen x.

Enraged Nina woke a sleeping Eddy.

'I thought it was over between you and Noleen?'
Eddy was groggy and took a while to rouse himself and understand Nina's question
'It is. She just sent me a text'.
'I know she did – I've just read it – were you planning to see her?'
'I don't know – I hadn't thought what I'd do yet.'
'So you were planning to see her. You haven't got over her have you?'
'We've been through for 3 years now and I hadn't made any plans to see her.'
'You were. I know you were. Otherwise why didn't you tell me about the text?'
'Because I didn't want you to get all upset. Look at you now – that's why I didn't tell you.'
'Me upset? Why should I be upset? Just because my partner is making plans to see his ex?'
'I wasn't planning to, Nina – I hadn't decided what to do. I knew you'd get upset. I just needed to think.'

The row continues into the early hours. Nina goes into the kitchen and starts throwing the newly bought wine glasses against the wall. Natasha wakes up, and hearing the familiar sound of her parents arguing, starts crying, and wakes up Jamie. Kate goes to look after her two young siblings. She is furious and says to Nina 'you're the most pathetic mother – you can't even go one night without upsetting the kids.'

Shamefaced, Nina and Eddy stop arguing. Eddy pointedly camps out on the living room sofa. Nina looks at the remains of the takeaway she'd been too relaxed and tipsy to clear. A shard of glass lies in the sweet and sour sauce of the take away, piercing the memory of the evening. She thinks 'Well done, Nina – typical you- messed things up again.'

Group Meeting

Nina has group therapy the next day and recounts the argument with Eddy. The response from the different members of the group varies.

Eileen: don't you trust him – all men are the same – disgusting – always wanting to go after someone else (Eileen has recently discovered that her husband has been having an affair with someone at his office). There are some murmurs of agreement.

But Sharon asks: I don't know – I'm not so sure he wanted to meet her.

Nina is furious: Oh listen to her. You're a real expert to talk aren't you – a real success with men.

(Sharon's relationship had recently broken down and her partner had left her). Sharon is visibly upset and her eyes moisten. Another patient in the group says to Nina: You shouldn't have spoken to Sharon like that.

Nina: Oh and who are you – are you telling me what I should and shouldn't say – so who do you think you are then? One of the staff?

The staff member in the group who had been trying to intervene comes in now. 'I think there are a lot of people in the group today who are having really strong feelings. Remember though that we said people need to feel safe to be able to do this kind of psychological work – let's try to slow things down a bit to allow us to think better.'

With some difficulty the discussion becomes less heated and there are ongoing ideas exchanged about what had happened between Nina and Eddy the previous evening.

That evening Nina returns still furious with Eddy, saying she knows Eddy was planning to see his ex girlfriend and start an affair. Eddy's patience runs out and he says he needs to get out of the house for a bit or he doesn't know what he will do next. Nina becomes alarmed at the prospect of Eddy distancing himself.

She pleads with Eddy: Don't go Eddy I couldn't manage that – if you leave me I don't know what I'd do to myself.

Her interaction with Eddy now is a mixture of special pleas, threats of self harm and ongoing suspiciousness of Eddy's fidelity.

Eddy feels trapped. He really doesn't want to be in the house with Nina at the present. Nor does he want her to harm herself in some way as she has done previously in similar situations when he has left the house. Frustrated he moves Kate out of her bedroom and camps in there smoking furiously. Kate, equally angry at being made to leave her room, goes out although she has an important French test the next day. Nina now does not have the authority to keep Kate in, and spends the evening fretting that she is not doing her homework.

Individual Meeting

Nina is in an individual therapy session with Linda a few days later. She is in tears.

'He's going to leave me I know. He's not said a word to me for days. Could you phone him now – tell him he can't leave me go on. Please phone him – here's my mobile – use it.'

Linda: I can see you're really upset and that's what I want to focus on.
Nina: Yes but I won't be upset if he agrees to stay with me and he'll listen to you.
Linda: Nina my job is to think about what's happening for you and to work with you as your therapist, not to make phone calls on your behalf.
Nina stops crying. An odd smile comes across her face.
Nina: So are you saying you refuse to make the call for me.

> Linda: Well yes I suppose I am really but its more about wanting–
> Nina: I don't care what you want – it's my therapy not yours. Obviously you don't want to help me because you can't even lift a finger to make a simple call. Well no one wants to help me. There's no point in carrying on is there. Nothing's going to change. I know what I can do – there's a lot of pills at home.
> Linda: Please stay.
> Nina: So you can say you kept me safe? You're just watching your own back now in case I kill myself. Call yourself a nurse? You're pathetic.
> Nina storms out of the room.

Team Meeting

Linda discusses what has happened with her team. Four team members are present for a brief meeting:

> Linda: I'm really concerned and think we should organise a visit to her home straight away.
> Mark: I disagree – she does this every other week – we can't just respond like this every time.
> Linda: But I could see the look in her eyes – she's really distressed, Mark. This time it may be more serious.
> Wanda: I'm worried too – she has seemed low over the last few weeks. I think we should do something soon to keep her safe.
> Mark: Last week Nina did something similar and we organised a home visit and what happened? She'd taken the children out for a picnic. I think we overreacted.
> Glenda: Ok everyone, let's think of what we do with these different views.

The team make a plan. Linda tries to phone Nina but there is no response. Linda starts organising for one of the services to visit Nina's home to check that she is safe and well. In the midst of this the local Emergency Services phone to say that one of the patients from the Personality Disorder service has been brought to hospital after overdosing on paracetamol tablets. The medical team have assessed her physical condition as stable and referred her to the psychiatrist. The patient is identified as Nina.

Nina is assessed by the psychiatrist who feels she is at ongoing risk of wanting to harm herself and arranges for her to be admitted to the psychiatric ward. This is planned to be a short admission. Nina settles in the ward where she is visited by Eddy who says he has texted his ex to say he cannot meet her. Nina immediately feels better. Linda visits her on the ward. Nina attends a group therapy session at the Personality Disorder service while still an inpatient and then is discharged from the ward within 4 days of being admitted.

A Week Later in the Individual Session

Nina is in more reflective mode: It's when Eddy says he's wanting a bit of distance – something in me just goes mad and says 'no you can't leave me' and then I go mental and start saying 'I'll kill myself if you do.'

> Linda: You say something in you goes mad – can you help me understand more what you mean by that?
> Nina: Well – goes mad – what more do you want me to say. I go mad.
> Linda: Yes but let's see if we can work out what may be going on in your mind, or what may you be feeling when you 'go mad.'
> Nina: Well all I can see is Eddy's leaving and I don't like it.
> Linda: When Eddy says he needs to get out of the house do you feel he's leaving you altogether?
> Nina: Yes – like he's just abandoning me.

The session continues. It becomes clear that Nina thinks that Eddy is in fact abandoning her and she then feels rejected and not worthy of being loved. This influences her behaviour. She becomes pleading and clingy and when this does not seem to work, she uses the threat of self harm to get her way. This pattern is identified as having occurred in all her intimate relationships.

Some time is spent clarifying with Nina whether she does find this pattern problematic. It's noted after all that it did achieve a positive result in that Eddy did stay in the house, albeit reluctantly. Nina does say she thinks it is jeopardising the relationship in the long term and that it's not something she wants to continue doing.

Linda also spends some time thinking with Nina what may have been happening for Eddy during the texting incident. Yes, it is possible that he kept quiet because he was planning a secret meeting with his ex partner – but are there other possibilities? Nina is initially prickly and sceptical. After a while however, Nina does consider it is possible that he genuinely didn't know what to do. Perhaps he felt torn – curious to see someone who had been important to him in the past, not wanting to hurt her feelings by brushing her off but also being aware that Nina would not like him seeing Noleen. With a cooler mind, Nina concedes that these other ways of understanding Eddy's motives are possible.

Time is also spent exploring Nina's assertion that she knows Eddy still loves his ex.

> Linda: How do you know?
> Nina: Well he didn't tell me about the text did he?
> Linda: Yes, though I think we have covered that – we've said maybe Eddy didn't tell you because he didn't know how you would take it.

> Nina: Ok. I just knew he still loves her.
> Linda: You just knew? Based on your feelings?
> Nina: Yes.
> Linda: Remember the lemon?
> Nina; What?
> Linda: The lemon.

There is a tense silence. Then Nina bursts out laughing. This is infectious and Linda starts laughing too.

To understand what they're laughing at we'll need to rewind to a session they had one month previously.

Nina had been discussing with difficulty how ashamed she felt at times about losing her temper with little Natasha. She had broken off suddenly and when Linda asked why, she said she had seen a look of contempt in Linda's face. Linda had explored this before asking:

> I'm sorry Nina, do you have lemons in your bag?
> Perplexed Nina pulled out a bag of lemons.
> What's that got to do with it for god's sake?

Linda explained that since childhood she'd responded to the smell of lemons by pulling a certain face as it affected her so much. They were able to retrace the session. When Nina had seen Linda's face twitch she had become convinced it was out of Linda making a moral judgement about Nina's mothering – she had just *known* it. Because she had so strongly felt criticised, it had become fact in Nina's mind. Discussion following this was that Nina's thinking could become quite concrete and fixed and that she could make assumptions based on external events, and that these assumptions could be wrong. These were identified as examples of difficulties in mentalizing. Since that time Nina and Linda had referred to the 'lemon' when they wanted a shorthand for Nina's concrete thinking.

To return to the present session. The situation has now relaxed. Nina is still laughing:

'Ok I get it.'

An Interlude During the Course of Treatment

One month after the hospital admission, Nina has remained stable. We catch up with her having a coffee with her twin sister Claire. The two are close and try to meet up at least every fortnight. Nina is telling Claire about how suspicious she'd been about Eddy. She now has sufficient distance from the episode that she is saying:

'So I really messed up big time there – getting so jealous. The poor man – I don't make it easy for him.'

Claire: Oh god Nina – I did something last week as well.

'Noo – not my sensible twin.'

'Well', says Claire, colouring a bit as she looks into her latte. Claire tells Nina that she'd met her husband Nick's attractive new trainee, Selma, at a work event. Claire noticed that Selma seemed very familiar with Nick, and this had upset her. She'd been quiet on the way home and caught herself at midnight googling Selma to see what she could find out about her. She spent the next day distracted at work and in the afternoon phoned Nick to say she needed to see him urgently. A perplexed and harried Nick found himself saying to Claire in response to her asking if there was anything going on between him and Selma – that there wasn't. He says that Selma tended to be over familiar with a number of his colleagues as part of her way of interacting. Claire concludes 'Nick kept on saying I'm not usually like this and he's right – I don't know what came over me.' The two sisters muse over how jealousy can affect thinking. 'Another coffee?'

'Something stronger?'

They link arms and cross the street to the bar.

Commentary

Nina is showing a number of features of Borderline Personality Disorder. Under stress she has become very suspicious of Eddy; she has a sudden shift in her emotions from feeling intensely happy while enjoying the meal with her family to being plunged into a pit of jealousy, anger and emptiness, only to feel better immediately after Eddy says he will not see his ex partner. Her impulsive behaviour is clear. Also clear is the intensity and instability of the relationship and her threats to harm herself in the context of feeling abandoned.

Let us also consider about the interaction between Nina and Linda. At the point when Nina accuses Linda of being incompetent, Linda actually thinks 'Is she right? Have I misjudged this?' Accompanying these thoughts, Linda actually does feel she has been incompetent, that she has nothing useful to offer her patient and also feels rejected. This in technical terms is a defence mechanism called *projective identification,* which in more everyday terms can be understood as 'giving bad vibes.' It is likely that Nina feels she is an incompetent mother and feels rejected first by Eddy, and then Kate. In the interaction with Linda she manages these difficult unwelcome feelings by passing them onto Linda. This is a way of managing difficult feelings that people with Borderline Personality Disorder often use, although at times of stress we can all use these mechanisms. We are all capable of passing on bad vibes – defence mechanisms are not just the province of Personality Disorder!

The impulse to self harm could be serving a number of psychological fantasies for Nina. This could have been a revenge fantasy where she may have thought that in some fantastical way she would still be around as an invisible observer after her death to witness how sorry Eddy felt for his 'heartlessness'.

Group Session

The group session shows a number of aspects. There is clearly identification with Nina's story by others in the group. This allows the others in the group to see how another person goes through an experience they can relate to. It also allows a useful amount of distance for the others in the group; thus being able to identify but not being so close that they can't see the main point. Of course, there may be such a strong identification with another person's experience that one's ability to think more dispassionately is affected by the strong feelings aroused, as occurs in this session. This is particularly the case with Eileen who identifies so strongly with Nina because her own husband has in fact been unfaithful. The facilitator tries to intervene to keep the setting safe and to moderate the strong feelings that can arise in these sessions.

As Nina hears the different viewpoints that other people have about her situation, she has the opportunity to widen her understanding of what may be happening in her own thoughts, feelings or intentions and that of Eddy's. Of course if she is too wound up and aroused, then she will have difficulty in entertaining any ideas other than her own.

The strength of group therapy is that patients can hear the experience and perspective of others who they can identify with. This allows a different experience to individual treatment, giving the patient access to other minds than the therapist. This is not to say whether group or individual treatment is better – more to say they can offer different experiences. The commonality of what they offer though is probably more important than their differences.

Prospective patients have an overriding fear of exposing themselves in a group setting. However for most patients the group setting becomes less of a threat than they had anticipated and comments are often made: 'it's really good for me to meet with people who struggle in the same way I do – I don't feel as though I'm the only one with my difficulties.'

Team Meeting

The excerpt from the team meeting shows that there are often different views among the treatment team. If there is only one person involved in the treatment then that clinician may have conflicting or split views within himself. This is not surprising given the complexity of personality, of Personality Disorder, of what motivates us to do the things we do. People with Borderline Personality Disorder also tend to segment different parts of themselves and so may present differently to different members of staff. Equally, different members of staff will have different buttons pushed related to their own personal history and how they react to various emotional triggers. These factors point to the need for any clinician working closely with someone at this deep level of personality to have had their own therapy so that they can be more aware of the baggage from their personal experience that they bring into the encounter (their countertransference). Even with the benefit of personal therapy, clinicians may bring in their own baggage, and hence the need for supervision.

While the workings of the team may not really concern you, there are two aspects that are relevant. Firstly, given the demands of working in this field, it does show that it can be useful if the individual knows that their prospective therapist has had their own therapy, and are in regular and intensive supervision. Secondly it's a reminder that just as different members of the team can respond differently to the individual with Borderline Personality Disorder, so can different members of the family or friends of the individual with Borderline Personality Disorder.

The Individual Session

The individual session shows a number of things. These include the need to understand events from a psychological point of view: if Nina just passed through treatment without getting a deeper understanding of herself then it's difficult to see how the treatment can really change her. However we shouldn't leave with an impression that the treatment is a mainly cognitive intervention, just to understand and change how she thinks. The emotional component is more difficult to capture. However the experience for Nina of having in Linda someone who will listen non judgementally to things she feels deeply ashamed about, who will clarify woolly or deceptive thinking, who will confront when necessary and at times make interpretations which may be uncomfortable for both, is what may be most important to Nina. Just the experience of Nina saying something she feels ashamed about and to have an experience of not being judged for it, could be the most important experience of the therapy for Nina. One patient said to me years after finishing psychotherapy: 'I don't remember much of my treatment. What I remember most is those silences when I had said something dreadful. The therapist would say something like 'Hmm' – in a way that somehow made it seem ok to say these things. That the therapist was listening in a way that wasn't saying I was this piece of shit. So then I started feeling able to think about these things in a different way – in a way that was less frozen.'

The individual session also points to the importance of building up a working relationship between patient and therapist. It indicates why therapy takes a long time. We repeat and repeat our unhelpful patterns and these need to be analysed in therapy. The aim will be an increasing ability to identify particular patterns of thinking, feeling and behaviour that we may have in certain situations. Having another perspective (in this case the therapist's) on what is happening can help the individual break out of a destructive pattern.

We Can All Lose It

The conversation with Claire shows that all of us, even supernormal successful Claire, can lose our ability to think clearly at times and respond to stress in disordered ways. It's just that, as in Claire's case, not everyone responds with the same intensity and frequency as does a person with Personality Disorder.

Meeting the Treatment Team

Nina is now more than halfway through the treatment programme. This seems a good time to ask her team about where they think they are, how they understand her treatment, what the direction is. So let's send in someone to interview them. In the meeting is a psychiatrist, group psychotherapist, psychologist and a psychodynamic psychotherapist.

What is the Therapeutic Work?

The therapeutic task is to engage Nina in a collaboration, where we try to describe and understand her problems and how these problems impact on her life and those around her. Steps towards this include empathy, support, clarification, confrontation, and interpretation.

Let us unpack these terms a bit:

Empathy involves Nina having a sense that what she has gone through, and is going through, is understood and appreciated at an emotional level.

Support involves Nina feeling that she is in a setting – this includes all aspects of the treatment – where she feels safe enough to tackle her problems in a fundamental way.

Clarification involves making clear to both Nina and her therapists exactly what her situation is. This is at both a 'real world' (the reality outside such as paying rent, needing to pick up the children from school) and a psychological level (such as if Nina feels she has to invite her mother to her birthday meal even though she'd prefer to spend it just with Eddy and the children, it may be worthwhile clarifying more why Nina feels this obligation so unquestioningly).

Confrontation involves identifying with Nina when there may be an inconsistency – 'you predict that your mother is going to set you and the children on edge and that it will spoil your birthday dinner having her present. You have also decided you are going to invite her anyway. It seems there's some contradiction here?'

Interpretation involves finding some psychological understanding or meaning behind the behaviour. So this may be: It may be important to have your mother present at your birthday dinner because you really still wish so much that she could for once be a proper mother and be less self absorbed and celebrate your birthday, something which she has rarely managed to do so far.

What has just been written may seem clear and simple, but if we consider how difficult it can be for an individual with Borderline Personality Disorder to establish a collaborative relationship, or to accept support, or not to see the therapists' attempt to clarify as being hostile – then you may get some idea how much time and effort this takes to establish.

In Nina's case it is very important that she experiences Linda as someone who is empathic and supportive. This is because, Nina, as a part of her Borderline Personality Disorder, becomes easily paranoid of others and mistrusts their intentions.

Who is in Your Team. What Roles Do they Take on? Is the Psychiatrist the Boss?

Personality Disorder Service teams are made up of people with different trainings and professional backgrounds, which may include nurses, psychotherapists, psychologists and psychiatrists. They may take on different roles depending on their training. The psychiatrist is not the boss and some services do not have a medical doctor in the team. The psychiatrist is trained in making a diagnosis and in prescribing medications, so this is a particular role he or she plays in the service. Psychiatric nurses usually bring in experience of working with individuals both as inpatients and outpatients when they have been in a psychiatric crisis, such as feeling at risk of harming themselves. Psychologists and psychotherapists have expertise in understanding the individual's problems from a psychological perspective and of treating their problems in a talking therapy. If the service you are being treated by is working well, the actual professional background of your therapist is less important than you being part of a well coordinated service where the particular strengths of the different professional trainings combine well to give you the best possible treatment.

What Type of Psychotherapy are You Using with Nina – Which is Best for Her?

We are using a psychodynamic model, in our case Mentalization Based Treatment . It is a useful approach at both the inner personal, and interpersonal level – but the other models emphasise other aspects and have a proven evidence base. Given the problems Nina has, a model which focuses on both her inner personal and outer or interpersonal level is appropriate. However it is difficult, given the evidence to date, to be too confident that one of the evidence based treatments is better for her than another approach.

The different emphases the different treatment approaches take to this is what differentiates them, for example a Cognitive Behavioural Therapy approach places more emphasis on core beliefs of the patient while a psychodynamic approach places more emphasis on the relationship dynamics between the patient and others, including the therapist.

Given that there are a number of problems at different levels (namely along cognitive, affective, behavioural and interpersonal lines), it would be difficult for one approach to effectively tackle all of these. The Cognitive Behavioural Therapy approaches (Schema Focused Therapy and Dialectical Behavioural Therapy) may be more successful with cognitive and behavioural outcomes. The psychodynamic (Transference Focused Psychotherapy and MBT) may be more successful at the intrapersonal (affective) and interpersonal level. But the evidence does not allow us to be too didactic about this.

What are Nina's Main Problems and What are the Implications for Therapy

Nina's core problems, as is consistent with people with Borderline Personality Disorder, are aspects of her inner self and interpersonal relationships.

Problematic aspects of self include a confusion about who she really is. This includes an unstable sense of self, and problems with managing her feelings. In Nina's case this shows in the uncertainty she has with the direction in her life, and in her sudden changes in mood.

Interpersonal aspects include a difficulty in tolerating closeness and intimacy, and problems in cooperative relationships. Nina shows this in the stormy relationship she has with those around her, including Eddy and Linda. It is in examining the relationship between her and Linda that a better understanding of her emerges. Thus when Nina repeatedly gets into a paranoid state with Linda, and accuses Linda of being rejecting, an understanding of Nina's inner world of a lack of trustworthy carers who rejected her at a fundamentally emotional level becomes clearer. But to get to this stage takes time. When Nina feels supported it is then easier to clarify and confront her with what she does.

The implication for therapy is that treatment needs to bring interpersonal difficulties to the forefront and find ways to manage these problems – hence the importance of maintaining the therapeutic relationship. Different psychological schools take different approaches to this. For example, the *deficit* school stresses the importance of not confronting the patient too early in the treatment whereas the *conflict* school holds that any aggression on the patient's part needs to be confronted early in the therapy and as a priority, despite this stressing the therapeutic relationship.

Can you explain more about psychodynamic concepts such as splitting, projection, projective identification and attachment theory through my increased knowledge of Nina?

Splitting may be described as separating off some feelings or aspect of yourself. For example at times Nina sees Eddy as all wonderful and good and at other times as all bad. Of course in reality he is neither all good nor all bad but Nina simplifies the complexity of this. This simplification ultimately does not help. Eddy cannot live up to being wonderful and good all the time which leads Nina to feel disappointed and let down. When Nina thinks he is all bad she can get scared of him. But she is shadow boxing with an image of an all bad Eddy which is at odds with reality.

Projection occurs when the individual experiences part of his own inner world as coming from another person. One example of this is Gregory the male model we met earlier. He is in fact envious of others, but this is an uncomfortable emotion for him to accept so he projects his own feeling of envy onto others. 'It is not I who am envious of them – it is they who are envious of me.'

Projective identification occurs when a person has a feeling that they are unable to bear, so they 'project' this feeling into someone else. So far the definition is similar to that of projection. The difference between the two defence mechanism is that in projective identification, as contrasted to projection, there is a *communication of emotions*. The individual resorting to projective identification induces in the other person the emotion that they cannot tolerate in themselves. The result of this is that the person who originally had the unbearable feeling is relieved of it while the person into whom this feeling was projected is left with the unwanted feeling.

Projective Identification is a defence mechanism that is particularly used by individuals with Borderline Personality Disorder. While temporarily relieving for the individual, it is an ungainly defence mechanism. The individual who has used it is left with a sense of lacking coherence as he is essentially disowning a part of himself. Just disowning that he feels envious doesn't solve the problem. He gets no deeper understanding of why he feels envious and so cannot process and work through this feeling. It also has an important negative impact on interpersonal relating and relationships, as can be seen in the example below.

Nina's Story Continued

Nina presents one evening to the emergency services in an agitated state, concerned she may cut herself. She is upset because she thinks her partner Eddy is having an affair. She is seen by a sympathetic female trainee psychiatrist. During the course of the assessment, Nina settles down. She no longer is expressing a desire to harm herself. The psychiatrist informs her she will discharge her and arrange that she has a follow up appointment. Nina, expecting she will be admitted, is outraged:

'What do you mean discharge me – I want you to admit me to hospital.'

The psychiatrist is flustered by the sudden switch in mood from this vulnerable woman whom she had grown to like in the meeting:

'But I've assessed you and I don't think there is a need to admit you.'

Nina becomes increasingly angry – and contemptuous. She finally says:

'You have no idea what you're doing – call yourself a doctor? Think I'm not at risk? Ok well let's see – I've got tablets at home and I know what to do with them. This is going to hit the newspapers, believe me.'

The psychiatrist watches Nina, who now seems glacially calm and composed. She wonders: 'Oh my god what have I done?'

One way to understand this encounter is that the feeling of incompetence and frustration that the psychiatrist is left with at the end of the encounter is actually the feeling that Nina was experiencing and which she manages to get rid of by causing the psychiatrist to take it on on her behalf.

Has Nina Made Any Progress in Changing?

This is an important question as it gives some idea as to how much progress Nina can make. The concept of change may be considered using a framework developed by a psychiatrist, John Livesley, who derived a 4 stage process in relation to Personality Disorder. He in turn drew from the work describing the steps through which change occurs in addictive behaviour.[75]

These stages are:

1. Problem recognition.
2. Exploration.
3. Acquiring alternative behaviours.
4. Consolidation and generalisation.

It's useful to think of the main tasks and responsibilities for both patient and therapist at each of these stages. As in the contract, it makes clear:

1. What the patient needs to do.
2. What the patient and therapist can expect of one another.
3. What is the scope (but also the limitations) of the therapist's role.

I appreciate what follows below is schematic and an oversimplification. It is really an attempt to map out key landmarks of what is a complex process.

Problem Recognition

This takes time for a number of reasons:

1. Problematic aspects of an individual's personality may not cause discomfort to the individual (they are 'ego syntonic'). This is not surprising. The main reason why we develop patterns of thinking, feeling and behaving (namely what constitutes our personality) is to avoid anxiety – even if only in the short term.
2. Individuals with Personality Disorder tend to externalise responsibility; 'Why is everyone else so difficult?'
3. Aspects of personality serve a function – so the individual may suppress or repress thoughts or emotions, leading to not recognising the problem.
4. The patient's social system may support him in not addressing his difficulties. An illustration of this is that Paul's parents provided a protective scaffolding for him. His overdependence on them is taken as a given and not challenged, so there is little incentive for Paul to think that there may be a problem.

The therapist's task then is to create the setting needed that is secure enough for the patient to acknowledge the very problems, thoughts and emotions that he has spent his life avoiding.

The patient's task is to recognise and accept their problem and commit to change. If the patient does not do this, he is not ready for the psychological work that will really lead to real change. Recognition is a problem.

Acceptance is a problem. Commitment is a problem. And even if any of these are achieved, they can be reversed. No wonder real psychological change does not always occur!

In Nina's case, the extended period needed to engage her, including the numerous times she broke off the assessment, point to her difficulty in recognising her issues as a problem. It was only when she truly acknowledged the impact of her issues on her children that she became more ready for the psychological work that could lead to change. This is an intensely personal decision on Nina's part. The individual needs to make the decision – it cannot be foisted upon her by the therapist.

Exploration

At this stage, the patient's task is to be open to self exploration and to collaborate in the process. The therapist's task is to help patients to increase their understanding of their thoughts and feelings and how this relates to their behaviour. This involves both providing a setting which allows this, while identifying and managing any obstacles to exploration.

In exploration it is useful to create connections, focus on general and specific maladaptive patterns, promote self observation, and identify maintenance factors. These aspects are described further as follows.

Create connections: these are connections both in time, and between thought, feeling and action. Too great a loss of connection can lead to *dissociation*. Dissociation occurs when there is a disconnect between an individual's thoughts, emotions, and behaviour in relation to what is happening in the real world. A patient once spoke movingly of being at his daughter's 5th birthday party. Despite a deep love for his daughter he was haunted by a feeling that he did not feel connected, in an emotional sense, with what should have been a special family event. 'I was there, seeing Roberta blowing out her candles – but I just didn't feel fully there – as though I was in some kind of glass bubble.'

Creating connections in time: this is both in present and in past time. In present time, people with Borderline Personality Disorder frequently seem to forget recent events or interactions. This may serve different functions. Sometimes what is forgotten seems more convenient to forget, for example if it was an unpleasant experience. By connecting things up temporally it is forcing the individual to confront something rather than avoiding it. In past time, again some unpleasant memory may be being avoided. Creating connections with the past may also help to clarify the meaning of something for someone in the present.

Creating connections in thought, feeling and action: Often we'll say 'that's just who I am' to explain why we do or don't do something. Or, as often ocurrs with people with Borderline Personality Disorder, the explanation will be 'it just happened' as though it's a black box why something happened. The problem with using these as explanations for behaviour is that they aren't explanations – they explain nothing. The aim of psychotherapy is to deepen understanding – to not accept that things 'just happen' and to think there is always a link between thinking, feeling and action (and 'non action' which in effect is an action. One could see an individual not attending their father's birthday party, while seemingly a non action, may in fact be an action of rejection).

Focus on General and Specific Maladaptive Patterns

The task here is to recognise repetitive maladaptive patterns. A clear example related to Nina is her repetitive threat that she will harm herself if Eddy leaves her. The task for Nina is to explore what is happening for her at times when she believes that Eddy will leave her. What has led her to believe this? Is it reasonable to believe this? Can she identify what her immediate thoughts are when she believes Eddy will leave her? What are the feelings that accompany these thoughts? What link is there with what she finally does do?

Promote Self Observation

A distinction may be made with self monitoring (awareness of an aspect of self and an evaluation of the experience) versus self consciousness (focusing attention on an aspect of self). Many people with Personality Disorder are exquisitely self-conscious, but have difficulty in evaluating their experience. This may lead to the individual doing a lot of agonising about something in a way that does not lead to increased understanding. In Nina's case this is not such a problem.

An example of self consciousness is in the case of Cressida, Nina's mother. For all her faults, Cressida has some awareness that her relationship with her daughters lacks real emotional contact. But when she is with Nina she is so conscious of her daughter's far more spontaneously loving relationship with her own children, that this is what she is most aware of; almost running an interior monologue comparing Nina's interactions with her own way of relating to them. Her attention is so focussed on herself (her observation of what Nina does and does not do is essentially in reference to herself) that she is blind to the experience she is actually repeating. We can think that she is self conscious but not self monitoring.

Identify maintenance factors: when Nina threatens to harm herself if he leaves, Eddy usually backs down and stay at home. Thus Eddy's response may have played a role in Nina continuing with her threatening behaviour, as she was rewarded for it.

There are many *obstacles to exploration*. The issues that need exploring may evoke negative feelings like fear, shame, guilt, or pain. These difficult feelings may be avoided in different ways such as suppression, repression, distraction, avoidance ('I don't want to talk about that'). These defence mechanisms are defined in the glossary.

Acquiring Alternative Behaviours

The patient's task is to be open to change, to identify alternative ways of behaving, and to test these out.

The therapist's task is to ensure that increased understanding leads to behavioural change. The therapist needs to be creative in identifying opportunities for the patient to experiment with changes in behaviour.

In Nina's case, a major task was to start exploring options for returning to some form of teaching. Even the small task of writing to the local community organisation to ask if there were any openings was a major step for her due to her low sense of what she had to offer and her fear of being rejected. Although it only took one hour to write the letter in the end, it took months of angst and self exploration before Nina felt able to finally put pen to paper.

Consolidation and Generalisation

Change takes time to consolidate: old patterns return, especially when we're stressed. New behaviours need to be consolidated during therapy so they have a greater chance of being continued after treatment has ended.

An important factor in maintaining change is the individual's explanation of the change process. Change attributed to internal factors and one's own effort is more likely to be maintained than change attributed to external factors.

The patient's task is to apply learning acquired in treatment to his everyday life. The therapist's task is to help ensure that this happens, dealing with obstacles along the way. The therapist may be able to give direction on more manageable first steps. The therapist can also usefully help the patient to anticipate problems that may occur along the way.

Nina's task was to continue to seek voluntary work after the initial non-responses and rejections. Whereas Nina's usual pattern would be to give up, in this case she persisted with her enquiries about voluntary work.

She was helped in this task by her realisation that making work enquiries was a particularly stressful ordeal for her and by anticipating the patterns of emotional responses that would be triggered in her by feeling rejected. When these patterns were indeed elicited, they were easier to recognise and to work with in therapy.

Nina's Story Continued: A Puzzling Development

Fast forward to 2 months later – Nina is meeting with Linda in an individual session.

Nina is in a good phase, and feeling more confident about herself. She and Eddy have been getting on better, that is until a week ago when Eddy seemed to become more irritable and short with Nina. He started finding fault with her and, at short notice, he cancelled the times that he'd promised to be at home to look after the children so that Nina could attend her course.

'Funny this is happening just at a time when things are going well for me and I'm feeling better about myself. And my course coordinator told me they may have a paid job for me when I finish because one of the teachers is going on maternity leave and they think I'm good.'

It emerges that this change in Eddy is no coincidence – on thinking this through with Linda, it seems that Eddy's attitude changed when Nina had come back with this good news.

Nina, feeling in a better state, is now able to explore the issue with Eddy. Eddy is initially dismissive of Nina's attempts to understand if he has changed but Nina is gently persistent. It gradually emerges that Eddy felt threatened by Nina's new found confidence and the prospect that she may also be a breadwinner. Although this is something that he has always encouraged Nina to do, the realisation that this might actually happen had suddenly made him feel threatened by the prospect of a partner who was out in the world and not as dependent on him as she had always been.

Commentary

What we're witnessing here is an important side effect of therapy. If the therapy 'takes' we can anticipate changes in the person undertaking it – after all that's why they embarked on it. This change will of course have a knock on effect on those around them, both because the therapy will change the person's sense of self, but also how he relates interpersonally. In Nina's case the effect of therapy seems to be a change in her perception of herself, so that she is now able to go out in the world, do a job and be respected for it. Eddy had picked up on this enhanced sense of self and had felt threatened by it. So undertaking a therapy is not a light matter – it can lead to profound changes in the individual and they may reconsider their life choices – including whether they remain with their present partner. For relationships to remain intact, adjustments may be necessary.

Key Points

- The stage the individual is at in the change process, will indicate the extent of real psychological work he is capable of doing.
- Given that psychological work is by definition personal, only the individual concerned can decide and commit to doing real psychological work. No amount of external motivation helps to make this decision or maintain the commitment. This is sometimes misunderstood by prospective patients, their families and referrers, who cannot understand why the therapist is not immediately offering therapy. The reason for this may be that the therapist is defining real psychological work as about the individual making changes in a significant way in his life. This is hard work and the therapist's pausing to consider and not immediately offering treatment is in acknowledgement of this, and to assess whether the individual is up for it.
- If real linking occurs between the patient's personal life outside and what they do in therapy, this allows for the translation of gains made in therapy into the patient's wider life. This has a potentially profound effect on the patient and his relationships – the entire fabric of relationships may change.
- Therapy consists of exploring how the individual thinks, feels and acts within the treatment framework. It is the sharing of minds, and emotions and understanding of impulses and behaviour within a controlled and safe setting which is therapeutic and enables the individual to change.
- Individuals with Borderline Personality Disorder cope with stress by using defence mechanisms which can generate a lot of discomfort for others, and in the medium to long term, for themselves.

CHAPTER 10

So What happened?

Let's find out what happened to the different individuals we met alongside Nina in the preparatory group.

Following Up the Lives of Nina's Fellow Patients

Gregory's Story Continued

If you remember, Gregory was the man who worked as a model and felt 'you can't trust anyone'.

Gregory dropped out of the programme after 2 months. He had become increasingly suspicious of his therapist, who he felt discussed his progress with his employers. His therapist addressed his concerns, clarifying that he had a duty of confidentiality to Gregory as his patient, but Gregory remained suspicious. Gregory reasoned that his agency wanted to get rid of him and he remained convinced that the Personality Disorder Service was in communication with his employers about him. Similarly, he had not managed to develop any sense of trust with the other group members, sometimes feeling that they discussed him behind his back.

Damian's Story Continued

Damian was the solicitor who felt he was destined for bigger things and was constantly disappointed that the bigger things didn't materialise. Damian stuck to the programme, but struggled to make use of it. He continued to use the groups to either offer advice to others, or to inform others of his ambitious plans. Then two things happened. His therapist left the service while Damian was midway through treatment. To his great surprise, Damian felt upset about this. To his even greater surprise he allowed himself to express this. At the goodbye session with the departing therapist he found himself moved when the therapist asked him if he wanted to end their final session with a handshake. Years later he would replay this moment with a sense of wonder and contentment. We all have ways of commenting on key moments in our lives. His comment, which he repeated to himself or to those he felt close to was: 'I just didn't expect Ken (his therapist) to offer this. I've always thought he's just doing his job – but when he offered the handshake I felt this prickling in my eyes because he was offering it like I was a person not a patient. I just stuck out my hand.' Damian looks at the floor and says quietly. 'You're not going to believe this – it's the first time I've ever just done something in the moment to show that anyone meant something to me.'

The second thing that happened was that Damian met a woman who, while not ticking all the boxes of his demanding list of criteria, he had sufficient sense to recognise as someone who was worth developing a relationship with. They have now been together for just under a year. Since these two events, he has allowed himself to a small extent to show his vulnerabilities and to be a bit less critical of his 'modest' job. He only has 10 weeks left in treatment and feels under considerable pressure to maintain his gains. He has, with some difficulty, been able to acknowledge his gains.

Commentary

'Life happens'. In this case two events conspired to accelerate Damian's progress. His therapist left, seeming to jumpstart his recognition that he had meant something important to him. He also met a woman who had qualities, which both attracted him but that also allowed him space to retreat when he felt the need. Clearly, events may also happen to decelerate progress. Given these events cannot be controlled it is important to be opportunistic regarding useful events. It may be helpful if negative events can be seen as challenges inviting a response, and to see if the response can be in any way productive. When Nina was not accepted for a course that she had applied for she was, as we could anticipate, devastated and felt rubbished. But when the meaning of this rejection was explored, it helped her to understand just why she felt as upset as she did, and to realise these feelings were extreme.

The underlying problem for an individual with narcissistic difficulties is to be able to deal with his intensely negative feelings (which include aggression, hatred, envy) and to allow his more positive feelings (which include liking, love, warmth) to emerge. It seems in Damian's case, he had used the therapy to deal with some of the negative feelings sufficiently to enable him to form some attachment to his therapist, and subsequently to the woman that he met.

Ronald's Story Continued

Ronald is the person who had a history of being antisocial and showed this in the way that he provoked other patients in the programme. He made little progress although he completed the programme. He continued being violent and at the time of discharge he had been charged for having assaulted a policeman who had tried to intervene when he had been threatening to staff in his supported accommodation.

Jason's Story Continued

Jason was the patient, who like Ronald, also had a history of being antisocial. However, differently to Ronald, Jason had made more use of the programme and had became less prone to angry outbursts. He also had started some initial meetings with his estranged wife with the hope of being able to see his 6 year old son again. At his exit meeting with his therapist he made the comment:

'You know, having Ron in the group was helpful in the end. I mean he was a real pain and I often didn't want to come because of him. But that time he was going on about how he'd beaten up that policeman and that it was because the policeman had been threatening and so of course he needed to defend himself by smashing in his face – and then he laughed about it –saying he'd heard that the policeman had just got engaged and he wondered how much his fiancé liked his face now – and I thought that's just sick man – and then I thought hang on, that's how I used to be – I mean about saying 'that's not my fault' – and I just thought – 'I don't want to carry on being like that' – you know?

But let's end of with Nina – what happened to her?

Nina's story Part 10–Goodbye to Nina

There are 2 ways the story could end:

Ending 1

Nina completes the treatment. At the end of the treatment she no longer feels depressed, and no longer had these sudden switches in mood. She emerges with a clearer sense of her identity – of herself as a person in control of her life. She goes on to complete her certificate in teaching English as a second language to adults and is enjoying her work in a college in East London. She has a deep sense of peace and inner contentment within herself now. She and Eddy are very happy in their relationship and look back at their turbulent past together with a sense of disbelief. Nina is also feeling confident in her role as mother and her children are doing well and thriving.

Ending 2

In this alternative ending, Nina also completes the treatment. Although she feels improved compared to when she started, this does not last. Her moods start fluctuating intensely again – so much so that she ends up hitting Natasha. She has started taking extreme views about Eddy again – veering from thinking he is the ideal partner to her, to accusing him of being too critical and neglecting of her. She has become increasingly convinced that Eddy is having an affair and planning to leave her.

When Eddy distances himself, Nina is desperate at the thought of being abandoned. She takes an overdose and needs to be admitted to the psychiatric ward. Social services are again involved and concerned about the welfare of the children as Eddy has again left the family home.

Neither of these endings occurred. This is what did happen.

Nina completed the treatment. There were areas of improvement. She was self harming less frequently and in a less risky way now. She no longer presented in acute ways to emergency services. Her moods still fluctuated but she felt more in control of them. She was better able to anticipate situations which would unsettle her and thus take precautionary steps to avoid spiralling out of control. In the heat of the moment she was more able to identify what she was thinking or feeling and to not be as overtaken by these experiences as had happened to her previously. Her children found her more in touch with them, more predictable and safer to be in love with, though they still experienced her as a mother who was more volatile and unpredictable than the other mothers at school. Eddy has still remained out of the house, although he comes every day and is a responsible father. Nina remains in love with him and misses him terribly.

Commentary

Studies on recovery show that individuals with Borderline Personality Disorder do show improvements. Improvements are made regarding their psychiatric symptoms, their self harm and their use of services. However the more inner side of themselves – how they feel about themselves, their sense of emptiness for example, has been shown to be more difficult to change.

Key Points

- Change, and improvement is possible. Nina's case is a vignette – but it is a composite of real patients. My experience is that profound change can occur – at a level which changes the individual's life qualitatively. For this to occur at least two ingredients are essential:
  - Willingness on the part of the patient.
  - Willingness and technical competence on the part of the service.

The *willingness on the part of the patient* is something the individual can best gauge and address. Some ambivalence on the part of the patient is to be expected. However, my experience has been that if there is no willingness or wish to change coming from the patient, then it is not possible for the service to achieve this on behalf of the patient – this needs to occur from within. The willingness to change then is the responsibility of the patient. There is no morality to this. If the individual is not at this point of willingness to change then this is just how the situation is. The push and pull factors which determine the willingness to change is unique to each of us – and that tipping point cannot be manufactured at will. There have been a small but significant number of patients in my service who at assessment either have not been ready, or during the course of treatment have discovered they are not ready, who have subsequently returned to the service in a state of greater readiness and thus been able to make good use of the treatment.

The *technical competence of the service* is something the patient can try to determine both on finding out whether the approach taken has an evidence base and what outcomes the service has to date for its work. The *willingness on the part of the service* is something the patient can test, hopefully giving the service enough time to prove whether it is willing to commit to its part of the relationship.

There is no one cause of Personality Disorder. The aim of 'changing personality' is to improve our lives in the three key aspects of our lives – love, work and play. It follows then that the treatment of someone with Personality Disorder needs to consider many factors. However this should not overawe us – we have a natural instinct for living what is a 'good' life (even if this instinct has been heavily battered in some of us). There is now sufficient technical knowledge and understanding of Personality Disorder that this nature can be nurtured.

CHAPTER 11

Epilogue

Nina's Story Part 11–A Life in Flow

Linda and Nina meet 6 months after Nina has completed her treatment as part of the routine follow up meeting. They are both acutely aware this is the last time they will meet.

Linda remembers the wan looking woman she met over 2 years ago. She still has the hawfinch tattoo but her hair is less stylish than before.

Nina says that on the whole she has maintained the gains made when she left the programme. If anything she feels even a bit better than at the time of leaving the treatment.[76] She is coping better with emotions – they change less rapidly and when they do change they do so with less intensity, though not always. She has only self harmed twice over the last 6 months (through cutting her arm superficially) compared to several times a month before she started treatment. She feels a bit more able to have a sense of herself – of where she's heading. However there are still periods when she feels a great sense of emptiness and loss of her sense of herself and her identity.

She is midway through training in her teacher's course; she is enjoying it, and is getting good feedback.

She also feels more confident in her role as a mother. Things are going well with the children. She says she has met Kate's new boyfriend. He is someone from her class at school and who seems nice and less wild than her previous boyfriends. Kate has settled back into a better school routine and is talking of training to be a psychiatric nurse. Nina now feels her relationship with Kate has turned a corner – that she feels Kate will confide in her more now.

Linda asks how things are between Nina and her mother.

'Oh we talk regularly and she visits her grandchildren sometimes.' Nina pauses 'But I get less upset by her now – I don't think I'll ever really be able to please her so I've sort of given up. I found out a bit about her own mother – apparently she forced my mother when she was a child to practice for hours a day on her piano and never got over her not finally becoming a concert pianist. And gran never thought Dad was a good enough catch for her daughter – she told my mother she thought he was just a plodding accountant who'd get a suburban house and drink tea in his slippers. Anyway that made me think maybe that's why my mother goes on with me like she does – she can't help it. She's just doing to me what her mother did to her. Maybe it's that thought that takes the sting out of that feeling she still gives me that I let her down'.

There are 10 minutes left for the meeting.

Linda feels she needs to ask: 'you haven't mentioned Eddy'

'Oh – things are ok – well we were talking last week about us maybe trying again – as a couple I mean. I think it's going to be ok between us. I hope so.' She looks shyly away

Linda: So things are ok on the whole then?

Linda nods. There's a long pause then Nina says 'I've been quite a bitch with you haven't I?'

Linda nods – 'well we've had our moments.'

'I just wanted to say thanks – for hanging in there.'

They both are silent for a moment, filled with memories of the fraught meetings they've had over the last 2 years

Linda nods 'it's time' and Nina hugs her in a manner which is both quick and longing, and hurries out of the room.

Annexure

Acronyms

CAT	Cognitive Analytic Therapy
CBT	Cognitive Behavioural Therapy
DSM 5	Diagnostic and Statistical Manual of Mental Disorders 5th Ed
DBT	Dialectical Behavioural Therapy
ICD10	International Classification of Diseases 10th Ed
MBT	Mentalization Based Treatment
MDT	Multidisciplinary Team
NICE	National Institute for Health and Care Excellence
NHS	National Health Service
SFT	Schema Focused Therapy
TFP	Transference Focused Psychotherapy

Glossary

Ambivalence

Having 2 opposing views about the same thing. In psychodynamic terms it refers specifically to having contradictory impulses or feelings towards the same person or thing. For example, you may both love and hate your father. This may result in contradictory, confused feelings. One person described setting off to her father's 75th birthday party. She had both strong feelings of love and dislike of him. She describes how she set off to the party, then returned home feeling she could not possibly go – then feeling very guilty at home and setting off again. After repeating this sequence three times, she finally set off and did eventually get to the party – but over two hours late!

Cognitive Behavioural Therapy (CBT)

Cognitive Behavioural Therapy was developed by Aaron Beck. In Cognitive Behavioural Therapy, cognition is paramount and this is what needs to be addressed in therapy. One's thoughts are what sets off the train of one's subsequent emotions, and how one responds. The treatment approach addresses cognitive errors (thought errors). The treatment is to expose the individual to the situation that sets off the cognitive errors and to work with the individual to prevent the usual and problematic response. This explains the term used when describing the strategy in Cognitive Behavioural Therapy, namely *exposure and response prevention*. The treatment is time limited, problem orientated, structured and collaborative, and homework is set in between sessions.

The evidence base is strong, with evidence for the effectiveness of treatment with Cognitive Behavioural Therapy for certain disorders such as anxiety disorders, and affective (mood) disorders.

Countertransference

The same as the transference (see below) but in this case the feelings of the clinician towards the patient due to the clinician's background experience. There is a second component to the countertransference however. This is the feeling the clinician has about the patient due to something currently happening in the encounter, which is not related to the clinician's own past. Both forms of countertransference however, do underline the importance for the clinician to be supervised – to both increase awareness of, and then process, this phenomenon.

For example, a young family practitioner saw a woman in her sixties in his practice. He felt anxious in her presence, unconfident of his diagnostic skills, and found himself apologising that the tests he was ordering would take the routine 2 weeks for results to return. This was all the more remarkable as he was a confident and competent doctor. On taking this encounter into supervision he was able to realise that this woman evoked similar feelings that he had experienced with his recently deceased mother. He had always had a strained relationship with his mother, who made him feel guilty that he could not have warmer feelings towards her. As a result he had overcompensated, striving ever harder to please her. In this case the countertransference was related to the 'baggage' that the young doctor took into the encounter due to his own history with his mother. However the countertransference was also a product of something which happened 'live' in the encounter with this patient, who had a regal bearing and managed to project any feelings of vulnerability into those around her, in this case even into her doctor!

Defence Mechanisms

These are the psychological mechanisms we all develop to manage inner conflict or anxiety. For example a young man faced with the difficult decision of having to choose between two desirable partners may manage this by a number of different manoeuvres: he may 'forget' his dilemma (repression), or he may pretend it doesn't exist (denial).

Anna Freud (Sigmund Freud's daughter) developed a useful conceptualisation of defence mechanisms, categorising them into different levels of maturity. These range from primitive to mature. The types of defence mechanisms used in Borderline Personality Disorder tend to be the more primitive ones, in particular splitting and projective identification (see definitions below). The more 'sorted' or 'well adjusted' or 'developed' the individual is, the less likely he is to resort too much to primitive defence mechanisms and the more likely he is to use more mature defence mechanisms, such as sublimation or humour.

Dissociation

This occurs when there is a disconnection between an individual's thoughts, emotions, behaviour, and what is happening in the real world. So in the period following the death of someone close you may experience being in a dreamlike state where you feel cut off from your emotions and from the external world.

Dissociation relates in particular to Borderline Personality Disorder in different ways. One way is in paranoia where individuals may become suspicious of others and their motives to a degree that is not warranted by the situation as it is. Another way is through the person with Borderline Personality Disorder experiencing himself to be hearing voices.

Evidence Based Medicine

A commitment to using the current best evidence in making decisions about patient care. There is evidence from research to support the efficacy of psychodynamic therapy. Effect sizes for psychodynamic psychotherapy are at least as large as those other therapies that have been accepted as evidence based.[77]

Formulation

The formulation is an attempt to distil the key psychological understanding of a person – pulling together key elements of his early history and life events, important early and later relationships, and how these play out in the present in the individual's coping mechanisms (his defences), relationships and difficulties. The benefit of a good formulation is that it sets out what the psychological work is, and anticipates problems in the treatment.

Mentalizing

Is what we all do all the time – when we're not too aroused, that is. It is the ability to identify what is going on in your own mind or heart, or that of the other person, and how this links in with behaviour.

Mindfulness

Mindfulness is a psychological and behavioural translation of meditation skills from Eastern (particularly Zen Buddhism) and Western spiritual practices. Its goal is to increase a number of areas, specifically attention to current experience, non judgemental awareness and the sense of one's true self.

Object

The psychoanalytic use of this term is confusing. In normal discourse we usually expect an object to refer to a thing. However in psychoanalysis, the term 'object' refers to a person or to an aspect of a person. An Internal Object is a mental representation which has acquired the significance of a person in the 'real' external world.

Presentation

This is a term used by clinicians when they want to describe the main problems the individual has.

Projection

Projection occurs when the individual experiences part of his own internal world as coming from another person. An example of this is when a successful established painter believed that a younger up and coming painter was envious and competitive with him. In fact it was the established artist who was envious of the early success of the younger artist, reminding him of his own early promise. Finding this emotion unacceptable, the older artist projected this feeling onto the up and coming artist.

Projective Identification

Projective identification occurs when a person has some feeling that he feels unable to bear and then 'projects' this feeling into someone else. So far the definition is similar to that of projection. The difference between the two defence mechanisms is that in projective identification, as contrasted to projection, there is a *communication of emotions*. The individual resorting to projective identification induces in the other person the emotion that he cannot tolerate in himself. The result of this is that the person who originally had the unbearable feeling is relieved of it while the person into whom this feeling was projected is left with the unwanted feeling.

In the example above, if the younger artist is blissfully unaware of any competitive feelings between himself and the older artist, this is projection. There has been no communication of feeling. However if the older artist casually name drops a gallery he has been invited to exhibit in, that he knows the younger artist has been unsuccessfully trying to make links with, and the younger artist suddenly feels 'oh my god, he's got in and I'll never make it there', then this is a different kind of projection. In the latter example there has been a communication of emotion – in this case envy.

This is a defence mechanism that is particularly resorted to by individuals with Borderline Personality Disorder, who use it frequently when relating to others. While temporarily relieving for the individual, it is an ungainly defence mechanism, leaving the individual who has used it lacking a sense of coherence, as he is essentially disowning a part of himself. But importantly it also has a negative impact on interpersonal relating and relationships.

Psychiatrist

A psychiatrist is a medical doctor who has gone onto a specialist training in psychiatry. Psychiatry is a branch of medicine which specialises in disorders of the mind. Clearly there is an overlap with many other areas of medicine, notably Neurology which specialises in disorders of the brain and central nervous system.

Accredited by: medical bodies (the General Medical Council in the UK) to practice as a doctor and by faculties or special divisions within medicine to be recognised as a psychiatrist such as the Royal College of Psychiatry in the UK.

Psychoanalyst

A psychoanalyst has a similar training to a psychodynamic psychotherapist but the training is more intense and equips the psychoanalyst to see a patient for psychoanalytic treatment (usually accepted as being 5 or at minimum 4 times a week).

Accredited by: Institutes of Psychoanalysis, for example the Institute of Psychoanalysis in London.

Psychoanalytic

A term that is often used interchangeably with 'psychodynamic.' Characteristics of this approach to therapy are: its exploratory nature, a belief in the unconscious, the emphasis on understanding meaning, the centrality of the dynamics of the relationship between patient and therapist.

Psychodynamic

See above re: psychoanalytic.

Psychopathy

Psychopathy is a Personality Disorder. The symptoms of psychopathy include shallow affect; lack of empathy, guilt and remorse; irresponsibility; impulsivity; and poor planning and decision-making.[78] The most common *expert-rater instrument* to comprehensively assess psychopathic traits is the Hare Psychopathy Checklist-Revised (PCL-R).

There is confusion between the DSM concept of Antisocial Personality Disorder and the Hare Psychopathy Checklist (PCL-R) assessment of psychopathy. The instruments are very different, and their labels cannot be used interchangeably. The DSM Antisocial Personality Disorder construct cannot serve as a proxy for a PCL-R score.

Psychotherapist

Although the term could be used generically as in 'a clinician who provides a talking treatment', when the term is used it usually indicates a clinician who uses a psychodynamic approach.

Psychologist

There are several different disciplines within psychology. The two which are most relevant to this book are clinical and counselling psychology.

The British Psychological Society describes a *clinical psychologist* as someone who 'aims to reduce psychological distress and to enhance and promote psychological wellbeing. They deal with mental and physical health problems including anxiety, depression, relationship problems, addictions and relationships.' It describes a *counselling psychologist* as someone who 'works with clients to examine mental health issues and explore the underlying problems that may have caused them. They work across a diverse range of problems, such as bereavement, past and present relationships, mental health issues and disorders.' The above definitions show there is an overlap in the kind of work and patients that clinical and counselling psychologists take on.

Accredited by Psychology organisations such as the British Psychological Society.

Schema

Schemas describe an organized pattern of thought or behaviour. It provides a system of organizing and perceiving new information.

Splitting

This is a defence mechanism which involves a separation of certain feelings or aspects of yourself. A young woman presented for therapy complaining of a series of failed relationships where she felt her partners were disappointing and not a match for her. It emerged in the therapy that she idolised her father. In fact the father, although loving, had been unfaithful to his wife for many years and had been a rather absent presence in the house. The young woman had in fact gone onto becoming a highly successful scientist (her father was a preeminent physicist). She had year after year won the science prize at her school and had said without any trace of emotion in her therapy sessions that she would have liked her father to see her at her prize giving, but that he'd always been at a conference or working on a tight deadline.

Unable to own up to herself that she had feeling of anger and disappointment with her father, the young woman instead only was aware of the loving feelings she had towards him. The function of this defence mechanism is then to protect the individual from awareness of feelings which are deeply uncomfortable. In this case the young woman would have to own up to having angry feelings towards her father and thus having to face the reality of a childhood which, although seemingly privileged, had been devoid of real love. The therapeutic work for this young woman was to become more aware of the anger she felt towards her father so that she could become more integrated in herself and thus become more able to start a more satisfying intimate relationship.

Trait

A distinguishing quality or characteristic of someone's personality; 'Keith has rather antisocial traits' may indicate Keith has some dissocial aspects to him but does not meet the general criteria for a Personality Disorder (so his dissocial aspect does not impact on his life or those around him significantly) or have a sufficient number of traits to be diagnosable as having a Personality Disorder. We all have personality traits.

Transference

The feelings an individual has towards another person that are largely the result of the individual's earlier experience. Put another way it is the process in which an individual displaces onto someone he is currently with, the feelings and ideas that belong to someone else earlier in his life. For example, Nina often experiences people who are in some authority position to be highly judgemental of her, due to her early experience of her critical mother.

Treatment frame

This is the way the therapist and patient agree at the outset of therapy to work together. For example it is in the treatment frame that emotionally important work occurs and is processed in the therapy. For emotionally important work to occur means that the treatment frame needs to ensure that the patient is able to use the sessions (by not using medications to the extent where the patient is sedated in the treatment sessions, by regular attendance and so on).

A Final Question on Different Disciplines: After All Your Explanation I Remain Confused About the Different Disciplines. Why Is That? and Does It Matter?

Good point. I find it confusing as well. From the above descriptions, the overlap between psychology and the other disciplines described in this glossary emerges, as well as the overlap between clinical and counselling psychology. To make it even more confusing, a clinician will have a core training such as psychology. The core training is the initial clinical training the individual does which gives him an identity with a particular discipline (whether doctor, nurse or psychologist). But the individual clinician may have an interest or further training in a particular approach. Thus although many clinical psychologists may use Cognitive Behavioural Therapy as their clinical approach, others have gone onto complete a psychodynamic training and may either be in settings where they use this predominantly or use different methods if clinically more appropriate. The underlying message then is that the core profession may at times give a clue to the psychological approach the clinician may take but this is not necessarily an accurate clue. There are some aspects though, which are more the domain of specific disciplines. Thus making a diagnosis and use of medications is more the province of psychiatrists as they are medically trained. Psychologists have more training in administering and interpreting structured interviews to assess aspects of cognition. This book underlines the contribution but also the limitations of diagnosis and medication to Personality Disorder. Psychiatrists are therefore just part of the set of disciplines which stand to contribute in working with patients with Personality Disorder.

A musical orchestra thus serves as a rough analogy for the Multidisciplinary Team (MDT) -Personality Disorder teams are composed of clinicians from different disciplines. The presence of each member can be seen as contributing to the work of the Personality Disorder service and to the clinical work for each individual patient. Each discipline may be seen as contributing the particular treatment in which they have greater skills, so a psychotherapist may have more expertise in managing a psychotherapy group. The metaphor with the orchestra has its limitations. There is more overlap of skills and contribution in a MDT – hence leading to professional jostling at times and confusion both amongst professionals and patients.

Does It Matter?

It matters if a clinician undertakes to do something he is not trained to do. This is an important point as the needs of someone with a Personality Disorder are complex and may tempt the clinician, in his therapeutic zeal to embark on a treatment which he is not trained or experienced enough to do. The implication for the individual seeking treatment is then to clarify what treatment is being offered, what is its evidence base, and how qualified the therapist is to deliver it. Even before this stage, the clinician has to have training to make the correct diagnosis or assessment and sufficient expertise and objectivity to recommend the appropriate treatment.

References

A very accessible inexpensive dictionary, which has informed definitions in this book is the one by Charles Rycroft. It's a really useful one for any half interested reader for the pithiness and incision of its definitions. The one by Laplanche & Pontalis is far more detailed and technical.

Rycroft, C. *A Critical Dictionary of Psychoanalysis*. London: Penguin, 1995

Laplanche J, Pontalis JB. *The Language of Psychoanalysis*. London: Karnac, 2004

Key Facts and Figures

Personality Disorder is diagnosed more frequently in males than females.

For specific types of Personality Disorder there is a gender difference.

Dissocial Personality Disorder is diagnosed more frequently in males than females.

Histrionic Personality Disorder is diagnosed more frequently in females than males.

The prevalence of each specific Personality Disorder ranges from 1–3% in community studies.

25–50% of people with 1 Personality Disorder have more than 1 Personality Disorder when assessed using structured instruments.

The prevalence goes up as one goes up the levels of care:

Prevalence in the Community: 6–13%.

Prevalence in Primary care (namely attending family medical practitioner): 10–30%.

Prevalence in secondary care (eg in psychiatric hospitals): greater than 50%.

Personality Disorder is higher in certain groups. These include: males, previously married, the unemployed, the young and the poorly educated.

Personality Disorder occurs frequently with other psychiatric disorders.

Suicide

There is a 5–10 times increased risk in someone with a Personality Disorder.

10% Borderline Personality Disorder patients commit suicide.

41% patients with recurrent deliberate self harm at an emergency department had a diagnosis of Borderline Personality Disorder.

Borderline Personality Disorder

70% of those diagnosed are female.

40–70% have a history of past sexual abuse.

75% have a history of having self harmed at least once before.

86% individuals show improvement of symptoms for longer than 4 years.

ICD-10 Classification of Mental and Behavioural Disorders Diagnostic Criteria for research World Health Organization, Geneva, 1993

F60 – F69 DISORDERS OF ADULT PERSONALITY AND BEHAVIOUR
F60 SPECIFIC PERSONALITY DISORDERS

G1. Evidence that the individual's characteristic and enduring patterns of inner experience and behaviour deviate markedly as a whole from the culturally expected and accepted range (or 'norm'). Such deviation must be manifest in more than one of the following areas:

1. cognition (i.e. ways of perceiving and interpreting things, people and events; forming attitudes and images of self and others);
2. affectivity (range, intensity and appropriateness of emotional arousal and response);
3. control over impulses and need gratification;
4. relating to others and manner of handling interpersonal situations.

   G2. The deviation must manifest itself pervasively as behaviour that is inflexible, maladaptive, or otherwise dysfunctional across a broad range of personal and social situations (i.e. not being limited to one specific 'triggering' stimulus or situation).
   G3. There is personal distress, or adverse impact on the social environment, or both, clearly attributable to the behaviour referred to under G2.
   G4. There must be evidence that the deviation is stable and of long duration, having its onset in late childhood or adolescence.
   G5. The deviation cannot be explained as a manifestation or consequence of other adult mental disorders, although episodic or chronic conditions from sections F0 to F7 of this classification may co-exist, or be superimposed on it.
   G6. Organic brain disease, injury, or dysfunction must be excluded as possible cause of the deviation (if such organic causation is demonstrable, use category F07).

Comments: The assessment of G1 to G6 above should be based on as many sources of information as possible. Although sometimes it is possible to obtain sufficient evidence from a single interview with the subject, as a general rule it is recommended to have more than one interview with the person and to collect history data from informants or past records.

It is suggested that sub-criteria should be developed to operationalize behaviour patterns specific to different cultural settings concerning social norms, rules and obligations where needed (such as examples of irresponsible behaviour and disregard of social norms in dissocial Personality Disorder). The diagnosis of Personality Disorder for research purposes requires the identification of a subtype (more than one subtype can be coded if there is compelling evidence that the subject meets multiple sets of criteria).

The Treatment Contract

An example of a treatment contract is the one used in my service.

Treatment Contract at DeanCross Personality Disorder Service, East London Foundation NHS Trust

Patient Name:

Welcome to the DeanCross Personality Disorder Service.

1. We are pleased you considering starting treatment with us. We know that trying to change longstanding patterns of thinking, emotions, and behaviour is not an easy task. There will be some difficult times for you in the months ahead.
2. Now that your assessment is finished, we would like you to read this contract so that you know what will be expected of you.
3. We want to help you get the best from your treatment, so we think it is helpful to have a contract with patients that sets out what your responsibilities as our patient will be, and what our responsibilities as the service treating you are.
4. This Treatment Contract[79] clarifies these responsibilities and give us a framework to work within. It will also help you to stick to the main work you set out to do. Once the treatment starts, the clarity of the contract will help us to identify any problems in the way we are working together.
5. The contract is not a legal document like a mortgage. It is a clinical document. We want you to think about it and encourage you to discuss it with staff.
6. There may be responsibilities that you think will be too difficult to accept at present. If you tell us about this we can support you in trying to make the necessary changes to meet the terms of the contract.
7. We know that some of the aspects in the contract may be difficult to achieve but we need to know before you start the treatment programme that you are willing to try to do what the contract sets out. Problems in

keeping to the contract need to be addressed before any other psychological work can be done.
8. You may decide that you do not want to agree to the contract at the moment and that's your choice. Your treatment can only start when the contract is agreed.
9. Some of the items in the contract are general points which apply to all patients and some are specific to you based on your assessment.

Patient's General Responsibilities

1. To have a fixed address and telephone number where we can contact you. Contact via email address is optional.
2. To get to DeanCross on your own initiative
3. To attend all parts of the programme regularly and consistently.
4. To let staff at DeanCross know in advance if a session will be missed.
5. To actively take part in all aspects of the treatment programme.
6. To inform staff if there is anything happening which may affect your ability to take part in the programme.
7. To reduce all forms of self-harm and violence to others, and to eventually stop this behaviour within the course of the programme. If self-harm or violence occurs, it is your responsibility to tell staff about it as soon as possible afterwards.
8. Not to threaten the therapy in any way for example through substance abuse, uncontrolled eating disorder, a passive lifestyle that defeats apparent efforts to change. Please note that these behaviours are viewed as self-harm which you are undertaking to reduce.
9. To plan for, and undertake activities, regarding the main areas in your life in love, work (or equivalent activities) and play during your time in treatment with us. The emphasis in the programme is on activity, so that we can work with you while you are actively making changes in your life.
10. To report thoughts and feelings freely, without censoring. To be honest and not deliberately withhold in sessions, for example by refusing to discuss certain subjects, by lying to the therapist either by omission or overtly, or by staying silent during sessions.
11. To try to reflect on what you tell the therapist and the group, and to think about their comments, and interactions with other patients and staff.
12. To use the programme to discuss issues which are of emotional importance to you.
13. To follow the crisis plan when necessary.

DeanCross' Responsibilities

1. Providing a safe setting.
2. Providing a stable environment.
3. To let patients know about changes to the programme in advance.
4. To work to help you gain a real understanding about yourself and about deeper aspects of your personality and difficulties.
5. To be clear about the limits of the service's involvement.

Specific Patient Responsibilities Based on Your Assessment

1.
2.
3.
4.

Signing the Treatment Contract

1. I have read and discussed the contract with staff.
2. I understand it and agree to try to keep the terms of it.
3. I have not thought of any other issues which I think should have been discussed and included in the contract.
4. I agree that if anything else emerges in the course of treatment, I will discuss these within my treatment.

Signed: (patient)
Signed: (DeanCross staff)
Date:

Relevant Resources

Books

Resources for families and friends of someone with Borderline Personality Disorder

Chapman AL. *Borderline Personality Disorder Survival Guide: Everything You Need to Know About Living With Borderline Personality Disorder*. Oakland: New Harbinger Publications, 2007.

Dobbs B. *When hope is not enough: a how to guide for living with someone with borderline personality disorder* 2008 Lulu.com http://www.tower.com/when-hope-is-not-enough-bon-dobbs-paperback/wapi/112280212).

Friedel, Robert. *Borderline Personality Disorder Demystified: An Essential Guide to Understanding and Living with Borderline Personality Disorder*. New York: Avon Publishing, 2004.

Kreger, Randi. *The Essential Family Guide to Borderline Personality Disorder: New Tools and Techniques to Stop Walking on Eggshells*. Hazelden Publishing, 2008

Kreisman, Jerold J. *I Hate You – Don't Leave Me: Understanding the Borderline Personality*. New York: Avon Books, 1989.

Mason, Paul T., Kreger, Randi. *Stop Walking on Eggshells: Taking Your Life Back When Someone You Care About Has Borderline Personality Disorder.* 2nd ed. New Harbinger Publications, 2010

Penney D, Woodward P. Family perspectives on borderline personality disorder. Ch 7. In Gunderson, JG, Hoffman. *Personality Disorder. Understanding and Treating Borderline Personality Disorder: A Guide for Professionals and Families.* American Psychiatric Publishing, 2005

Porr, Valerie. *Overcoming Borderline Personality Disorder: A Family Guide for Healing and Change*. Oxford University Press, 2010

Internet

1. Emergence http://www.emergenceplus.org.uk/ Emergence is a service user-led organisation supporting all people affected by personality disorder including service users, carers, family and friends and professionals. This is a comprehensive useful website.
2. Tara (www.TARA4Borderline Personality Disorder.org) The Treatment and Research Advancements Association for Personality Disorder, TARA APD, is a not-for-profit organization whose mission is to foster education and research in the field of personality disorder, specifically but not exclusively Borderline Personality Disorder (Borderline Personality Disorder).
3. http://bpdresourcecenter.org/ The mission of the Borderline Personality Disorder Resource Center (BPDRC) is to promote Borderline Personality Disorder education and connect those affected by Borderline Personality Disorder to established resources for treatment and support. Provides a useful link to other online resources http://www.bpdresourcecenter.org/resources/online/.
4. https://www.youtube.com/watch?v=967Ckat7f98 "Back From the Edge" offers guidance on treating Borderline Personality Disorder. The video was created by the Borderline Personality Disorder Resource Center at New York-Presbyterian.
5. http://www.dmoz.org/Health/Mental_Health/Disorders/Personality/ DMOZ is the largest, most comprehensive human-edited directory of the Web. It is constructed and maintained by a global community of volunteer editors. It was historically known as the Open Directory Project (ODP).
6. http://www.bpdcentral.com/ Randi Kreger has addressed concerns of people who have a family member with borderline personality disorder (Borderline Personality Disorder) and narcissistic personality disorder (NPD) through her best-selling books, informative website, and popular online family support community Welcome to Oz.
7. http://www.bpddemystified.com/ This website has been developed by Dr R Friedel for people with borderline personality disorder, for those who think they may suffer from it, for their families, and for psychiatrists and other mental health care providers who strive to help them. Website contains useful links
8. http://www.borderlinepersonalitydisorder.com/ Website of the NEA. Borderline Personality Disorder National Education Alliance for Borderline Personality Disorder is a nationally recognized organization dedicated to building better lives for millions of Americans affected by Borderline Personality Disorder (Borderline Personality Disorder).

NEA.Borderline Personality Disorder works with families and persons in recovery, raises public awareness, provides education to professionals, promotes research, and works with Congress to enhance the quality of life for those affected by this serious but treatable mental illness. NEA-Borderline Personality Disorder maintains an extensive library of audio and video resources at no charge, sharing reliable, current information from leading research professionals. This is a good source for hearing leading experts talking. http://www.borderlinepersonalitydisorder.com/resources/media-library/bpd-videos-by-topic/

9. http://outofthefog.net/ Out of the FOG is an information site and support group offering help to family members and loved-ones of people who suffer from personality disorders. Out of the FOG was written and developed by people who have experienced a relationship with a family member, spouse or partner who suffers from a Personality Disorder.

10. http://www.mind.org.uk/information-support/types-of-mental-health-problems/borderline-personality-disorder/#.U_obwqNuWSo Mind is a leading mental health charity in England and Wales and has extensive information on personality and personality disorder.

11. http://www.rcpsych.ac.uk/healthadvice/problemsdisorders/personalitydisorder.aspx. Information leaflet on Personality Disorder by the Royal College of Psychiatrists.

Notes and References

1. These are referred to as Accident and Emergency (A&E) Departments in the UK and the Emergency Room in the USA.
2. Livesley J. *Handbook of Personality Disorders Theory Research and Treatment*. New York: Guildford Press, 2001.
3. The ICD-10 (International Classification of Diseases) is the standard diagnostic tool used to classify diseases and other health problems, including mental health conditions. The ICD-10 was endorsed by the Forty-third World Health Assembly in May 1990 and came into use in WHO Member States as from 1994. It is the main diagnostic system used in the UK and many other countries but not the USA, which uses the Diagnostic and Statistical Manual of Mental Disorders (DSM). The 11th revision of the classification has already started and will continue until 2017.
4. Moriya N, Miyake Y, Minakawa K, et al. Diagnosis and clinical features of borderline Personality Disorder in the east and west: a preliminary report. *Compr Psychiatry* 1993; 34: 418–423.
5. Prichard JC. *A treatise on Insanity*. London: Sherwood Gilbert and Piper, 1835, p 6.
6. http://www.psychiatrictimes.com/articles/toward-credible-conflict-interest-policies-clinical-psychiatry.
7. American Psychiatric Association. Diagnostic and Statistical Manual of Mental Disorders (Fifth ed.). Arlington, VA: American Psychiatric Publishing, 2013.
8. Lewis G, Appleby L. Personality disorder: the patients psychiatrists dislike. *Br J Psychiatry* 1988; 153: 44–9.
9. This is a major area of work in my service, namely clarifying whether a clinical depression is present which merits treatment per se and which is 'on top of' the depressive symptoms which often accompany Borderline Personality Disorder.
10. Gunderson JG. Borderline Personality Disorder: ontogeny of a diagnosis. *Am J Psychiatry* 2009; 166: 530–539.
11. National Institute for Mental Health for England. *Personality Disorder: no Longer a Diagnosis of Exclusion. Policy Implementation Guidance for the Development of Services for People with Personality Disorder*, Gateway Reference 1055. London: NIMH(E), 2003.
12. I have used the ICD-10 definitions except for Borderline PD, Narcissistic PD and Schizotypal PD where I have used the DSM-5 definitions. The DSM-5 definition of Borderline Personality Disorder is simpler to understand than the ICD-10 definition, and Narcissistic PD and Schizotypal PD do not appear in ICD10.

13. The distinction between neurosis and psychosis is a red line for psychiatrists. While someone with neurosis may be suffering enormously, the crossing into a loss of contact with reality (i.e. psychosis) is an important distinction to make, requiring different management, including medications. The fact that Borderline Personality Disorder is a condition where at times it is difficult to make a clear distinction between neurosis and psychosis points to the complexity of the condition.
14. Rey, JH. Schizoid phenomena in the borderline. In J Le Boit and A Capponi (eds) *Advances in the Psychotherapy of the Borderline Patient*, New York: Jason Aranson, 1979, 449–84.
15. *Ibid* 14.
16. Deutsch H. Some forms of emotional disturbance and their relationship to schizophrenia *Psychoanal. Quart* 1942; 11: 301–21.
17. Winnicott D. *The Maturational Processes and the Facilitating Environment.* London: Hogarth, 1965.
18. In mirroring the infant, the care giver must 'mark' (i.e. exaggerate or slightly distort) the response so that the infant can understand this response as part of his own emotions rather than that of his caregiver (Fonagy P et al. *Affect regulation, Mentalization, and the Development of the Self.* New York: Other Press, 2002).
19. I am not arguing for an 'anything goes' approach to treatment. It is critical that the approach taken is coherent and consistent with a particular model of the mind and of how change occurs. However there are common factors in different psychological approaches.
20. More information on this can be found at http://www.legislation.gov.uk/ukpga/2005/9/contents.
21. It is of interest that Freud conceptualised psychosis as a form of extreme narcissism, where all interest is turned inwards and away from the external world. This helps us to understand why the expert psychiatrists in the Anders Breivik case had such different views. It also does point to the ability of someone with personality disorder, particularly Narcissism, to be out of touch with reality.
22. Buchanan A, Leese M. Detention of people with dangerous severe personality disorders: a systematic review. *Lancet* 2001; 358: 1955–9.
23. Tyrer P, Duggan C, Cooper S et al. The successes and failures of the DSPD experiment: the assessment and management of severe personality disorder *Med Sci Law* 2010; 50: 95–99. DOI: 10.1258/msl.2010.010001.
24. Zanarini MC, Frankenburg FR, Reich DB, Fitzmaurice F. Time to attainment of recovery from borderline personality disorder and stability of recovery: A 10-year prospective follow-up study. *Am J Psychiatry* 2010; 167: 663–667.
25. Zanarini MC, Frankenburg FR Reich DB et al The Subsyndromal Phenomenology of Borderline Personality Disorder: A 10-Year Follow-Up Study.*Am J Psychiatry* 2007; 164: 929–935.
26. Leishsenring F, Leibing E. The effectiveness of psychodynamic therapy and cognitive behaviour therapy in the treatment of Personality Disorders: a meta-analysis *Am J Psych* 2003; 160: 1223–1232.

27. The effect size is a simple measure for quantifying the difference between two groups, in this case between treatment and control groups. An effect size of 0.8 is considered a large effect size, 0.5 is a moderate effect and 0.2 is a small effect. One study has reported an effect size of 1.46 for psychodynamic psychotherapy treatment Personality Disorders. (Leishsenring F, Leibing E 2003). To contextualize the impressive size of this effect size, compare it to the effect size of antidepressant medication – one of the highest being 0.31 (Turner, EH et al Selective publication of antidepressant trials and its influence on apparent efficacy. *New England Journal of Medicine* 2008; 358: 252–260.)
28. Department of Health. *Borderline Personality Disorder: quick reference guide* 2009.
29. Department of Health. *Antisocial Personality Disorder: Treatment, management and prevention. NICE Guidelines* 2009.
30. It is not surprising that patients develop a moralistic tone to the diagnosis of Borderline Personality Disorder. The Cluster B Personality Disorders, in which group Borderline Personality Disorder falls, is defined and diagnosed by traits that evoke failures of morality or virtue (Pearce S, Pickard H. The moral content of psychiatric treatment. *British Journal of Psychiatry.* 2009; 195: 281–2.). Not only patients, but clinicians also develop a moral tone to the diagnosis of Borderline Personality Disorder. A useful approach suggested to enable clinicians to hold patients responsible without blaming them, is to pay attention to their past history. This attention will allow compassion and empathy as against a blaming attitude. (Pickard H. Responsibility without blame: empathy and the effective treatment of personality disorder. *Philosophy, psychiatry, & psychology* 2011; 18 (3): 209–223). A successful therapy will allow the patient to have sufficient compassion and empathy for himself, so that he is freed from the crippling sense of blame, (which in effect allows no change to occur) to that of responsibility and a real attempt at changing things.
31. Bouchard, J, Loehlin JC. Evolution, and Personality. *Behavior Genetics* 2001; 31: 3.
32. Torgersen S et al. A twin study of Personality Disorders. *Compr Psychiatry* 2000; 41: 416–425.
33. Shiner, RL. The development of Personality Disorders: Perspectives from normal personality development in childhood and adolescence. *Development and Psychopathology,* 2009; 21: 715–734.
34. Roberts, BW. DelVecchio, WF. The Rank-Order Consistency of Personality Traits From Childhood to Old Age: A Quantitative Review of Longitudinal Studies. *Psychological Bulletin* 2000; 126 (1): 3–25.
35. Kandel ER. A new intellectual framework for psychiatry. *Am J Psych* 1998; 155: 457–69.
36. Bowlby J. *Attachment and loss, vol 1. Attachment.* New York: Basic Books, 1982 2nd ed.
37. Ainsworth MI, Wittig, BA. Attachment and the exploratory behaviour of one-year-olds in a strange situation. In BM Foss (Ed.), *Determinants of infant behaviour* 4: 113–136 London: Methuen, 1969.

38. Main, M, Goldwyn, B. Interview-based adult attachment classifications: Related to infant-mother and infant-father attachment *Developmental Psychology* 1995; 19: 227–39.
39. Agrawal HR; Gunderson J; Holmes BM; Lyons-Ruth K. Attachment studies with borderline patients: a review. *Harv Rev Psychiatry* 2004; 12: 94–104.
40. *Ibid* 38.
41. Bowlby, J. *Maternal care and mental health* p 13. World Health Organization Monograph (Serial No. 2), 1951.
42. Lorenzini N, Fonagy P. Attachment and personality disorders: a short review. *Focus* 2013; 11(2): 155–166.
43. The formulation is an attempt to distil the key psychological understanding of a person – pulling together key elements of his early history and subsequent life events, important early and later relationships, and how these play out in the present in the individual's coping mechanisms (i.e. his defences), his relationships and difficulties.
44. Gunderson JG, Chu JA. Treatment implications of past trauma in borderline Personality Disorder. *Harv Rev Psychiatry* 1994; 1: 75–81.
45. Feurino L 3rd; Silk KR. State of the art in the pharmacologic treatment of borderline Personality Disorder. Curr Psychiatry Rep 2011; 13: 69–75.
46. There is a clinical condition called Rapid Cycling Bipolar Affective Disorder, where the changes in mood occur more frequently than in the usual Bipolar Affective Disorder. However it is still possible to distinguish Rapid Cycling Bipolar Affective Disorder from Borderline Personality Disorder as in the former the changes in mood, although more rapid, are not anywhere as rapid as the emotional shifts in Borderline Personality Disorder. Rapid Cycling refers to patients who have experienced at least 4 episodes during the previous 12 months. In Borderline Personality Disorder we are talking of mood shifts which can occur several times within a single hour.
47. A useful paper on this issue is Pickard H. Responsibility without blame: empathy and the effective treatment of personality disorder. *Philosophy, psychiatry, & psychology* 2011; 18 (3): 209–223.
48. Chanen AM, McCutcheon LK, Jovey M, et al. Prevention and early intervention for borderline personality disorder. *Med J Aust* 2007; 187 (7): S18–S21.
49. Lenzenweger, MF, Castro DD. Predicting change in borderline personality: Using neurobehavioral systems indicators within an individual growth curve framework. *Personality Disorders: Theory, Research, and Treatment* 2012; 3 (2): 185–195.
50. The National Institute for Health and Care Excellence (NICE) provides national guidance and advice to improve health and social care in the UK.
51. Rosenfeld, H. Afterthought: changing theories and changing techniques in psychoanalysis. In H.Rosenfeld *Impasse and Interpretation*. London: Tavistock 1987.
52. Gabbard GO. Two subtypes of narcissistic Personality Disorder. *Bull Menninger Clin* 1989; 53: 527–532.
53. *Ibid* 52.

54. Gunderson J, Weinberg I, Choi-Kain L. Borderline Personality Disorder *Focus* 2013; XI (2): 129–145.
55. Bateman AW, Fonagy P. Effectiveness of psychotherapeutic treatment of Personality Disorder. *Br J Psychiatry* 2000; 177: 138–143.
56. de Groot ER, Verheul R, Trijsburg RW. An integrative perspective on psychotherapeutic treatments for borderline personality disorder. *Journal of Personality Disorders* 2008; 22(4): 332–52.
57. Bateman A, Fonagy P. *Psychotherapy for Borderline Personality Disorder: Mentalization Based Treatment.* Oxford: Oxford University Press 2004.
58. Bateman A, Fonagy P (Eds). *Handbook of Mentalizing in Mental Health Practice.* Washington: American Psychiatric Press, 2012.
59. Clarkin, JF, Yeomans, F, Kernberg, OF. *Psychotherapy of borderline personality: Focusing on object relations.* Washington, D.C.: American Psychiatric Publishing, 2006
60. *Ibid* 59.
61. Kernberg OF. *Borderline Conditions and Pathological Narcissism.* New York: Jason Aronson, 1975.
62. Young J. *Cognitive Therapy for Personality Disorders: A Schema Focused Approach* 3rd Ed Sarasota Fl: Professional Resource Press, 1999.
63. Young J, Klosko J, Weishaar ME. *Schema Therapy: A Practitioner's Guide* Guilford, 2003
64. Kellogg S, Young J. Schema Therapy for Borderline Personality Disorder. *J Clinical Psychol* 2006; 62(4): 445–458.
65. Linehan M. *Cognitive Behavioral Treatment of Borderline Personality Disorder.* New York: Guilford Press, 1993.
66. Ryle A, Kerr I. *Introducing Cognitive Analytic Therapy: Principles and Practice.* Chichester: Wiley, 2002.
67. Waldinger RJ, Gunderson JG. Completed psychotherapies with borderline patients. *Am J Psychother* 1984; 38: 190–202.
68. Bateman A, Fonagy P. Assessing the severity of borderline Personality Disorder *Br. J. Psychiatry* 2013; 203: 163–164.
69. Tyrer P, Merson S, Onyett S. et al. The effect of Personality Disorder on clinical outcome, social networks and adjustment: a controlled clinical trial of psychiatric emergencies. *Psychological Medicine* 1994; 24(3): 731–740.
70. Gunderson JG, Bender D; Sanislow C et al. Plausibility and possible determinants of sudden "remissions" in borderline patients. *Psychiatry* 2003; 66: 111–119.
71. This simile has its weakness in relation to psychiatry as the discipline does not yet have the same biological measures as exist in physical medicine but the principle of a doctor establishing a diagnosis and treating this diagnosis is the same.
72. Zanarini MC, Frankenburg FR, Hennen J., et al. The longitudinal course of borderline psychopathology: 6-year prospective follow-up of the phenomenology of borderline personality disorder. *American Journal of Psychiatry* 2003; 160: 274–283.

73. Gunderson JG, Berkowitz C. *Multiple Family Group Program at McLean Hospital.* The New England Personality Disorder Association, 2006. http://www.borderlinepersonalitydisorder.com/wp-content/uploads/2011/08/Family-Guideline-running-doc-15-Nov-06.pdf
74. Bateman A. *Family Guidelines. Multiple Family Group meeting at Halliwick Unit, St Anne's Hospital, London.*
75. Prochaska J, DiClemente C. Stages and processes of self-change in smoking: toward an integrative model of change. *Journal of Consulting and Clinical Psychology* 1983; 5: 390–395.
76. This finding is in fact in keeping with research. In a review of Randomised Control Trials, Shedler found that patients report an ongoing improvement in their symptoms after treatment (Shedler, J.. The efficacy of psychodynamic psychotherapy. *American Psychologist,* 2010; 65(2): 98–109.)
77. Shedler, J. The efficacy of psychodynamic psychotherapy. *American Psychologist,* 2010; 65(2): 98–109.
78. Kieh KA, Hoffman MB. The criminal psychopath: History, neuroscience and economics. Jurimetrics: *The Journal of Law, Science, and Technology* 2011; 355–397.
79. Thinking around the contract, and aspects of specification of the contract are based on Clarkin JF, Yeomans FE, Kernberg O. *Psychotherapy for Borderline Personality focusing on object relations.* Ch 6 Assessment Phase II Treatment Contracting pp 179–220. Washington: Am Psychiatric Publishing, 2006.

Index

A
abusive behaviour
   response of family towards individual with personality disorder 139
acting out 49, 119
adolescents
   borderline personality disorder diagnosis 65–66
affective disorders *see* mood disorders
aggression 18, 104
   self harm 58
agoraphobia 51
alcohol problems 50
   impact on personality disorder treatment 61–62
alternative therapies 124, 125–126
ambivalence: terminology 177
anankastic/perfectionist personality disorder
   case illustration 80, 87
   ICD 10 and DSM-5 diagnostic criteria 79–80
antidepressants 53, 94–95, 120
antisocial/dissocial personality disorder (ASPD) 9, 19, 38, 95
   case illustration 78–79, 167
   Department of Health (UK) guidelines 27–28
   ICD 10 and DSM-5 diagnostic criteria 77
anxiety 50
   diagnosis 50–51
anxiety disorders
   versus borderline personality disorder 51–52
anxious/avoidant personality disorder
   case illustration 81–82
   ICD 10 and DSM-5 diagnostic criteria 80–81
anxious/preoccupied attachment style 37–38
Appleby, L 13
attachment
   deactivation 38
   importance for progress of therapy 18, 27–28
attachment theory 15–17, 36–40, 136
   Adult Attachment Interview 37–38, 39
   Infant Strange Situation procedure 37, 39
   infants and children 35, 36–39, 136
auditory hallucinations 56–58
avoidance
   social phobia versus borderline personality disorder 51
avoidant personality disorder 95

ICD 10 and DSM-5 diagnostic criteria 80–81
avoidant/dismissing attachment style 38

B
Bateman, Anthony 16, 97
Beck, Aaron 106
bipolar disorder
    treatment 54
    versus borderline personality disorder 53–54
borderline personality disorder (BPD)
    see also classification of personality disorder; diagnosis of personality disorder; personality disorder; treatment for borderline personality disorder; treatment for personality disorder
    adolescents 65–66
    books on 195
    'borderline' condition between psychosis and neurosis 14
    case studies 33–34
        Nina's story 3–6, 16–17, 25–26, 31–33, 34, 45–46, 60–61, 69, 151–152
    conflict view 17–18
    criteria for psychiatric diagnosis 10
    deficit view 15–17, 18
    Department of Health (UK) guidelines 27–28
    evidence based therapy 27–28, 95–113
    facts and figures 188
    family getting help 140–141
    identity diffusion 17–18, 104
    improvement and recovery 26–29, 168–169
    Internet resources 196–197
    link with post traumatic stress disorder 52
    mentalization 15–17, 40–41
    psychiatric perspective 13–15
    psychoanalytic approaches 15–18, 113
    valid psychiatric disorder 12
    versus anxiety disorder 51–52
    versus bipolar disorder 53–54
    versus mood/affective disorders 52–55
    versus schizophrenia 55–57
    whether occurrence of sexual abuse relevant 41
Bowlby, John 15, 36, 39, 136

C
capacity
    Mental Health Act test for assessing 22
    moral 9
childhood sexual abuse 34, 41
children
    attachment theory 35, 36–39
    personality development 34–35
classification of personality disorder 10–12
    DSM-5 system 10–11, 72–79
    ICD system 10–11, 72–79
clinical depression 50, 120, 121
cognitive analytic therapy (CAT) 27, 98–99
    application of CAT to a patient 112–113
    framework 112
    key concepts 111
    mechanisms of change 111

patient therapist relationship 112
relationship to other
   treatments 112
techniques 112
theoretical background 111
treatment goals 112
cognitive behavioural therapy
   (CBT) 27, 95, 156
dialectical behavioural therapy
   (DBT) related to 110
relationship to schema focused
   therapy (SFT) 108
terminology 177
complementary therapies 124,
   125–126
complex post traumatic stress
   disorder 52
confidentiality 141
contract for treatment *see* treatment
   contract
coping mechanisms 16, 19, 50, 107
   see also defence mechanisms
countertransference 119–120
   case illustration 119
   terminology 178
culture
   relevance to diagnosis of
      personality disorder 7
cyclothymia 55

D

dangerous and severe personality
   disorder (DSPD) 23
defence mechanisms 47–49, 104,
   162
   see also splitting
   case illustrations 47–49, 151
   projective identification 101,
      104, 119, 151, 157–158
   terminology 178–179
delusions 56

denial 49
Department of Health (UK)
   antisocial personality disorder
      (ASPD) guidelines 27–28
   borderline personality disorder
      (BPD) guidelines 27–28
dependence
   cultural influence 7
dependent personality
   disorder 40
   case study 70–71, 83, 88–89
   ICD 10 and DSM-5 diagnostic
      criteria 82–83
depression 50
   versus borderline personality
      disorder 53, 94–95,
      120, 121
depressive aspects 9
Deutsch, H 15
diagnosis of personality disorder
   see also classification of
      personality disorder
   argument for retention of
      clinical diagnosis 12
   Clusters A, B and C 9, 72
   criteria for 10–12, 72–79,
      189–190
   cultural factors influencing 7
   difficulties 12–13, 41–42
   stigma attached to 11–12, 13
   whether condition meets formal
      criteria for a medical
      diagnosis 87–88
devaluation 13, 18
Diagnostic and Statistical Manual
   of Mental Disorders
   (DSM-5) 10–11, 72–79
   antisocial personality disorder
      77, 182
   anxious/avoidant personality
      disorder 80–81

borderline personality disorder 13–14, 57
criticism of 11
dependent personality disorder 82–83
histrionic personality disorder 76
Infant Strange Situation and Adult Attachment Interview links between 39
narcissistic personality disorder 84
obsessive-compulsive personality disorder 79–80
paranoid personality disorder 72–73
schizoid personality disorder 74
schizotypal personality disorder 75
dialectical behavioural therapy (DBT) 27, 98–99
application of DBT to a patient 110–111
framework 110
key concepts 109
mechanisms of change 109
modification of cognitive behavioural therapy (CBT) 110
patient therapist relationship 110
techniques 110
theoretical background 108–109
treatment goals 109–110
dismissing attachment style *see* avoidant/dismissing attachment style
disoriented/disorganized attachment style 38
dissocial personality disorder *see* antisocial/dissocial personality disorder (ASPD)
dissociation 18, 57, 160
terminology 179
distortion 49
drive theory 103
drug problems 50
impact on personality disorder treatment 61–62
DSM *see* Diagnostic and Statistical Manual of Mental Disorders
dysthymia 55

E

eating disorders 50
environment
nature versus nurture debate 33–36, 39
evidence based medicine: terminology 179
evidence based psychological treatments
borderline personality disorder (BPD) 27–28, 95–113
cognitive analytic therapy (CAT) 27, 111–113
cognitive behavioural therapy (CBT) 27, 95, 156
common characteristics of treatments for BPD 95, 96
dialectical behavioural therapy (DBT) 27, 108–111
mentalization based treatment (MBT) 27, 34–35, 40–41, 46, 97–103
personality disorders generally 95, 98–99
schema focused therapy (SFT) 27, 106–108
transference focused

psychotherapy (TFP) 27, 34–35, 41, 46, 103–106

F
family
  role in helping individual with personality disorder 131–143
Fonagy, Peter 16, 97
formulation 45–49
  terminology 179
Freud, Anna 47, 178
Freud, Sigmund 47, 103

G
generalised anxiety disorder 51–52
genes
  nature versus nurture debate 33–36, 39
group therapy
  advantages 117, 152
  case scenario 117–118, 146–147, 152
  versus individual therapy 116–118, 152

H
Hippocrates 8
histrionic personality disorder
  case illustration 69, 77
  ICD 10 and DSM-5 diagnostic criteria 76
homosexuality 11
hospital admissions 118–119, 141
  case scenario 148, 158

I
ICD 10 *see* International Classification of Disease (ICD 10)
idealization 13, 18, 49
identity
  as if/false self personality 15
  DSM-5 criteria for diagnosis of borderline personality disorder 13–14
  self 9, 13, 15
identity diffusion 17–18, 104
impulsive behaviour 13, 14
individual therapy
  case scenario 147–148, 149–150
  value of 153–154
  versus group therapy 116–118, 152
infants
  attachment theory 36–39, 136
insanity
  personality disorder distinct from psychosis 6, 8–9, 22, 55–57
International Classification of Disease (ICD 10) 10–11, 72–79
  anankastic/perfectionist personality disorder 79–80
  antisocial personality disorder 77
  anxious/avoidant personality disorder 80–81
  dependent personality disorder 82–83
  F60-F69 disorders *Text* 189–190
  histrionic personality disorder 76
  paranoid personality disorder 72–73
  schizoid personality disorder 74
  schizotypal personality disorder 75

interpersonal relationships 9
   as if/false self personality 15
   case illustration of patient with problem with 156–157
   DSM-5 criteria for diagnosis of borderline personality disorder 13–14
   splitting 13, 17–18, 35, 48

J
Japan
   cultural influence on diagnosis 7

K
Kandel, E R 35–36
Kernberg, Otto 17, 35, 103–104

L
law
   Mental Health Act test for assessing capacity 22
Lewis, G 13
Linehan, Marsha 108
Livesley, John 158–159

M
madness *see* insanity
major depressive disorder (MDD) 11
manipulation 49
medicalization of mental health 11, 12
medication
   bipolar disorder versus borderline personality disorder 54
   borderline personality disorder (BPD) 121
   depression 53, 94–95, 120
   drug trials on effectiveness in treatment of borderline personality disorder 27
mentalization 15–17, 40–41, 97, 100–101
   case illustration 16–17, 26
   terminology 179
mentalization based treatment (MBT) 27, 34–35, 40–41, 98–99
   application of MBT to a patient 103, 156
   example of patient from a MBT perspective 46, 103, 130–131
   framework 102
   key concepts 97–101
   mechanisms of change 101
   patient therapist relationship 101–102
   relationship to transference focused psychotherapy 102–103, 105
   techniques 102
   theoretical background 97
   treatment goals 101
mindfulness 109, 125
   terminology 180
mood disorders
   versus borderline personality disorder 52–55
moral capacity 9

N
narcissistic personality disorder 13, 19, 38, 84–87
   Anders Breivik 22
   case illustrations 84–86, 161, 165–166
   concept of narcissism 86–87
   DSM-5 diagnostic criteria 84
National Health Service *see* NHS
nature versus nurture 33–36, 39
neurosis

versus psychosis and borderline personality disorder 14
NHS
   use of ICD classification of personality disorder 10–11

O

object: terminology 180
object relations theory 103, 104
obsessive-compulsive personality disorder *see* anankastic/perfectionist personality disorder
offence
   individuals with *dangerous and severe* personality disorder 23
   Mental Health Act test for assessing capacity 22

P

paranoid personality disorder 13, 38
   case illustration 71, 73, 165
   ICD 10 and DSM-5 diagnostic criteria 72–73
passivity 56
patient
   see also therapist/patient relationship
   willingness to change 169
perfectionist personality disorder *see* anankastic/perfectionist personality disorder
personality
   as if/false self 15
   children's early experience influence on 34–35
   conflict view 17–18
   deficit view 15–17, 18
   enduring 29, 34
   four main dimensions 10, 14
   meaning 6–7
   nature versus nurture debate 33–36, 39
   positive qualities 46–47
personality disorder
   see also borderline personality disorder (BPD); diagnosis of personality disorder; treatment for personality disorder
   classification 10–12, 72–79
   distinct from psychosis 6, 8–9, 22, 55–57
   facts and figures 187
   historical view 8–9
   meaning 6, 7
   Mental Health Act test for assessing capacity 22
   society and the dangerous and violent individual 23
Pinel, Phillipe 9, 22
post traumatic stress disorder (PTSD) 52
   link with borderline personality disorder 52
preoccupied attachment style
   see anxious/preoccupied attachment style
presentation 18, 130
   anxiety disorders versus borderline personality disorder 51–52
   terminology 180
pretend mode 17, 100, 131
Prichard, J C 9, 22
primitive defence mechanisms 104, 178–179
privacy 140
prognosis for borderline personality disorder 26–29, 168–169

projection 48
    case illustration 157
    terminology 180
projective identification 101, 104, 119, 151
    case illustration 151, 157–158
    terminology 180
psychiatric nurse: role 155
psychiatrist
    role 155
    terminology 181
psychic equivalence 17, 26, 100, 131
psychoanalysis
    treatment for borderline personality disorder 113
psychoanalyst: terminology 181
psychoanalytic: terminology 182
psychodynamic: terminology 182
psychodynamic therapy 27
psychologists
    role 155
    terminology 182–183
psychopathy: terminology 182
psychosis
    distinct from personality disorder 6, 8–9, 22, 55–57
    versus neurosis and borderline personality disorder 14
psychotherapists
    role 155
    terminology 182

R
reaction formation 120
repetition compulsion 59–60, 161
Rey, Henri 14–15
Ryle, Anthony 111

S
schema: terminology 183
schema focused therapy (SFT) 27, 98–99
    application of MBT to a patient 108
    framework 108
    key concepts 106–107
    mechanisms of change 107
    patient therapist relationship 108
    relationship to cognitive behavioural therapy 108
    techniques 108
    theoretical background 106
    treatment goals 107
schizoid personality disorder
    case illustration 74–75
    ICD 10 and DSM-5 diagnostic criteria 74
schizophrenia
    versus borderline personality disorder 55–57
schizotypal personality disorder
    case illustration 76
    ICD 10 and DSM-5 diagnostic criteria 75
secure/autonomous attachment style 37, 38–39
self harm 13, 14, 58–59
    psychological motives 152
    response of family towards individual with personality disorder 139–140
self identity 9, 13, 15, 100–101
    as if/false self personality 15
    attachment theory 15–17, 35
    case illustration of patient with problem with 156

DSM-5 criteria for diagnosis
of borderline personality
disorder 13–14
sexual abuse 34, 41
social phobia 51
society
individuals with *dangerous
and severe* personality
disorder 23
somatising 49
splitting 13, 17–18, 35, 48
case illustration 157
terminology 183
sublimation 49
suicidal behaviour 8
case illustrations 5, 21, 33
DSM-5 criteria for diagnosis
of borderline personality
disorder 13
suicide: statistics 187
suppression 49

T
teenagers
borderline personality disorder
diagnosis 65–66
teleological mode 17, 100
therapist
own therapy and supervision
119, 153
selection 115–116
therapist/patient relationship
101–102, 105, 108, 110, 112,
115–116
case illustrations 119–120, 151,
156–158, 171–172
countertransference 119–120
individual sessions 153–154
projective identification 119,
151, 157–158
treatment contract 60–61

thought interference 55–56
trait 6, 29, 34
terminology 184
transference: terminology 184
transference focused psychotherapy
(TFP) 27, 34–35, 41, 98–99
application of TFP to a patient
105–106
example of patient from a TFP
perspective 46, 105–106
framework 105
key concepts 104
mechanisms of change 104
patient therapist relationship
105
relationship to mentalization
based treatment (MBT)
102–103, 105
techniques 105
theoretical background
103–104
treatment goals 105
treatment contract
example 191–193
purpose 60–61
treatment for borderline personality
disorder 27–28, 40–41, 54,
95–113
see also cognitive analytic
therapy (CAT); cognitive
behavioural therapy
(CBT); dialectical
behavioural therapy
(DBT); mentalization
based treatment (MBT);
schema focused therapy
(SFT); transference
focused psychotherapy
(TFP); treatment for
personality disorder
assessing progress 158–164

case study: Nina's story 93–95,
    117–118, 123–124,
    129–131, 145–164,
    167–168, 171–172
choosing a treatment 113–114
common characteristics
    of evidence based
    treatments 95, 96
drug trials 27
exploration 160–161
group or individual therapy
    116–118
hospital admissions 118–119,
    141, 158
improvement and recovery
    26–29, 168–169
medication 121
problem recognition 159–160
psychoanalysis 113
seeking treatment 114
selecting a therapist 115–116
treatment contract 60–61
treatment for personality disorder
    see also treatment for
        borderline personality
        disorder
    case illustrations 21–22
    considerations before starting
        therapy 19–20, 28
    deficit versus conflict approach
        18, 157
    difficulties 41–42
    drug and alcohol dependence
        and 61–62
    identifying the need 19
    responsibility of the patient
        63–65, 66
    when to start 21–22
    whether cure possible 28–29
treatment frame: terminology 184
treatment team
    competence 169
    composition of clinicians from
        different disciplines 185
    meeting the team 154–158
    team meeting 148, 152

U
unresolved/disorganized
    attachment style 38

V
voices (auditory hallucinations)
    56–58

W
World Health Organisation
    International Classification of
        Disease *see* International
        Classification of Disease
        (ICD 10)

Y
young people
    borderline personality disorder
        diagnosis 65–66
Young, Jeffrey 106

Z
Zen philosophy 109